# The Colour of Sunset

## Travels Through
## Southeast Asia

John Bell

NEWEST PRESS

© Copyright John Bell 2000

All rights reserved. The use of any part of this publication repro-
duced, transmitted in any form or by any means, electronic,
mechanical, recording or otherwise, or stored in a retrieval system, without the prior consent of the publisher is an infringement
of the copyright law. In the case of photocopying or other repro-
graphic copying of the material, a licence must be obtained from
the Canadian Reprography Collective before proceeding.

**Canadian Cataloguing in Publication Data**
Bell, John, 1962-
The green light of sunset

ISBN 1-896300-13-8

1. Bell, John, 1962- —Journeys—Asia, Southeastern. 2. Asia,
Southeastern—Description and travel. I. Title.
DS522.6.B44 2000    915.904'53    C00-910228-0

Cover design: Bob Young
Cover photgraphs: John Bell
Author photograph: Alistair Eagle

COMMITTED TO THE DEVELOPMENT OF CULTURE AND THE ARTS

NeWest Press acknowledges the support of the Canada Council for the
Arts for our publishing program. We also acknowledge the financial sup-
port of the Government of Canada through the Book Publishing Industry
Development Program (BPIDP) for our publishing activities.

NeWest Publishers Limited
Suite 201, 8540-109 Street
Edmonton, Alberta  T6G 1E6
(780) 432-9427
www.newestpress.com

1  2  3  4  5  04  03  02  01  00

PRINTED AND BOUND IN CANADA

*This book is dedicated to all of my travelling companions in Southeast Asia. I value your collective contribution to this journey and to my life.*

# Table of Contents

# Introduction

There are times when change is inevitable. There are times to move on, even if pain and challenge make us face our own reality and explore our passions. I made such a move—one that has sometimes seemed a move in all directions! Most importantly, it was a step inside. Through the course of this adventure, I learned a great deal about who I am. My best and my worst in stark reality. From this experience, I gained a new understanding of passion, creation and discovery.

The journey I made spanned four months: November 1994 to the end of February 1995. The destination was across the Pacific Ocean. I travelled to Thailand, Malaysia, Singapore, and the Indonesian islands of Sumatra, Java and Bali. Southeast Asia had always intrigued me. Many of my friends had gone through these countries, capturing the scenic beauty in photographs and stories.

In 1983, I travelled to Europe and North Africa. Europe was often a standard choice for a first trip as young people ventured off to find themselves and see the world. Only a backpack, a decent guidebook, a desire for adventure and good common sense were required. That five-month trip left me in awe of the experience. I had always promised myself that I would take another such trip, this time somewhere in Asia. I felt attracted to its beautiful places, its cultures and philosophies and the many temples and Buddhas throughout.

I took this journey alone, leaving home, leaving a marriage and setting a new course for my life. An instinctive call to venture out on my own came from deep within. It was a voice I could not deny. I yearned for change. I felt compelled to rediscover myself and face the fear of being alone.

I took with me one small packsack filled with bare necessities and an acoustic guitar in a padded nylon bag. The guitar helped me meet new friends and share music with those I met. As well, it kept me company at times when I travelled alone. A hidden waistbelt carried money, traveller's cheques and an airline ticket. The open-ended ticket took me first to Hong Kong and Bangkok. From there I continued overland to Singapore, my next departure point. Similar arrangements were made for the extension into Indonesia, ending with my flight home from Bali. A *Lonely Planet* guidebook stowed in my pack helped me fill all the spaces in between.

I wrote this book as a way to share this adventure. I hope that anyone who reads this account will feel the sense of the adventure I experienced on the road.

I began my adventure on the eighth of November. It was a cold, wet day. The rain came down in light showers throughout the morning. My wife Jill and I shared tears. Our last moments together were strained and tense. We had both felt our separation coming for a long time but that day we faced its curt reality. We were in a panic, trying to stuff all we had to say into those last few minutes. Still, we were down to small talk by the time we reached the terminal. Strange to feel so comfortable with the words that do not mean a thing. At the gate, however, my heart sank. Non-passengers could go no further. Tears and sadness overcame me as I turned to say good-bye. I didn't want to let her go at that moment, only to stay and hold her close to me.

Something I found hard to identify, a knowing, a sixth sense, a driving force beyond me, was calling me to leave. Calling me to be alone on a soul-searching quest. My decision to listen to the voice in my heart was one of the single most important I have ever made.

I chose to be free, regardless of the consequences, to reach out and test my faith in myself. I chose to go to an alien world and to rediscover what I had allowed to be overshadowed, forgotten, and set aside. I put trust in life to unfold as it would. I stood at the crossroads; the paths of fate. As I made my choice, there could be no other path for my soul to take, no matter what was to be.

Here then is my adventure to the far side of our world, to the tropical wonders of Thailand, Malaysia and Indonesia . . . to the beginning of my own road of change.

# CHAPTER 1: HONG KONG

## Into the Jaws of the Dragon

*Tuesday, November 8, 1994*

I was in for a lengthy flight. I had to psych myself into enjoying a gruelling fourteen-hour ordeal in a sardine can. It seemed, at first, as if I had the space of a king aboard the 747 but after a few hours the grandeur faded. I grew impatient in my window seat. I spent quite a bit of time studying as many maps of Hong Kong as I could find, getting a sense of familiarity with the city I was flying toward. I occasionally watched the TV screen displaying a partial map of the world, with North America and Asia sitting like bookends at the edges. A tiny plane jetted its way across the vast expanse of ocean in between. The further the plane moved from the edge of my own continent, the more apprehensive I became.

I was leaving all that was familiar to me. The more I thought about leaving Jill and being on my own on this adventure, the more I wanted to be back home. The feeling was amplified as I observed other passengers in the aircraft. For the most part, people were travelling with someone else or in small groups. I watched them converse and laugh with their friends. My only personal contact was with the flight attendant as she pulled her cart of beverages and snacks up and down the aisle of the plane. Her friendly smile rolled by with the rattle of glass bottles and I found myself soaking up her glance as if she were an old friend. Finally, I leaned back in my seat, closed my eyes and began to concentrate on the exciting places I was to see and experience. This helped my feeling of nervousness become less apparent. I ate the tasty Cathay Pacific food, drank considerably, snacked on about a million packages of dry peanuts, and waited. Sleep came only in short naps interrupted by either a loud conversation nearby or another visit from the flight attendant with the offer of yet another snack.

At one point, I woke from a light slumber without any interruption. Wondering why, I shifted uncomfortably in my seat and grumbled to myself about being exhausted. As I sat in a crumpled pile under an airline blanket, I felt compelled to look outside. I slid the shade up to see a black night. The stars were clear and I gazed into deep space. A bright light caught my attention far below and I looked down on a scene full of light and movement. The centre of a vast city pulsed and flowed with a current of electricity and colour. Glancing briefly at the map on the TV screen, I saw that we were over the edge of Japan and I thought this must be Tokyo. It was a sea of light like I had never seen before. The pulsing lights and flow of the traffic danced in the darkness. On the outskirts of the main city I saw whole islands, lit and glowing in the blackness. I continued to watch, mesmerized by the sea of lights. Fatigue eventually overtook me and I fell back to sleep.

I finally woke to the sound of animated conversations. Passengers were being asked to take their seats and prepare for the descent into Hong Kong's Kai Tak airport. I sat up in my seat and stared out the window, watching our progress toward the Asian metropolis. The coastline approached and I began to see the congested streets of the city. It was now 8:30 PM, a day ahead of my departure from Canada.

As we flew closer to the ground the first thing I noticed was the dense concentration of buildings. The terrain was very rugged and a few sharp peaked islands reached in vain to touch the bottom of the jet. Passing over the last mountain, I saw the central city looming ahead. Another cluster of tall buildings blanketed the ground. The jet banked a steep right turn, dropping down over the towers of the city of Kowloon. As we skimmed along the tops of the tenements, I looked down into the lives of thousands of city dwellers. The jet was so close I could look into the apartments and see people sitting at the dinner table or even looking up at us. Closer, closer, then the buildings vanished and the Kai Tak airport replaced the scene below the aircraft. A few seconds later the wheels touched down on a strip of pavement only wide enough for the landing gear. I looked out my window to see the wing out over the water as the plane came to a stop at the end of the runway.

Collecting my packsack and guitar from the overhead compartment, I followed the other passengers down the narrow aisle and out onto the tarmac. Descending the stairs, I was greeted by a brisk wind that made me catch my breath. The crowd walked into the belly of a large bus that carried us to the door of the terminal. Walking into the arrivals area, I felt edgy and nervous. A blank stare and the loud thud of a rubber stamp greeted me at the immigration counter when I presented my papers under the glass window. Walking down the steps toward the exit doors I could feel my nervousness growing stronger.

I walked the last few metres toward the doors as strange faces and Chinese signage swirled around me. Then, all at once, nervousness turned to exhilaration. I tightened the grip on my luggage as I approached the end of the large hall. The doors out into the Asian night opened like the jaws of a dragon and its breath hit me like ice.

A line of taxis stood waiting, the drivers yelling and waving to anyone who might be a potential customer. I found the closest available driver and hopped into the rear of his car. Getting the driver to understand my destination ended up taking longer than the actual ride. Reading no English, the driver was at a loss as he stared at the name of the hostel I had scrawled on a small piece of paper. Handing him a map of the city, he found the equivalent spot and soon smiled in confidence that he could deliver me to the right place. He lurched out of the long line of cars and sped around onto a road leading toward the forest of towers I had seen from the plane.

From the back of the cab I could see many rickety-looking buildings covered with bamboo scaffolding. Looking into some of the windows as we passed by, I saw just how small some of these apartments really were. Living rooms looked like closets. My view was occasionally interrupted by a sharp jerk of the car that sent me to the other side of the automobile. The cab careened wildly over and under viaducts. I felt a little safer when I finally found the other half of my seatbelt. At last the cabbie stopped near a bright neon sign marking the STB Hostel, next to the entrance of a busy night market. Although my first impulse was to explore the area, I chose to check in, take a hot shower and sleep. A tall steel door opened with a small amount of force and revealed a narrow hallway. Beside the elevator at the rear of the building, a steep staircase led me up to the top-floor hostel. As I climbed the stairs, I heard jovial laughter and random conversation grow steadily louder. I stepped out of the stairwell into a brightly lit office and lobby full of old, tattered couches and chairs, occupied by resident guests. Music played from an unseen stereo and some people were playing ping-pong in an adjacent room. The steady knocking of the ball against paddles sounded as precise as a clock. I glanced at the small clock above the clerk's desk. It was now close to 10:00 PM local time, and there were a few other travellers who had arrived just before me. I waited for the next available clerk who booked me into a dormitory bunk.

After a hot shower I returned to my room and got acquainted with the few roommates who were in the large room furnished with ten bunk beds. I asked questions about the city and area before climbing into my bunk. I lay down on my back and immediately fell into a deep sleep.

*Thursday, November 10, 1994*

I woke early, excited about my first full day in Asia. Once I had stowed my baggage in the hostel storeroom, I packed up my essential papers and headed out on a quest for breakfast and drinking water. The sun was bright as I walked down Nathan Road. Hungry and not having any idea where I might find something to eat, I decided to weave through the streets until I found a restaurant. Following the smell of food, I came across a small café. As I walked inside to have breakfast with the locals, a cloud of tobacco smoke, grease, and loud conversations swirled around my head. I noticed most of the patrons eating an identical meal: fried chicken breasts in lots of grease, noodle soup and milky tea. I decided to follow suit, ordering the same from the small man behind the counter. Afterwards, the meal weighed heavy in my stomach.

I continued south to the port of Kowloon to catch the ferry connection to Hong Kong Island, just across the harbour. I watched the busy marine traffic until I saw one of the big brown ships sail into nearby dock and then walked to the gangway. I joined in the queue down the long ramp, paid the equivalent of thirty cents for my ticket and was directed onto the vessel. The five-minute ride across the harbour was like a mad cartoon show. Ships bouncing and bobbing made me dizzy as I sat on the wooden bench and stared out the upper deck window. Diesel tugs, Chinese junks and giant freighters fought for space in the narrow waterway. The air was misty, aided by the evident pollution.

I stepped off the dock onto the island, finding the geography very steep. I looked up to see the thin track of the Victoria Peak Tram climbing to the summit viewpoint. Along the edge of the island, virtually every piece of land was covered by huge office buildings fighting for space, a steel world of towers and towering sums of cash.

I made my way into the maze of streets and alleys. I didn't have to go far before I began walking uphill in a very literal way. One byway, Ladder Street, was nothing but flights of stairs. Clambering up the steps and onto the cross streets, I walked past a multitude of tiny little shops. Crooked alleys disappeared into the gloom. Dust and incense swirled in the air as hectic traffic had me moving cautiously at every intersection. I heard a truck backing out of a small alley. The back-up beacon was a bad musical version of "We Wish You A Merry Christmas." The song seemed so out of place to me that I laughed out loud.

I followed my map to the Botanical and Zoological Gardens. There I saw some orangutans from Borneo. It was sad to see them on display, so solemn as they sat quietly in their iron cage. They looked bored. Several adult humans stood nearby with their children. The kids were very excited and took much more interest in the apes than their stoic-looking parents. When I walked up behind the group the children began to take as much interest in me as they had in the orangutans. With my red hair, I got long inquisitive looks from the kids, their tiny black-haired heads angled up at me. One child stared at me, stared at the apes and back again with a funny look on his face. I smiled back and imagined him thinking that I had escaped the enclosure. Soon the young boy became shy and moved to hold the hand of his mother while continuing to stare at me. I gazed through the fence and the lonely apes stared back with sad faces. I began to think about seeing them in the wilds of their home jungles and decided to put Sumatra on my list of destinations.

The peak tram up to the island's summit was next on my list. Looking like a San Francisco street car, the tram tracked up through the lower parts of the city at an astonishing forty-five degree angle. At times I thought it might tip over backwards. Soon the steep pitch gave way to a shallower slope, the train car crawling up the side of the mountain. Occasional glimpses of the surrounding view showed our elevation above the bay. Slowly the train reached the peak and pulled into the tiny summit station. The view was breathtaking as I walked out onto the open boulevard of tourist shops. I perched myself on the edge of the mountain. Boats, ships and planes did a hectic dance below me. Across the water the city of Kowloon lay nestled up against the expanse of hills and farmland. Beyond the dry hills in my sight sat the Chinese border. Banks of dense cloud hung over the distant land like a dark shroud.

I sat on the mountain peak for about an hour and, once the novelty had worn off, re-entered the tram platform for the return journey. Rattling down the steep slope of track, I braced myself against the bench seat in front of me and listened to nervous laughter from two older women riding on the other side of the tram. The steeper the pitch, the louder their laughter.

The hot and sunny morning gave way to a muggy afternoon as I walked out of the station at the foot of the mountain. A light breeze tried to cool the air, but I still felt the sun on my fair skin. The downhill grade of the streets made the walk to the pier much easier.

I bought another ticket and joined the line of people waiting to board the ferry back to Kowloon. The exhaustion of the day's walking and the heat had me sitting down heavily on the hard wooden bench on the ship's upper deck. Staring out the window, I gazed at the murky water. I was conscious of all the pollution floating in the chuck under and around the ship. Madly bobbing through her course, the ferry pulled into the port with surprising swiftness.

There are a number of clubs, restaurants and shops on the south end of Kowloon. Packed into only a few small blocks, the area has almost anything that one would desire. The odour of cooking food swirled in the air. It was so intoxicating that I felt compelled to walk a few laps around the block. I finally stopped at one small restaurant for a delicious bowl of wonton soup.

After the small snack I headed back toward my hostel along a main street near Kowloon Park. When I had walked by this morning, most businesses were closed. Now I paraded past a long line of busy shops. At one point I was distracted by a sign hanging at near head level: "Topless Bar." It hung over a narrow doorway which lead below street level.

My curiosity came alive as I peered down the dark stairway. I chuckled to myself, almost nervously, wondering what one could see in a club like this.

The stairs led off the bright, sunny sidewalk down into the basement. It took a few seconds for my eyes to adjust to the dim light and I stumbled down to the foot of the stairwell. To make matters worse, the wallpaper was dark in design, adding to the atmosphere of the club. Once the light returned to my vision, I found the entrance to the club and opened the door.

A pretty young woman stood behind the bar in a very short mini skirt and skimpy leather vest. Only two small buttons held her vest closed, her dark skin and breasts left slightly exposed. When she saw me coming through the door she called toward a back room. Four other women appeared from the next room and beckoned me to join them at the bar. Scantily dressed, they smiled alluringly and took their places on the stools in front of me.

"Welcome sir. How are you today?" The woman who spoke was the tallest of the four and quite attractive. She eyed me slowly up and down and I wondered whether she would have preferred to talk to a man in a suit instead. By the look on her face she didn't seem too impressed by my cotton shorts, sandals and T-shirt.

Despite my attire, she continued with her spiel, "You look so hot. You could use a drink, perhaps?" She signalled to the woman behind the bar who promptly filled a pint glass with amber gold.

"Love one," I said, settling onto a stool next to her. With this, all the women pulled their stools into a semi-circle around me and talked jovially to me and amongst themselves.

"Why not buy us all a drink today?" one of the other women asked. "They are very cheap—each only sixty Hong Kong dollars" (about twelve dollars). With this she popped the top button of her almost non-existent vest with two fingers. The alarm bells started to ring loudly and I knew that anything that I would see or do in here would come with a very high price tag.

"Sorry, I can only afford one drink," I said to her, reaching for my glass.

"What do you mean you can only afford one drink?" she came back, indignant. She then proposed that I buy one for the bartender alone. After I refused the second offer, the women started to speak to me in an angry tone. They knew that I would not give them any "extra" business and they were noticeably upset.

I continued to smile and sip my beer amid stone cold stares and angry words until the glass was empty. Pulling the money out of my wallet, I paid for my drink and slowly stood up to make my exit. As I departed I wished the women a happy day and closed the door behind me. I listened to the fading sound of curses as I left the club and walked up the stairs into the light of the street.

When I climbed the stairs to the hostel's lobby, I was invited to join a group of people who were going out for dinner at a local Australian pub. We filed out onto Reclamation Street and strolled into the dusk southward toward the port of Kowloon. Our destination was close to my topless bar experience. I laughed silently to myself as our group walked past the shingle hanging from the wall.

Turning the corner, we reached Ned Kelly's Last Stand. Run by Aussies, the pub's theme revolved around a famous outlaw bushman and his band of men. Large black and white photos of the gangsters adorned the walls, mixed with the timber frame decor and old artifacts you would typically find in a pub. Food portions were a bit small and the beer expensive, but overall it was good. I found the entertainment the most hilarious aspect of all. It was so bizarre to be in Hong Kong, sitting in an Australian pub having a beer while listening to five Chinese guys playing Dixieland jazz. The group was called Ken Bennet and the Kowloon Honkers.

After dinner we headed out into the evening to search out adventure amidst the crowded street markets. A sea of people surrounded us as we wandered through the stalls, block after block. There were endless piles of almost every item in the world for sale at the roadside booths. Vendors gawked at us with a vague look of surprise and wonder, their faces mirroring our own expressions.

At one corner we saw some guys selling watches. Suddenly, within ten to fifteen seconds of a warning whistle from a buddy, they disappeared around the corner into a small van. Trays of watches were quickly hidden and the men soon returned to the same spot with loads of new merchandise, this time white collared shirts. No sooner had they made the switch when policemen wandered by to inspect the booths in this corner of the market. The vendors sat on their stools, cool as anything.

Further along we came across a huge hardware market. The majority of items consisted of refurbished equipment and materials, in what looked like a well-organized junk yard. Rebuilt motors and others in disrepair, scrap iron, aluminium, car parts and old tires. Everything seemed to be covered with the same amount of dirt, grime and dust. Brisk winds tossed debris and dirt into my face as I made my way through the narrow paths.

Amidst the junkheap were food markets and my nose filled with the scent. The smell of rot also cut through with a vengeance and the occasional sight of rats made me think twice about buying anything uncooked. At one point I saw a large crowd observing something interesting. The sound of their excitement had me curious and I pushed my way through the crowd to see what was happening.

An old man sat beside a large covered basket. A huge cutting board and cleaver lay on a table in front of him. His most recent sale had just been bagged and the old man now looked out into the crowd for his next customer. An elderly woman waved at him with a single finger held up into the dusty air. With a nod the old man reached into his crate and pulled out a good-sized snake which twisted wildly in his grip. As the man brought the snake's head down onto the cutting block, the creature must have known its fate, fighting and wrapping itself tightly around the man's forearm. With a swift chop the head rolled and the body fell limp on the small table. A few quick slices and the snake was gutted, peeled, placed in a bag and handed to the old women. My curiosity was noticed by an old man standing beside me. "Good soup!"

After a time, I felt overwhelmed by the scenes around me. My senses were overloaded. We wandered on for two hours through the maze of alleys and darkness. Dim lights dangled from wires and swung in the breeze. On the way home I stopped at a small street vendor to inspect his selection of fine juices. Upon closer inspection of his cart, my eyes picked up an image through the vapour-coated window, a cool icon of refreshment: Heineken $1.00. Two dollars would quench my thirst and I handed the money to the man. Nestling one of the cans into my pocket, I lifted the other high in the air to signal my companions of a great discovery. Pulling back my finger, I felt the cool snap of the can echo off the walls of the alley. The air was silent for just one moment more. I clambered after my mates as we headed home.

I sat with a small group of late nighters who had settled into the lower lobby of our hostel sharing tales of discovery and adventure. Many had been on the road for some time and would return home in the next few days. Others, like me, had just arrived and listened attentively to stories of places we might see on our own journeys. Topics included Nepal, Thailand, Sumatra, Bali, with a few more obscure place names thrown in. I listened and my excitement grew, my imagination picturing the exotic destinations.

I later retrieved my guitar from the dorm and joined my new friends in the lower lobby. We sang songs for about two hours, all the while trying to avoid being run over by the many people coming out of the elevators. A few other travellers joined us as they came home from a night out. Finally an old man came down to tell us that the rest of the population in the small tower did not intend to let our rowdy rendezvous ruin their night's sleep.

I lay in my bunk after my first Asian adventure, looking out a small set of windows. I focused all of my attention on the distant sounds of the city. As I listened the night noise grew louder until I could hear people in the market a few blocks away ending a busy day of commerce. As the street grew quiet I felt a sense of uncertainty as I contemplated my next move—my next adventure. I closed my eyes and felt the fear of being alone grow stronger. I began to see that I was being challenged to face my fear, to see how much I had let it affect my decision-making in the past. I breathed deeply and realized that I was in the right place—a place where I could learn more about myself. I dispelled my worries with a willingness to face the darkness, to stick my neck out into the unknown and to grow.

# CHAPTER 2: BANGKOK, THAILAND

## Destination: Khao San Road

*Friday, November 11, 1994*

I sat back in my airline seat and watched the coastline and the buildings of Hong Kong disappear.

I was due to arrive in Bangkok just before nightfall. I much preferred to find my way to a safe haven with the aid of daylight and the immediacy of darkness made me feel hesitant. My stomach churned slightly as I researched my travel plans through the city with the aid of my Lonely Planet guidebook and a torn map given to me by an English girl at the airport in Hong Kong. She had no more use for it as she was headed back to London after six months away. It was tattered and torn and dangled from my grip. I would use it only to get into the heart of Bangkok and then it would become trashbin material. A few missing pieces of map made the fun all that more real as I cross-referenced my locations in my guidebook.

The jet dropped, piercing a thin layer of cloud I thought would surely block the sun from the ground. However, after breaking through the cloud cover, I glanced up to see a clear blue sky. We had only gone through a layer of humidity and were now ready to fry in the sun. My view from the window opened up to a thick forest of palm trees and small fields. Large buildings popped out of the foliage below, just before the plane touched down on the tarmac.

As I stepped off the plane I walked into the wall of heat that a friend had warned me about. The description had left me only slightly prepared and I could tell it was going to be a warm experience. Air-conditioning in the terminal provided a short reprieve from the temperature as I slowly made my way to the immigration desk.

On the plane I had practiced some Thai phrases to use with the locals, muttering them to myself as I stepped one person closer to the desk.

*"Sawadi-khrap."* I hoped that my guess at the pronunciation of the standard greeting didn't turn out to be something like "Hello, dirtbag" or some other insulting remark that would result in a vacation from Hell in a Thai prison. Smiling, I presented my passport and papers to a small woman behind the glass enclosure. Her tiny hand pulled them

toward her inspecting eyes. A look of casual boredom was returned to me when the stamped papers were handed back through the round cut in the glass panel. Without glancing at me at all, she nodded her head and gestured for me to carry on. I shuffled after the crowd of passengers ahead of me, descending the large staircases leading to the exits.

Deciding to take local transport, I inquired about the fare and the proper connections in a short conversation with a young woman sitting in a booth near the last exit. I thanked her for her help and she smiled, sending me on my way. I turned, following others to the exits leading to the dusty roadway in front of the terminal. I fingered the few coins I would need to reach my goal—Khao San road, a large area of good accommodation, fantastic cuisine and abundant bargains. My book recommended this area highly, as had friends who had travelled here before. I strolled down the edge of the sidewalk, searching for a bus stop. Finding none, I decided to watch how the locals got a ride on a bus. People waited in groups by the roadside waving at whichever bus they wished to ride in. I tried to blend into the crowd, but the looks I was getting assured me that I was not about to get away with it.

Dirt and grime blew into my face as I waited for the right bus to fight its way through the slow-moving traffic. The chorus of vehicle horns was deafening and the smell of exhaust made me nauseous as it hung thick in the air. I soon saw a few banged-up old buses lumbering out of the distant dust, completely packed with passengers. People flagging them down would squeeze themselves tightly into the doorways as they opened. It was hard to believe that so many people could fit inside these vehicles. Guessing that I may not get anywhere unless I was willing to pry myself into one of these things along with everyone else, I waved down a number six transit and fought my way in through the doors. My packsack and guitar fit snugly in front of me. I handed the conductor the fare and she handed me a small piece of paper the size of a large postage stamp. I took the ticket from her and stuffed it into the deepest corner of my pant's pocket so it wouldn't become lost.

Rush hour in this city of nine million people was a slow crawl. Once we had left the airport the roads became more clogged with vehicles. Lengthy, stalled jams had me roasting in the warm tropical air. I must have been on the bus for an hour when I began to wonder where my stop was and whether I had already passed it, heading deeper into the unknown city. I pulled my map and book out again and reread my directions. I was to stay on board until I reached a big traffic circle containing a huge monument. There, I was to make a connection to the Democracy monument, near Khao San road. As we crept along I began to see that every single intersection had some kind of large monument in its centre. I started to study the small picture on the map, hoping to be able to recognize that particular monument, but to no avail.

I felt a hint of panic. I had actually wondered how long it would be before my fear would rear its head. I felt myself riding the wave of emotion as it carried me into a much more reactive state. I began to study the map again and began asking people around me, with the aid of the map, where I was.

"Khao San road?" In vain I tried to ask the shy and staring locals, holding the map in my outstretched hands. Only a few people tried to read my map and lend assistance. Most others would turn away after a quick shake of their heads. One girl tried her best to help me but finally handed the map back to me, shaking her head. No one was able to help and I wondered just where I would end up on my first night in the city. As more and more monuments went by the windows, I knew that I would have to make a decision soon.

The universe must have heard me screaming for assistance because just as I was having visions of bedding down in a ditch, another Westerner stepped onto the bus in front of me. Since he carried no baggage, I knew he had to be familiar with the city. I caught his eye and raised my head to indicate that I wished to speak with him.

"Excuse me, do you know how to reach Khao San road? I'm afraid I am slightly lost."

"Actually, you're not." His voice, with it's thick American accent, bellowed out as he instructed me to keep on for a while longer. "The place you want is in a section of the city called Banglamphu."

He then spoke briefly with some of the locals in Thai and they reconfirmed that, indeed, the connection was still ahead. He even asked them to tell me where to get off, as his stop was before mine. He went on to tell me that he had been working in Thailand for three years. The stranger's assistance turned my apprehension into a burst of confidence. I relaxed and observed the world outside. I watched through the windows as the bus passed run-down residential neighbourhoods, busy stores and cafés, garbage piles, numerous street carts and lines of people waiting at local bus stops. After some time a girl with a bright smile urged me to get off the bus for my next connection. I thanked her and shuffled to the rear door.

I descended into a hot, dusty intersection and, after dodging vehicles beeping and bumping their way through the traffic circle, ran to the number nine bus I had been told to take, hopped on and paid again.

Democracy monument. We had reached the centre of Banglamphu. Night had descended as I stepped off the bus onto the dirty sidewalk. There were many people seated on benches and milling about in bunches under the street lights, all staring at me as I again pulled out my trusty travel book. A friendly policeman walked over to lend assistance.

"Khao San Road?" I inquired when he stepped within ear shot. Nodding his head, he pointed his finger across the busy intersection to a small alley.

"Go there and left. The next street over." His English was good. I waved and thanked him for the help. He smiled and carried on along his beat.

The gloom of darkness had fallen as I began my search for a place to stay. Traffic was still swelling through the roadways as rush hour continued. Dodging vehicles, I scrambled across the wide street to the opening of the alley. I walked quickly and immediately began to see other travellers. I made another left and came upon a scene that amazed me.

A wide street opened in front of me, lined with rickshaws, tuk-tuks (motorized rickshaw-like taxis with three wheels and room for four or five passengers), small cars and motorbikes. Beyond, crowds of people were gathered in the open spaces along the road. The smell of food drifted into my nose, making me hungry for a meal. I made my way down the street, following directions toward a guest house suggested to me by a friend who had been here a year earlier. The listing in my book verified that the hotel was situated just past the opposite end of this busy street. I took the opportunity to explore Khao San along the way. As I expected, the volume of foreign tourists was enormous. A centre for hotels and shopping, Khao San Road was alive with people. Colourful clothing hung on racks which almost blocked the sidewalks. Music stores offered racks of cassettes and CDs. In order to attract buyers, these shops had their own stereos cranked up to top volume. A stereo war was in full force. Squeezing through the thin spaces between people and merchandise, I was bombarded by vendors trying to sell me their wares. I graciously shook my head, knowing I would have plenty of time to buy once I had settled into a room.

Near the centre of Khao San, I passed the Hello Hotel. Like many others, it had a large restaurant on the main floor. Tables and chairs spilled out to the edge of the roadway. The lack of seating space indicated that this was a popular hangout. Listening to the variety of languages spoken, I guessed the majority of travellers to be German, Swiss, or Dutch. Crowded tables competed for space with the multitude of street vendors who squeezed in beside them. The smells of chicken, meat, fish, fresh fruit, and juices emanating from these vending carts made me drool. I could wait no longer. Purchasing fresh guava juice, I poured it into my mouth and my taste buds delighted in the sweet flavour. The wide smile of the young woman who sold it to me was as refreshing as her product. Feeling refreshed and relaxed, I walked to the end of the crowded roadway and searched for the street leading to my hotel.

The noise, scents and lights of Khao San faded quickly as I reached the last intersection feeding into the street. Across from me, the stone wall of a temple complex blocked my path. I crossed the roadway and followed the wall until I reached the first sidestreet. What I found was a crack in a wall of darkness. An alleyway leading into nothing. I plunged into the dimly lit path.

The dim light came from small lanterns hanging from a few vending carts parked next to the temple wall. Many people sat by the wall, chatting in groups, inspecting me as I wandered by. As I walked further into the lane the residual light dissipated and soon I was shrouded by the black night. It was so dark that I had to feel my way down the road with each step. Stumbling in the blackness, I kept on, guided by a distant light at the far end of the block. I could see that the road made a sharp left turn there, around the edge of the temple. Conscious of the slight security offered to me by the distant beam of light, noises in the darkness around me made me nervous. Muffled voices and the sound of shuffling from both sides of me made me turn to find the source. Barely visible, groups of people stared at me from their sitting places along the sides of the road. The sound of snuffling and scratching reached my ears and I jumped out of my skin when I was touched by something I could not see. My leg bumped into something short and solid. I froze momentarily to investigate. A cold, damp dog's nose inspected the top of my foot. The animal soon lost interest and continued into the blackness. Rounding the corner onto the next back road, I saw a sign marking the "Merry V" hostel and sighed with relief.

I climbed up to the third floor and found my tiny room. It had a small bed, a bedside table with lamp and a wastepaper basket in the corner. A thin sheet covered a mattress that was worn and stained, looking like it had not been cleaned for decades. I pulled my sleeping sheet (a bed sheet sewn together to resemble a sleeping bag) from my pack and laid it out over the mattress cover, preferring to have another layer between me and the bed. I lay quietly on my small bed, taking slow, deep breaths as I stared at the ceiling fan and the screen of mosquito netting which surrounded the upper windows like a jail cell.

## Tropical City
*Saturday, November 12, 1994*

I awoke to the sounds of Bangkok coming alive. I strolled to the end of my hallway and stared down from the open window. The sun was bright but the air still cool.

The most prominent noise came from small packs of mangy dogs crying for their meal. They were wretched creatures, some of them with only small bits of hair left on their bodies. The tropical heat encourages their skin to infect and the fur to fall out. These dogs do nothing but wander through the streets scrounging for food. Their lives are filled with disease, hunger and, at best, a slow death. I am sure the occasional local or tourist shows some pity but, for the most part, the creatures are ignored. During my time in Thailand I met some Thai people who believed that if a person did something wrong in his life, he would come back in his next life as a dog. I wondered what these souls had done to end up like this. Being repulsed by some of these vile creatures, I decided to keep my distance from any I came across.

The rest of the city was waking and the beeping of car horns and the roar of motorcycles grew louder with the rising sun. Many people used motorcycles and to see the way people drive here would have even the calmest driving instructors praying for their lives. Most commonly sighted were entire families on one bike, with Dad at the helm, baby sprawled on the fuel tank, Mom on the back-end sidesaddle and, mashed in between parents, a young son or daughter. I also couldn't help noticing that the only helmets were on the parents' heads.

Cool morning shower . . . the first of many. Refreshing for only a few minutes, these showers became numerous, as many as ten each day. Still, the humidity stuck like glue to my skin.

I sat on the verandah of the guest house drinking thick, sweet coffee. I could already feel the temperature getting warmer, even at this early hour. I was joined by two Canadian women who were waiting for visas to enter Viet Nam. Having a few days to wait, Paula and Valerie were looking for things to occupy their time while here in Bangkok.

"How about joining me for a trip to the snake farm," I suggested.

"Sure, where is it?" inquired Val.

I pointed with my coffee spoon to the location on the map. Paula knew of the best way to get to that section of the city—the riverboat transit system. I followed the pair to the boat dock, only a short jaunt from our guest house. Taking places on the small wooden benches by the water, we waited for the express boat.

Paula pointed to the long white boat approaching from a distance. "There it is," she said. "The best way to travel Bangkok—and the cheapest."

The boat pulled alongside the dock. Throwing the engine into reverse, the captain backed into the floating platform stern first. Other passengers were getting ready to jump onto the back platform before the boat sped back into the busy river traffic.

I was just about ready to leap when Paula reached out and grabbed my arm.

"Wait just one second before you jump onboard." She grinned as she held onto me.

I stepped back from the edge of the water. As the boat approached the dock, the engine roared to slow the craft and prevent a hard contact. In doing so, a soupy mix of oil and water spewed out of the large pipe in the transom. Splotch! It splashed against the edge of the foot rail and sprayed into the air. Another unfortunate traveller had taken my place by this time and she and her belongings were sprayed by the ugly mess.

Once safely and cleanly on board, we sat in seats along the side rail and watched the city go by.

Stepping off the pier, we walked down a narrow street toward the snake farm. It wasn't long before a businessman dressed in a dark pin-striped suit emerged from some crack in a wall, telling us about good deals on a variety of items from his cousin's business. Pushing his business card into my face, he insisted that we go to his shop for gems, gold and textiles.

"Actually we are headed for the snake farm." I handed the card back to him. I felt agitated. I was in no mood for a sales pitch this early in the morning.

"Snake farm closed today, this better for you," he retorted. I thought to myself that the only thing it was better for was his wallet. He was very persistent and finally persuaded the women to accept his offer. I did not want to shop and felt uncomfortable with the salesman.

Paula and Valerie wanted me to tag along so I finally agreed to join them, keeping my feelings to myself. Upon our agreement, the man whistled and a small tuk-tuk roared out from around the next corner—what a coincidence. Once we were seated in the back, the salesman spoke quickly to the driver and sent us on our way. The driver took us only about five blocks, parking in front of a large store which was part of a huge shopping complex.

I knew nothing about gems but decided to fake being interested as I strolled through the store, inquiring about prices on certain items. Aside from selling gems, the store was stocked with beautiful fabrics, carvings, and gold. The women's interest outlasted mine. I was again anxious to leave. After turning down many a "good deal," we decided to return to our original itinerary.

It was now early afternoon and, as this was my first day in the tropical sun, I started to feel the heat burning my skin. Moreover, the stifling humidity was heavy and sticky. I could feel myself getting edgy and impatient. I knew it was because of the temperature but I was conscious of how I was acting around my companions. Without a lot of cover from the scorching sun, the walk felt lengthy as we followed a map to our destination. Heat and dust were rising with the help of passing traffic. Small patches of shade provided rest stops and an excuse to drain yet another bottle of water.

When we arrived at the farm, the show we had hoped to see had just finished and the complex was being closed for the day. I laughed at the irony as we sat by the entrance in the shade of a large grove of trees, contemplating what to do next. Undaunted by the gem store delay and the farm closure, we hailed a taxi which delivered us to the Dusit Zoo in the city centre.

The zoo was a welcome haven with lush greenery and shady trees. We headed straight for a small café and lunch. Paula and Valerie told me about a place they had just returned from.

"Kanchanaburi is a small town in the mountains toward Burma." Paula spoke favourably of the small town just three hours east of Bangkok. "It is the home of the Bridge Over the River Kwai and it has access to beautiful hiking. It is a nice quiet place to relax."

The infamous bridge was originally built during the Second World War by Allied prisoners of war captured by Japanese soldiers. Destroyed by Allied bombers and then rebuilt after the war, the crossing is now a major tourist attraction and, along with the town's local museum, is a grim testament to the horrors of war.

The more the women spoke about Kanchanaburi, the more I wanted to go.

## Grand Palace
*Sunday, November 13, 1994*

I wandered into the early morning traffic searching for a temple called Wat Pho which had a traditional massage school on its grounds. My guidebook mentioned that visitors could receive a traditional massage at an inexpensive price. When I finally reached Wat Pho, I first paid a visit to the central temple and its famous reclining Buddha before searching out the massage school.

I was greeted there by an old man who smiled graciously as he led me into the building. I asked for an hour-long massage and was led into a large room adjacent to the entrance hall. Many mattresses, each with fresh white sheets, lay on the floor. Most of them were occupied. Some of the students were obviously Western while others were local. They were busy working on each other, practicing their techniques.

I was introduced to an old man dressed in white. He smiled and bowed, his hands held as if in prayer, and I nodded back to him. As he led me to an empty mattress, I noticed his hands looked very strong. I was right.

The old man dug deeply, hunting for tight muscles. I breathed deeply as he worked the tense areas in my back, shoulders and legs. He was totally silent as he concentrated on his task. The pain of tightness soon gave way to relaxation as my muscles responded to the healing work. After what seemed only a few minutes, I felt the old man gently shake me back into consciousness—the hour was complete. I emerged from the temple gate with smooth, flowing steps. The massage had loosened any and all tension in my body. I felt calm and content, even as the day grew warm.

After Wat Pho I went to explore the detailed buildings at the Grand Palace. Deeply etched mosaics and gold leaf covered almost everything. The ornateness of the culture's architecture fascinated me. The thing that struck me most was the age of it all—thousands of years—and the ties to the ancients.

The most popular thing to see was the Emerald Buddha, residing in Wat Phra Kaeo at the centre of the Grand Palace. This is the most sacred Buddha image in Thailand, apparently carved from jade. People lined up to gaze upon it and pray. It was difficult to find a place to kneel or sit. In the centre of the large room, the green Buddha sat on a tall altar covered with gold, incense and offerings. Other Buddha images I had seen in various temples were quite large and heart-stopping. The Emerald Buddha was less than one metre high and was almost hard to see on top of its altar. The size of it disappointed me slightly—all the hype for this tiny Buddha. I stopped my judging and took a place on the floor.

Throngs of people surrounded me, praying and placing offerings. Thick incense smoke permeated my nasal passages as I knelt on the carpeted floor with the devoted. Following example, I walked to the bottom of the monument, lit three sticks of rich-smelling incense and stuck them into a large, sand-filled pot. Thin trails of smoke drifted past my face as I gazed up at the tiny green figure staring out into the crowd at its feet. My offering smouldered and smoked its way to the short wooden ends as I closed my eyes and asked for guidance, protection and peace on my journey.

## Wat Arun

*Monday, November 14, 1994*

Wat Arun, the Temple of the Dawn, sits along the banks of Bangkok's river, Chao Phraya. I made my way down to the riverside pier near the guest house and waited for the express boat. Dodging the spray of slime from the tail pipe, I jumped onto the deck and paid my fare. The early morning rush hour traffic zoomed by and I turned my face into the cool breeze.

The boat negotiated all the stops along the route and finally approached the distant monolith shining in the sun. Wat Arun contains one tall, round-tipped pagoda or *"phra prang"* and four smaller ones, each a corner of the complex. The architecture of this particular temple had always intrigued me; it seemed the quintessential Thai structure.

The riverboat pulled into the stop directly across from the temple and the morning sun bathed the richly carved contours of the building. A small boat filled with orange-robed monks waited to cross the river. I hopped down the gangway and sat myself down opposite the monks in the centre of the boat. They smiled and were silent as the boat sailed. On the other side I followed the holy men up the trail to the gates and entered behind them.

The *prang* shone in the sunlight, narrow ribs striping the giant spire with shadow. I approached the base and looked straight up at the tip. A very steep staircase led up the side of the *prang* to a high viewpoint overlooking the city of Bangkok. The stairs were at such an angle that a rope had been installed to aid the climb to the viewing deck. I looked out over the river for a few minutes. High above the city I felt a strange separation from the rush of life below. When it came time to descend, I chose to come down backwards to avoid vertigo. I overheard some Japanese tourists joking amongst themselves as they stared over the edge of the staircase. Amid their foreign conversation, I distinctly heard the word "bungi" mixed in with the laughter. I rappelled down to the shallower stairs and returned to the river dock.

## Snake Farm

The snake farm is a small section of Bangkok's Thai Red Cross Centre where inoculations take place. The snake serum production centre collects poison from a large number of venomous snakes, among them the lethal King cobra. The venom is then used to produce antidotes for bite victims.

The reptiles sat coiled in their enclosures, eyes watching intently, tongues extended as if tasting my presence. I stared at the beautiful creatures. Despite the snakes' beauty, a remote, unconscious fear of being bitten had my eyes darting into every corner, in case any residents had slithered free. In the centre of the complex, uniformed guides were directing people toward a small amphitheatre.

The lecture started off with information about the facility and its mandate. Then trainers began bringing some of the resident snakes into the open.

"These first snakes are the Siamese cobras." The guide described the two creatures now slithering onto the inner floor of the arena. The handler calmly guided the creatures into the centre of the floor. The man then began to slowly circle the cobras and the snakes' heads immediately lifted from the floor, hoods extended as they both followed every move the handler made. I watched the hypnotic dance. The cobras moved in exact synchronicity, flashing their tongues with a hiss. They would occasionally attempt to strike but for the most part remained quite calm. After a few minutes one of the snakes was taken back to its cage.

The handler then carefully grabbed the other by the head and neck and performed the milking technique used to extract venom. The creature twisted and contorted its body, attempting to release itself from the man's grip. Its open mouth and fangs were forced onto the side of a small glass container in the handler's other hand. Immediately, milky-white liquid began to stream down the glass surface. A small pool of liquid death gathered in the bottom of the vessel.

"This snake might scare you," said the host. "This snake is the King cobra, biggest of the cobras. This particular specimen is almost four metres long." The crowd of spectators gasped audibly as all eyes focused on the giant serpent sliding silently into the arena. It stopped in the centre and looked up at us with piercing eyes. I stared into the face of hissing death.

"Cobras, in general, are only able to strike from where they have lifted themselves into the hooded position. However, the King cobra can still move forward with great ease as well as strike." The guide had a hint of caution in his voice.

The giant serpent emitted a hiss like an overloaded steam vent as it stood facing us. A black forked tongue waved frantically in the air and the long, tapered tail twitched slightly next to the trainer's foot. The man stood ready to react at any sign of trouble. The cobra's stare was cold as ice and the guttural sound of hissing made my skin crawl. The snake swayed to an eerie rhythm, scrutinizing the crowd, as if looking for a weak link at which to strike first. During the show, the keepers had allowed some of the tourists to take photographs from the edge of the floor area. Cameras were clicking as the monster silently stared back. A scary demonstration of the snake's speed came next.

The King shifted its body and sprang toward the people in the front row. The tourists fell back on themselves in panic and haste, their cameras flying through the air. Some cameras made audible cracking sounds as they hit the cement floor. Others were caught in the air by people in the seats behind. Fortunately, the trainer had been able to grab the snake's tail just before it reached its target, preventing the great beast from striking one man in the leg. The snake had missed only by a few centimetres. The near-victim gazed, sheet-white, from his reclaimed seat in the stands.

A series of other snakes were paraded in front of us, including non-poisonous species. Finally, we were shown two large Burmese pythons. One was passed around and dangled around various necks, including mine, for photos while the other was put through the rigours of a feeding demonstration. The keepers force fed eight or ten chicken legs down the serpent's gullet using a pair of long metal tongs. I felt sick watching the raw chunks of chicken carcass being rammed down the python's throat.


## Patpong

During the Viet Nam War this district was a favourite stop-over for soldiers seeking R & R away from the battlefront. Since that time, Patpong has grown into a major centre for the Thai sex trade, selling the services of young girls forced into prostitution.

When first planning my trip to Thailand, I had entertained fantasies about going into some of the brothels. That was until my research revealed that at least eighty percent of Thai prostitutes are HIV positive (along with Hepatitis B and C). The majority of the clientele are foreign tourists on sex holidays. The mostly older men come specifically to engage in sex with these young girls. The thought made me ill and I had finally come to the decision that I would not take part in the "rape" of these young women. And yet I was strangely compelled to enter the seedy area.

"Hello, hello, you want good time today?" A woman in skin-tight blue pants sat at the bar sipping her morning breakfast. She looked as if she had just finished the busiest night of her life. A smouldering cigarette dangled from her lips.

"Thanks, anyway." I put on my best fake smile and walked past her. She continued to attempt to entice me with her wares but I ignored her calls.

I walked past a maze of club marquees, lights flashing dimly in the daylight, not knowing what to expect. Without warning a young man emerged from a small doorway.

"Hey, you want to meet some beautiful women today, sir?" He walked up to me and engaged me in conversation. "Very nice girls for you, sir," he continued, urging me to follow him into his brothel. The temptation was strong as he described the women kept in reserve for special clients.

"How much?" I asked.

"With nice lady for good time—one thousand *baht*," he replied, tugging my sleeve.

"Look, okay?" I asked him. "If I don't want, okay?"

Nodding his head in agreement, he pulled me toward the door of a small hotel across the street. The temptation was too great. I felt like a fish drawn to the bait.

"Yes, okay sir," he said reassuringly. I followed him up a narrow stairway and down a dimly lit corridor leading toward the back of the building. At the end of the passage I was directed into a small lounge. The entire room was done in red-coloured paint and furnishings. Ushered to a couch, I was handed a cup of hot tea. After a few moments I was led to the other end of the room where a window allowed me to look into another room. Looking through the glass, I saw an entire roomful of gorgeous young women dressed in nothing more than bikinis. They all sat on tiered benches which faced the window. Each woman had a large numbered tag attached to her clothing that was big enough to be read from across the room. Their bodies were sleek and dark, their complexions flawless. They were so young. I guessed the oldest to be no more than eighteen or nineteen years old.

The expressions on the faces of these young women ranged from fear and depression to boredom and absolute exhaustion. Many of these girls are sold to brothels by their own families and are kept there against their will for years. I looked into their faces and could comprehend only a hint of the painful lives they lived. The longer I looked the more I wanted to leave this place, the strong desire for sex extinguished by feelings of compassion. I knew I could never bring myself to abuse any of these caged beauties. I finally turned to the young pimp and handed my mug to him.

"Sorry, I just can't decide. Maybe some other time." I walked out of the room and down the stairs to the street. The man followed me outside, offering discounts and special deals to draw me back inside.

# CHAPTER 3: KANCHANABURI, THAILAND

## Early Train
*Tuesday, November 15, 1994*

My morning path through the alleys was accompanied by the smell of fresh bread and fruit on the market shelves. I bought a bag of huge pineapple chunks to quell my rumbling stomach, tripped over a dog or two and walked down to the dock, searching for the boat to the opposite bank. The express boats continued to mar the pier and any unwary patrons with their slimy sludge. A friendly Thai woman sat down beside me on the wooden bench and greeted me with a bright smile.

"Where you go?" she asked, staring at the folded map in my hand.

"Kanchanaburi," I replied. "Do you know which boat I should take to get to the train station?"

She pointed across the water to a small dock on the far bank. "You need go there. Your boat coming soon."

Directing my eyes with her finger, I could see a small boat slowly making its way downstream. It seemed to be going back and forth across the river like a yo-yo, stopping at every pier along the route. Finally, the tiny vessel nudged up to the dock and the woman ushered me to the gunwale, telling the conductor where I needed to go.

"Thank you," I said and turned to wave to her from the deck of the boat. The tiny woman just smiled and disappeared into the large dockside crowd.

As the boat floated lazily toward the far bank, I noticed a large water compound full of large boat houses. Sticking out of one end of the protective frames, the guilded prows of the Royal Barges sat silent in the morning sun. These large ships carry the King and his entourage. The barges' dragon heads shone in the daylight, waiting patiently for their Royal master.

The Thon Buri station was just a short walk from the dock on the opposite bank of the river. I found my way to the ticket office by the main door and joined the queue. An old man sat behind the glass, trading tickets for cash, his face expressionless.

"Kanchanaburi." I held up one finger to indicate that I was a solo passenger. I dug the equivalent of two dollars out of my wallet and slid the coins under the window. He handed me a ticket and, with a slight nod of his head, indicated that my train was at the main platform.

"What time?" I pointed to my wristwatch to help him to understand what I was asking. He clearly understood and, with a slightly more urgent nod of his head, he again indicated the train I was to board. This time I looked over and saw the back end of the train begin to move slowly out of the station. Jamming my ticket between my teeth, I sprinted down the platform, packsack and guitar tossing loosely in my grasp.

Running alongside the train, I threw my belongings into the open door of the last car. With my arms now free, I gripped the brass railing and hauled myself into the train. I gathered together my belongings, found my way into the car and sat down with a loud sigh on a cushioned bench. My timing had been perfect. The train was gaining speed as it left the dusty terminal and snaked westward out of the city.

I leaned out the window, watching the groves of palm trees passing by and feeling the cooling breeze on my face. My view and my seat were great, at least until the conductor entered the car. He stared at my small ticket and told me I was in the wrong car. I possessed a third-class ticket but had found my way into a second-class coach. I was escorted to another car containing only bare wooden benches.

We passed through the village of Nakon Pathom, home of the tallest Buddhist monument in the world, a *prang* nearly one hundred and thirty metres high. I could see the tip of the spire sticking up above the trees as the train rolled through town. Reading further in my guidebook, I learned more about Kanchanaburi, the Bridge Over the River Kwai and the surrounding area. It sounded perfect and I longed for a quieter setting in which to rejuvenate my senses.

It being Tuesday, it was my day to ingest my favourite thing of all—Larium. This malaria medication is quite a foul experience. Warnings from the health department that gave me the stuff told me of people losing their hair after taking it for more than three months. The stories made me wonder if I wanted to take it at all. I ended up ceasing treatment close to the end of my journey, mostly because of its awful taste. Today, however, I would learn that use of this medication required a substantial amount of water.

I had sipped only a few mouthfuls as I swallowed the bitter pebble. With only a little moisture to assist its descent, the pill became stuck halfway down my oesophagus and began to burn, making me feel really sick. My head began to swim as the combination of Larium and my hangover pinned me to the wooden bench. I felt a sense of urgency as I tried to come up with remedies for the problem.

The trouble with the pill was that it disintegrated as soon as I put it in my mouth. I tried to wash it down with more water, but with no result. I continued to feel ill as the medication roasted a hole in my chest wall. I ate some food but it did not do much to alleviate the discomfort. I finally decided that all I could do was just deal with the feeling and soon it would pass. Bracing up against the window, I was cooled by a slight breeze.

My sick feeling worsened whenever the train passed by farms. I could smell the animal excrement amplified by the tropical heat. About halfway to Kanchanaburi we had the fortune of stopping right next to a pig farm.

The unmistakable aroma of swine shit swept over me like a wave of revenge set upon me for some wrongdoing in this or, perhaps, a former life. I would have been able to stand it had the train not decided to stop there for half an hour.

I kicked up dust as I climbed off Kanchanaburi's train platform and headed for the river. A young man on a rickshaw bicycle taxi pulled up beside me, offering transport. I accepted his offer and hopped into the back of his limo. He happily took me to the River Guest House, my chosen riverside accommodation. Pulling up next to a high wall of stairs on the banks of the Kwai, the driver pointed to a quiet bungalow nestled along the river's edge, standing on stilts in the shallow water. All the huts were connected by a maze of elevated boardwalks. The sun reflected brightly off the surface of the river.

On the far side of the bungalow a large floating deck was tied to the boardwalk. I found myself a comfortable spot on the platform and watched life float by on the current. A small group of kids were splashing in the river off to my right. Every once in a while someone would paddle past me, giving me a curious glance. In the distance a range of mountains paralleled the river and grew hazy in the heat. Further upstream I could just make out the contours of a railroad bridge spanning the river.

"That must be the bridge!" I thought to myself.

Across the river sat numerous and very popular floating discotheques. These large barges are roughly fifteen by thirty metres and carry a bar, sound system and light show onboard. Patrons from Bangkok charter them on weekends, cruising up and down the River Kwai. I had read that the party crowds created a lot of noise at night, especially on weekends. Workers were busy moving one of the barges as I watched from the deck, a noisy boat pulled the vessel by a long cable. With the volume of the towboat's engine, the lead line to the barge needed to be quite long in order for guests to hear the music. The afternoon waned and the river continued to buzz with activity.

## Companions

"Need a beer to cool you off, mate?" a thick English accent asked from behind me.

"Hey, thanks." I turned, grasped the cool can and shook the hand of the man attached to the voice. He stood tall and thin with very tanned skin. Dark sunglasses hid his eyes. A blonde woman stood with him on the boardwalk. They were both dressed in shorts and shirts and carried bags of beverages and snacks. They had come to the river's edge to enjoy the last hours of the day. I made room on the platform and introduced myself. When they learned that I was Canadian, they scoffed at the sheer number of us they had met here in Asia.

Stuart and Melanie were on the start of an eighteen-month journey that would see them return home to England in the spring of 1996.

"We started up in Chiang Mai about a month ago." Melanie described their itinerary. "Next week we're heading south to the Thai Gulf Islands, eventually ending up in Australia."

"We should be able to get some work down there to make extra money," said Stuart. "I want to stay there for six or seven months."

"Where will you go after Australia?" I was intrigued by their plans.

"Back through India, Afghanistan and Saudi Arabia," replied Stuart. Recalling a trip I had taken to Egypt back in 1984, I suggested a stop at the pyramids.

"Well, I really want to go to Yemen," said Melanie.

"Yemen? That's on the southern tip of Saudi Arabia, isn't it?" I asked.

"Yeah, man," she said, giggling. This phrase was Melanie's

favourite for as long as I knew her. She promised to use it until she stepped onto Yemenese territory. The happy laugh which accompanied the words had me in stitches.

"One of the islands we want to visit has good scuba diving. We want to do a course when we get there," Melanie said, excitedly.

"You're welcome to join us if you like. I'm sure we would have a great time down there," said Stuart. I immediately had a good feeling about these two strangers. I felt compelled to join them on their journey. I thanked them for the offer and agreed it would be the perfect sojourn for all of us as we headed southward.


## Erewan
*Thursday, November 17, 1994*

"Hurry up, you twerps, the bus is going." Melanie was sticking her head out of the window of a wretched old bus in the middle of the small town's bus station. Stuart and I had been distracted by sights in the busy market square on the way to the bus depot. We jogged across the roadway, paid the fare, and took the seats Melanie had saved for us.

We were taking a two-hour trip west of Kanchanaburi for a day of hiking in Erewan National Park. The description given to me by Paula back in Bangkok remained clear in my mind and both Stuart and Melanie had expressed interest when I told them about the place. This lush area has a wonderful system of hiking trails and good swimming in the river's many pools. The bus drove through lush green forest, the landscape rugged and beautiful. Part way into Erewan National Park we passed a few large private mansions sitting along the edge of a large lake. High fences enclosed the properties. On the hillside behind the buildings the fence had become nothing more than a trellis for the mass of vines sneaking in from the dense forest beyond.

"Look at those bloody houses!" exclaimed Stuart.

"Looks like only a few people get to live like that around here." I pictured an average house in any small village, nothing close to these huge homes. The mansions faded into the distance as the bus continued to climb into the mountains. Many new passengers joined us as we passed through several small villages further upriver. Locals always interacted with us, bright smiles accompanying their friendly questions. The valley narrowed and the bus finally entered the Erewan park gate and a large parking lot.

The air was cool and moist as we walked into groves of trees. The dense deciduous trees were alive with small birds singing loudly as we made our way to the park centre building. We could see the movement of branches but it was hard to spot the creatures as they flew from tree to tree.

The Erewan River forms a large pool near the gates of the hiking trail where we began our walk. From here the trails snake along the edge of the water and up into the forest behind. We hiked past a series of waterfalls into a large area of layered pools formed from solidification of minerals in the water. The river spilled down through the waterway as if over a multi-layered staircase stretching far back into the forest.

Leaving the trail, we walked into the stream of refreshing water and climbed through the maze of layered steps along the hardened edge of each pool. Our sandals found a solid grip on the water-covered ledges. Following the flow of water, we reached the upper pools. We climbed for another short distance and came upon yet another open glade full of crystal clear pools. We eventually passed through seven distinct levels. Returning to a large open group of pools halfway back to the gate, we stripped to our shorts and dove in for a refreshing swim. Our delighted shrieks echoed through the surrounding trees. Strong currents pulled us over small ledges and threw us into the pools below.

At one point, Melanie let out a scream. She had been swimming in the largest pool and encountered a school of fish. They had closed in around her in the water and begun to gently nibble at her legs. I told her to count her fingers and toes when she came out of the water. She laughed nervously. It wasn't long before Stuart and I experienced the same thing. The gentle nibbles of tiny mouths caressed my legs as the tiny fish surrounded me. I hoped that there were only these fish in the water and kept my eye out for anything larger lurking below.

A group of English tourists came upon us and, when they saw us swimming, immediately decided to join us. One member of the party was quick to enter. Standing up to his waist in the cool water, he told his friends how wonderful it was. Meanwhile, the fish had discovered him and were creeping toward his naked legs. Having had no warning about the curious residents, the man suddenly ceased his revelry and now possessed a look of shock as the first fish approached his bare skin.

"What's that, then?" One fish began to nibble on his hairy legs and then another.

By this time, his imagination had probably conjured up a few alligators or water snakes. We could see him attempt to reach the edge of the pool. As he did so, he lost his grip and his balance and tumbled back into the deeper water. He panicked and fought his way out of the tranquil pool. By this time we were all in fits of laughter. I could have sworn he came out of the water with a booster rocket tied to his butt, what with all those gaping jaws gnashing the water under him.

The day had faded to dusk by the time we returned to Kanchanaburi. The dust swirled around the bus as it pulled into the station. I shook my two companions to life and sleepily they followed me out the rear doors.


## Loi Krathong

The large town square surrounding the depot was bustling. Locals were busy preparing for a big event, an annual festival. We had all heard about the event and were excited to see it finally arrive. It was time for the festival of Loi Krathong.

This festival is celebrated throughout Thailand. It is a water festival and takes place on the full moon in November each year. The heart of the festivities revolves around the *krathongs*—small, colourful floats that celebrants set on the river at midnight. Bearing burning incense and candles, the tiny floats represent an offering to the rivers, to give thanks for the recent rains and bountiful harvests. Each *krathong* is made from a slice of banana tree decorated with flowers and leaves. Participants place their *krathongs* into the river after saying prayers, allowing the current to carry them away.

Walking toward the river we could see people setting up tables on the roadside. On these tables were hundreds of tiny decorated *krathongs* adorned with candles and incense sticks. The smell of rich food carried on the warm breeze, mixing with the exhaust fumes of the many vehicles delivering last-minute items to their appropriate places. Time was short and soon the event would begin. The sun fell away and left a dark sky until a brilliant full moon lifted itself out of the horizon's hiding place.

River Guest House was a noisy place when we descended the stairs from the upper road. The staff were having their own version of a celebration, lighting a barrage of fireworks over the river from the float. Shouting from the verandah followed the loud cracks of powder.

"Let's head back uptown and check out the riverside festivities," I suggested to my friends. It was guaranteed to be an event to be part of.

We walked back to join the local celebrants in the festivities. The upper road ran through the temple grounds, leading into the town centre. The main street turned parallel to the river and down to a large park by the riverbank. A second street cut to the left, into a shopping area. Well lit, the alley held a lot of promise for what we needed to purchase—fireworks.

Almost every store carried them and the variety was almost infinite. I wandered through a maze of tables covered in boxes filled with explosive items. I fished through the boxes and collected a few firecrackers, including small paper triangles, cherry bombs, and smaller ones with angled wings attached to them. Painted blue with yellow stripes, these were designed to look like bees. They looked like fun so I took a few extra along for good measure. Other fireworks sold here seemed best left alone. One set of giant clay pots with giant fuses resembled cannon balls.

"Maybe another time," I thought to myself. Equipped with enough ordnance to last the entire evening, I followed my friends down to the riverbank.

We stopped to watch a kickboxing match in progress. After a time I felt restless and reached into my small bag, pulling out one of the bee-shaped firecrackers. The majority of the crowd was facing the ring in front and a large open space was created behind us.

Stuart's attention was diverted by the fight as I caught Melanie's eye. I flashed the small bomb at her with a wink. She smiled and pointed down to a spot just two metres behind her boyfriend's heels. I placed the device on top of an empty beer can and held my lighter to the wick. Melanie engaged Stuart in conversation just as the first stage of the propellant went off. I had no idea what this thing was going to do and Stuart had no idea what was in store for him.

The "bee" lifted itself off the surface of the can with a shower of bright white sparks emanating from one end of the small cardboard tube. The wings on the cylinder acted like a propeller, sending it up into the sky. I recall that Stuart's breathing corresponded with the flyer's first stage—a long, slow inhalation of cool night air. Sparks were now landing around him as he slowly turned to investigate. He never did see the device because just as he turned, the main load of fuel exploded. The second stage was a much bolder shower of coloured sparks that lifted the cylinder ten to fifteen metres straight up. The shower of fire sent Stuart to the ground in a heap. He scrambled up, grabbing onto Melanie only to find her in fits of laughter. When the smoke had cleared, we inquired as to whether perhaps Stuart had wet himself in the middle of the scene. He told us that these fireworks were a sure-fire cure for low blood pressure.

The excitement gained momentum as midnight neared. People prepared to launch their *krathongs* into the river's current at the stroke of twelve. By now most had been sold and the once-full tables dwindled to just a few along the river road.

"It's hard to decide which one to buy. They are all so beautiful." I was taking my time to pick my *krathong*. The fresh flowers smelled sweet and the rich colours were sublime. Once we had chosen, we made our way down to the riverbank and took our places as midnight approached.

"What are you going to ask for, John?" asked Melanie as she sat beside me on the sandy bank. She was cradling a large *krathong* that the couple had bought. She had just lit the sticks of incense and the smoke began to waft past our noses.

"I have been thinking a lot about why I am here alone and where this journey will take me," I said.

"Are you afraid to be alone?" Stuart inquired.

"Sometimes I feel more at fault than afraid. I feel that I am to blame for everything that happened between my wife and me." I sat on the ground, thinking hard. "I feel like I am in exile as a way of punishing myself, by running from my relationship." Melanie put her arm around my shoulder. "Don't blame yourself for this. These things happen all the time and people forget that it takes two people to create this kind of situation." Her voice was gentle and this helped to quell the nervous feeling in my guts.

"All the events that brought you to this place at this time are for a reason. All you have to do is to discover what that reason is. Look for positive things rather than the negative ones that make you feel the way you do now." Her voice was like that of an old sage I would have expected to see in a secluded temple. She smiled back at me.

"Sounds like a good opportunity to find your own soul again," Stuart added. "Did you ever feel that you had lost yourself in the relationship?" When he asked me that, it seemed that he had taken the thought right out of my mind.

"That's it! That is exactly how I feel," I replied with excitement. The discussion had grounded me. "I had to leave to find myself again." I felt as if a huge weight was lifting off my shoulders.

Looking up I could see many local people launching their little boats into the stream. The midnight hour had come. Accompanying the release of *krathongs*, groups of people started to sing songs and hug each other.

Melanie, Stuart, and I followed the throngs to the river's edge. I set my *krathong* into the cool water. Incense and paraffin smoke rose past my face. Closing my eyes, I wished that my soul might be at peace. I trusted that I was in the right place and that I wanted to learn from the experience. I also asked God to look out for me on this journey and to keep me safe. I let the *krathong* slip out of my hand into the current and breathed deeply. It was a beautiful and serene sight. The tiny lights on our *krathongs* joining hundreds of others now set adrift in the river. Reflections from the water doubled and tripled the bright lights with a flashing twinkle. A few of the floats eventually tipped over, snuffing out the burning wax and disappearing in the darkness.

"Use this time to explore your dreams, too," Melanie said as she watched the lights.

I was at a loss for a moment. "Sometimes it feels like I have no dreams," I said.

Melanie was puzzled and asked me why I felt that way. I thought for a moment and then spoke. "Sometimes I feel like I am drifting just like these *krathongs*, with almost no sense of steering my own way." I added that I also felt I had been well blessed by a rich array of experiences so far in my life.

"Dreams are the fuel of the flame of human spirit. They are the things that keep you alive," Melanie said to me.

With this, I felt slightly uneasy, feeling that I was just wasting time. I tried to look past the feeling that I had run away from my problems and to go further inside. I yearned for my own voice, for my own unique power that would put me in the forefront of my own life. The first thing that came to my mind was my dream to play music professionally and make a difference in other people's lives, a dream that felt like an impossibility. Through talking to my companions, I felt more conscious of my lack of connection to my own power. I was inspired with a purpose. I would use these experiences to get in touch with my soul and get used to being in my own skin. With that, I would have the tools to rekindle the fire of creation. I felt renewed and refreshed at having met these good friends. It was only the beginning.

## Monk

I spent the next few days exploring the town. I rented a bicycle one hot Sunday and rode to a local temple that was at first hard to find. Even though I was navigating flat ground, the cycling was tough due to the heat. I took a few wrong turns but the scenic groves of trees and open fields by the river were enough reward.

When I finally arrived in the temple grounds I saw a long staircase ascending the side of a small mountain. The steps led to a small dark cave overgrown with thick foliage. The grounds were filled with busy souvenir shops and food vendors always ready to serve visitors. I leaned the bike against a tree and hoped that no one would "borrow" it, forcing me to walk home. Glancing around to see if I had been noticed, I walked to the steps.

At the top of the stairs the cave opened into the side of the rock wall. On the floor next to the entrance was a brass bowl containing small paper packets and sticks of incense. Ahead of me, inside the cave, a small monk stood in prayer. He reached down and picked out one paper packet and three sticks of incense before walking further. Taking my example from the monk, I reached down to the brass bowl at my feet.

Following the old man into the cavern, I watched as he approached a golden Buddha. Carefully, he opened the small envelope, revealing pieces of gold leaf. Placing smoking incense and a burning candle into the sand of yet another pot, he rubbed the gold onto the statue with his fingernail. The golden figure looked ragged from the many golden flakes placed by worshippers. As the monk rubbed the gold onto the statue, he noticed me watching from a distance. He turned and gestured me to join him. I walked up and stood beside him in front of the gold Buddha. The monk was friendly as he mumbled something in Thai, lightly chuckling. He guided me to the idol and prompted me in his best sign language to light the incense, apply the gold, and then pray. The old man stood in silent prayer for a few moments. I performed the ceremony as he had shown me and when I looked up from my prayers, the monk had disappeared. I closed my eyes and continued my own ceremony. Aside from praying for a safe journey, I jokingly prayed that my bicycle would still be outside the cave.

Emerging from the shady refuge, I found my transport had been blessed by the gods. I happily jumped onto the seat and pedalled back up the riverbank road into town.


## Remnants of War

Most tourists I had met in Kanchanaburi were German or Dutch. I found quite a number of the Dutch visitors wanted to visit the local war museum. It seemed they were most passionate about remembering the fallen soldiers of the war. During World War II the Japanese had imprisoned a huge number of Allied prisoners here, using them to build a major railroad supply line into Burma. Working under terrible conditions and given little food, many prisoners died at the side of the tracks from exhaustive overwork.

The J.E.A.T.H. (Japan, England, Australia, America, Thailand, Holland) Museum has a concise display of artifacts and many photographs of life in the camps. It looked like a horrid place.

"Why does it take a museum like this to remind us of the tragedy of war and the terrible things that are done to our fellow human beings?" I thought to myself. I returned to the silent riverbank and thought long of young lives tortured and lost.

Further upriver, the Death Bridge was now a major tourist attraction. The old relic's grim historical significance was being sold to visitors in the form of placemats, key tags, ashtrays and T-shirts. The countless souvenir shops nestled next to the bridge along the banks of the Kwai.

I walked to the middle of the span and stood looking down into the slow-moving water. I imagined the thunderous noise of Allied bombers flying in low over the trees and destroying the vital link over the river. Faint marks on the concrete supports showed evidence of the attack. The small holes made by exploding shells and bullets had been repaired when the bridge was rebuilt after the war. Despite the suffering of the prisoners during construction, the railway increased transportation and agricultural production in the area.

It had been a wonderful, restful stay here in Kanchanaburi. It felt like a small lifetime here by the river. I found the peacefulness of this place had calmed my fears, leaving room for positive growth. The memory of Kanchanaburi would remain long after my next adventure.

# CHAPTER 4: PASSAGE TO BANGKOK

*Monday, November 21, 1994*

I stared out the window of the train as the rhythmic sound of the wheels and tracks lulled me into a half-sleep. Small villages along the railroad provided only brief stops as the train made its way toward Bangkok.

"One more day," I thought to myself. "I should have stayed one more day." I regretted my departure from the quiet town on the banks of the Kwai. I pictured the lush forests of Erewan and the cool, refreshing water. I could have easily stayed longer, relishing in the tranquility of the river. However, it was time to move on. I stared back and saw the mountains around Kanchanaburi become obscured by thick haze and distance.

Despite my return to the city, my stay would only be a few days. Since I was heading south, I wanted another chance to do some more shopping. I loved the markets of Khao San Road and since I would keep heading southward, this would be my last chance to take advantage of them. I also wanted to catch up to my friends and make sure our travel plans were set in place. Melanie and Stuart had returned to the city the day before and my task was to find them in the maze of guest houses. Melanie had left me a short list of potential hotel choices before leaving Kanchanaburi. They had to arrange extensions on their visas before heading south and planned to be in Bangkok until Friday.

I climbed off the train and was greeted by a typical Bangkok afternoon. The sweltering heat was heavy in my lungs as a brisk wind blew dust and dirt into my face. I found my way back to the river and returned to the hotel district of Banglamphu. I found space in a small hotel next to the Merry V. My Green Guest House room was a bit smaller, a bit dirtier, but I soon called it home.

As I sat out front of my hotel, planning the search for my friends, I overheard some people who had just returned from Koh Phan-Ngan, one of the Thai Gulf Islands we were planning to visit. I listened in.

"The full moon party was the most unbelievable thing I have ever seen." One young woman was telling her friends of her experience attending the party at Hat Rin. "There must have been seven thousand people on the beach."

"What about cops?" inquired another young woman seated next to her.

"All over the place but they were easy to spot." She laughed. "They were the only ones on the beach wearing proper shoes and carrying walkie-talkies." A collective chuckle rose from the table.

"Just be careful with drugs if you indulge down there," the first young woman warned her friends. "There's no mercy if they catch you and the first thing they want is your cash."

Apparently there had been a lot of publicity around the country about the notorious reputation of the drug scene. Any and all types of drugs used to achieve some sort of buzz could be purchased at a bargain basement price. As a result, police would patrol the area searching for people in possession of illegal substances. Many other areas of the country apparently lose a great deal of tourist business once a month as throngs of party devoted travellers take part in their own version of walking to Mecca. There was a rumour that extra police were being sent to Hat Rin to cash in on the poor unfortunates caught in the act. I also heard that the arrest and jail portion of the equation can be avoided if you have enough money to bribe the police into letting you go. The typical fine for being caught with even a burned-out roach in your hands was said to be well over two thousand dollars US. Lack of sufficient funds was likely to gain you a free trip to the legendary Bangkok Hilton, the nickname of a large prison in Bangkok where foreign travellers do time for drug offences. Not a good place to end up on a holiday.

## Sights and Sounds
*Tuesday, November 22—Thursday, November 24, 1994*
It wasn't hard to find my friends. I began my search on crowded Khao San Road and went first to the Hello Hotel where I saw the pair sitting at a large table in the restaurant, amongst a crowd of other travellers. By the time I joined them they were well on their way to completing their first bottle of Mekong whiskey.

"Here, John, do your best," slurred Stuart as he passed me the semi-empty container and a fresh glass of cola. My body shuddered as I recalled my previous experience with this witch's brew. Reluctantly, I mixed a refreshment for myself and pulled a chair up to the crowded table. The early evening air was cool and I ordered a meal so that the Mekong would be held at bay for at least a short time.

"Pretty nasty stuff, really," Melanie said as her bloodshot eyes examined the remnants of her cocktail in the bottom of the tumbler.

"Mel, that's the understatement of the month," I chortled.

The night continued with (unfortunately) more bottles of the evil liquid being uncapped at our table.

Occasionally we would take breaks and wander through the crowded marketplace. Even at this hour there was a buzz of business. Day and night the vendors were hustling, dealing and smiling. My senses were flooded with sights, sounds, smells, and tastes of everything from food to brightly coloured clothing.

Clothing, jewelry, fabrics, T-shirts, knick-knacks, books, stickers, flags, toys, postcards, and electronics passed by my eyes as I walked the narrow sidewalks. After a while my head begin to spin, the dizziness accentuated by the whiskey.

All of this mixed with the strong and healthy aromas of a great variety of foods being sold by street vendors.

Of all the foods, I discovered a dessert that could not be missed. A tiny woman stood by a small stand with a large, flat grill. I watched as she served a customer in front of me. She produced a small ball of dough that she began to slap repeatedly on a wooden cutting board. The dough ball slowly expanded into a large thin crepe. She threw it onto the hot grill and deftly sliced and tossed bananas on top of the cooking dough. When enough bananas had been added, she folded each of four edges into the centre, flipped it over, and grilled it until each side was golden brown. When she finished, it was pulled off, cut up, drizzled with sweetened condensed milk, and handed over with a smile. I promptly approached her and ordered two, paid and wandered down the road, the warm sweetness sticky on my fingers.


*Wednesday, November 23, 1994*

In the morning, I functioned rather slowly. It was no surprise considering how I was feeling. I was never quite sure whether it was the alcohol in the drink or the chemicals apparently added to prevent spoilage in the heat. Either way, it was causing a bit of a low energy response from my body.

Stuart and Mel wanted to discuss our Friday departure. We picked a place just a stone's throw from my hotel, just at the corner. I made our appointment just on time. I could see the two of them entering the door as I walked up to the gate.

Our conversation turned to our departure southward. Melanie had heard that Koh Tao's weather had been fairly stormy recently. A debate revolved around the boat crossing which could be really rough if the weather was foul. We finally decided to undertake the trip and make it an adventure. We would travel to Chumphon by train and take a night boat to the small island of Koh Tao. Now that we had plans in place, the feeling of excitement began to grow in my belly.

Large posters for a Muay Thai (Kick Boxing) event that evening caught my eye from the corner of the restaurant. "We have to see this," I told my friends.

I took a walk to the stadium which was only a short distance from the main tourist office. As I walked by the office gates, I passed an attractive woman standing out front. She was busy studying a map of the city. I paused to offer assistance.

"Hello, my name is Catherine," she said as we introduced each other. The words poured out of her beautiful mouth like honey. I stared at her lips until she noticed and I shook my gaze to meet her eyes. She was Swiss, tall with shoulder-length brown hair. Her body was strong and healthy. Looking very much a "woman from the mountains," she looked like she could climb a peak before breakfast on her way to a triathlon. Her smile was infectious and bright.

Introducing myself, I soon learned that she was also heading for Koh Tao where her boyfriend worked as a divemaster. I informed her of our group's plan to make the night boat in Chumphon on Friday and invited her to join us on the journey.

"That sounds great. I may see you there. Thanks again for your help." She reached out and gently held my hand for a moment, looking into my eyes for a few intense seconds. I felt hypnotized by her beauty. Finally she broke her gaze and turned. I stood there watching as she slowly walked away down the street. I felt my knees melting under me as I carried on to the stadium.

All the way home I could not stop thinking about Catherine. It was as if her image had burned into the cells of my memory. I wondered why I felt such a sudden flood of emotion after meeting this person for only a few minutes. I was aware of my obvious physical attraction to her, but the feeling seemed to go deeper than that, a connection that I could not put my finger on.

I neared the Democracy Monument. As I walked across a wide street the clear image of Catherine was shattered by the sight of a dead dog near the roadside. I had seen this particular dog on the streets in the days before and always been repulsed by it. As I walked past a row of cars, I noticed the carcass lying in front of a small vehicle on the side of the road. I remember noticing that it had ceased to be a dog. It was now only a corpse, void of life energy. A stiff form with flies descending upon its eyes as the process of decay began to consume it in the heat. My next thought was that the struggle had finally ended for this spirit, sent to live out this life of suffering in a world where no one cared. I silently wished him peace and wondered how long his difficult life had been.

### Muay Thai

The inside of the stadium looked like a gladiator pit. The ringside seats at floor level were flanked by tiers of benches eight levels deep. All of this was enclosed inside a giant cage of fence wire which extended almost to the ceiling. Outside this area, cement steps served as extra seating.

There was a loud buzz in the air. I felt as if I was at the Thai version of an NHL hockey game. As we walked into the stadium we were each handed a list of the evening's competitors. The list showed ten fights, the fifth and sixth of which were highlighted. We figured these must be the featured acts. People began to file in carrying armloads of beverages and I thought to myself that tonight was going to get a little wild. The building held about eight thousand people and we could feel the growing energy, as if the air were turning electric. We could see a few people placing cash bets for their favorite fighters.

The sound of horns and drums officially opened the evening. Following that, the national anthem blasted out of the speakers. Fiercely proud of their King and the Kingdom, the Thais stood tall and sang their national song. I could feel the enthusiasm that they exuded and reflected on how I had seen some Canadians react to their own anthem with almost indifference. I picked up on the energy of people around me and rose to stand with them.

As the first fighters entered the ring there was a great roar from the spectators who were ready for a night of good kick-ass fun. The two fighters walked around the ring responding to the cheering throngs of fans. They both took part in a brief ceremony before the bout began. Each walked a circuit around the ring, stopping in each of the four corners, praying, and performing what looked like a ritual dance. As they passed a corner, they took several coloured ribbons from their armbands and hung them from the corner posts. When they were finished, the referee started the match.

The first two bouts were strictly boxing. In the third pairing, however, the legs began to fly. By the time the fourth round came along, the betting was getting heavier and tempers had begun to flare. The audience had clearly taken a dislike to something or some-one, possibly the referee. Cups full of ice and drinks began to shower down on the heads of lucky people in the one-thousand *baht* ringside seats. These projectiles were obviously aimed at the ring but the air time was never long enough.

"Ouch," I thought as a large plastic cup crashed into a man sitting ringside. Weighted by ice, the cup flew right-side up through the air and broke apart as it landed on the man's head. The sudden shock and shower of ice cubes made him jump. He turned and screamed at the area of the crowd from which it had come. People around him howled with laughter. We sat observing the scene from outside the cage, glad to be isolated from the craziness.

The next two rounds featured the best fighters. I watched in amazement as the men kicked with absolute precision, the force of the blows being completely absorbed or deflected. The exciting contests continued on into the seventh and eighth fights. By the end of the eighth round, we had seen enough and respectfully made our way down the crowded stairwells to the exits. We also wanted to avoid the rush after the last fight. I had expected the event to be very brutal, but had seen otherwise.

**Patpong II**
Piled in the back seat of a careening tuk-tuk, Stu and I held on for our

lives as the driver barrelled through the dark streets of Bangkok. Coerced by two drunk fellows from my hotel, we had been talked into joining their detour to Patpong to investigate the sex scene.

David, a humorous Englishman, had teamed up with Chris, a Dane whom we had met first in Kanchanaburi. Recruiting us as part of their men's club, they dragged Stuart and me into the chariot and shouted directions to the driver amid drunken laughter. Melanie happily saw us off, laughing as she returned alone to the hotel.

I always felt nervous crawling into one of these three-wheeled death traps and I wondered if Thais ever felt the same way. The tuk-tuk shot through spaces far too narrow and bounced off the occasional car along the way. The driver, his head down, was sure to get us to our destination safely, at least according to him. Amid our criticisms of his ability from the rear, we hung tightly onto our seats.

Upon arriving in Patpong, the driver immediately raised his price from his original quote. We dropped the exact amount of his original offer on the seat and left him knowing that we hadn't arrived in Bangkok yesterday.

"Good time, good time, sir?" I hadn't even placed both feet on the sidewalk when a greasy little man took me by the arm, hoping to rent one of his girls to me for just the right price.

"No, thanks," I said, shrugging him off. Three more salesmen circled us like vultures.

"Let's go to one of those clubs over there," suggested David, pointing across the road. "I hear the shows are terrific." He rubbed his hands together with excited anticipation.

A friend who had travelled here a few years ago had warned me to be careful which nightclub I chose to patronize. Promising a minimal fee at the door, some clubs extort more money out of you when you want to leave, threatening your well-being if you do not cough up. Having heard similar reports in recent days, we chose with caution.

There were several nightclubs in a row, all with crowded doorways. Flashing lights and neon danced around most entrances, giving the street a Mardi Gras atmosphere.

"You want to see the show?" asked a young man from his tiny booth.

He guaranteed us that we would have no hassles or rip-offs. He went on to explain that a company called the King's Group had purchased many of the clubs in an attempt to alleviate the very extortion racket we were trying to avoid.

"No problem, sir, no rip-off from King's Group. It's okay, just good time." He sounded reassuring. After paying our cover charge, we were directed to the door of a club called Pussy Galore. I laughed out loud at the name flashing brightly above the doorway.

"Well, this is it." I looked over at Stuart. We had arrived. All of the stories and rumours of Patpong's reputation were about to be confirmed. I felt a mix of emotions as I approached the door. I was intensely curious, sexually driven, and repulsed all at the same time. Loud music poured from inside the club. I penetrated the entrance as if it were a path of no return.

Entering a hallway, I noticed a large sign hanging from the wall. It was a list or menu of the various shows performed by the resident girls: Girl with Boy, Girl with Girl, Girl with Snake. Besides these acts, numerous anatomical acrobatics were listed: Smoking Cigarette, Writing Letter, and Shooting Balloon. I walked on to a steep staircase leading up to a noisy upper floor bar.

The first thing I noticed were the girls onstage in the centre of the room. About twenty-five girls, not many older than eighteen (some looked a lot younger) danced erotically, dressed in almost non-existent bikinis and high heels, looking quite bored. Each wore a round numbered badge pinned to the strips of material on her body. The numbers were large enough to be seen from across the room. Around the stage area men, mostly foreign travellers, were seated. They all looked older than forty-five. Some had two or three girls sitting with them, sharing drinks. I watched as the men groped and fondled the bodies of the young women.

"What a bunch of pigs," I thought. These men were only here to exploit and abuse girls for their holiday fun.

I was standing next to a row of older men ogling the girls on the stage. I saw one man hail a waitress and make quick pointing gestures to one of the dancers.

"Send me number twenty-three," he said in a thick German accent.

The waitress nodded and disappeared behind the stage. Before long, a beautiful young girl broke ranks with her workmates and walked over to the waiting man, her face expressionless as stone. Sitting beside him, she faked a smile as he handed her a drink and began to fondle her small breasts through the fabric of her bikini. She winced slightly but only for a moment. The man winked at his friends beside him.

"I think she'll be a good one." His eyes swept over her body from head to toe.

The man's comment enraged me and I stared at him with disdain. I thought about the high number of his fellow countrymen who come here looking to taste the sweet youth of Thailand. I saw this man as a symbol of all men who come here to, essentially, rape young girls. Deeper down, I recognized him to be only a reminder of my own sexual urges. Inside, I was as hungry for these young women as he was. My anger toward him was a reflection of my own struggle to keep my distance from the temptation of sex. I felt I wanted to protect this girl from the man's groping hands. I also felt like landing a heavy chair over his thick head. I finally chose to ignore him and followed my friends to an empty table in the back of the club.

Once the dancing was finished, some girls began to perform various stunts amid cheers of encouragement from the audience. A succession of women took the stage one by one and began to pull long strings of items out of their vaginas. Strings of flowers and beads were proudly shown off to the crowd after complete extraction. Some women came to the stage with large dildos and began playing with them sensually.

Finally, another woman climbed slowly up onto the platform and began pulling on yet another long string. This time, I looked hard and elbowed Stuart.

"Do you see that?" I said.

Stuart examined her stunt and turned to me. "No, can't be," he replied.

"I sure as hell hope not, for her sake," I said.

The young woman sat with legs spread toward her audience. Gingerly, she tugged at the bundle tucked inside her. I watched in horror as a string of razor blades was being carefully extracted one by one. When done she took a piece of paper, cutting it with each blade to prove that they were not fake.

As I sat and drank my beer, trying to further comprehend what was occurring before my eyes, I began to wonder about the numerous balloons hanging from the walls. At first, I thought that they were meant to create a kind of carnival atmosphere. I turned and began to speak with my companions, taking no notice of the girl who was making her way to centre stage.

BANG! The sound startled me as a balloon exploded over my head. I moved my eyes toward the girl onstage. She stood smiling at our table. Once I saw her, I soon understood what all the balloons were for. I watched as she calmy reloaded for another shot.

She stuck a straight pin through a small piece of folded toilet paper, making a sort of dart. This she inserted into the end of a normal drinking straw. When her straw was loaded, she picked her target and turned so that it was directly behind her. She then bent over so she could see between her legs, inserted the straw into herself, made a quick squeezing motion, and nailed another balloon. BANG!

At this point, I knew that I had seen everything. We all shook our heads in disbelief. She then picked another target that was on our side of the room. I prepared to hit the floor, ready to avoid a veritable AIDS missile flying in my direction. Fortunately (and strangely), she was extremely accurate with her craft. I suddenly had a bizarre vision of this woman's resumé.

The night got stranger by the minute as we were approached by numerous women selling their company. Even though the women were attractive and temptation had me teetering on the edge, the fear of AIDS had me convinced that I needed to stay away from them.

"Oh, come on. It'll be great. It's been awhile for me, anyway." David laughed as he searched the room for a suitable choice.

He picked one women who I thought may have been a wrestler at one time. She had a very muscular body. Despite her firm build, the many years of exploitive service hung heavy on her face. David started buying her drinks and soon was sure that he wanted to spend the night with her. Chris also chose a companion and the pair of men and their women disappeared for the remainder of the evening.

Stuart and I laughed with bewilderment as we watched the drunken strangers go off into the night. At 2:30 AM, after more beer and bizarre side shows, Stuart and I were ready to head home. Walking out into the street, we bargained for a ride.

I haggled with the first driver I saw and quickly talked him down to a normal price. We climbed into the backseat and the smoky tuk-tuk jerked forward, away from the Patpong circus, at the usual high speed. As we sped along the road and as I was carried away from the senseless scene, I felt sick thinking about the exploitation going on here. I felt sorry for all those women. I also felt a sense of guilt for supporting the place as a visitor. I was glad to have the experience behind me.

Stuart slumped in sleep against the railing and I occasionally checked to make sure that he wouldn't fall out of the cage. The weaving and bobbing continued as the driver sped through the night. There was almost no traffic in some parts of the city. The ever-present whine of the tuk-tuk motor echoed off the cement towers of a large industrial compound. The stench of the burning oil made me cough as I hung out the side of the machine to breathe cleaner air.

Suddenly, the tuk-tuk stopped. The driver cut the engine and the humid silence engulfed us under the amber streetlights. I felt a slight sense of fear as the driver turned around to face me. The sudden stop had woken Stuart from his slumber and he sat up.

"What's going on, John? Why did we stop?"

The little man pointed to us both as he spoke. "Ladies . . . you want ladies?"

Stu looked at me and we both broke out in a chuckle.

"No, we don't want a lady. We just want to go home to Khao San Road," I said.

"No, you want lady. I have lady good for you and your friend." He had confidence in his product.

"Look, I told you. We just want to go home." I started to get impatient.

Our verbal sparring continued for a good five minutes and all the while the man saw his commission from the local whorehouse get closer and closer to zero. He became increasingly insistent as the debate went on but finally backed down and let out a loud, deep breath. He slowly turned around in his seat, started the engine, and jerked back out into the middle of the roadway.

As we sped through various traffic circles, we soon began to recognize the landmarks close to home. I found it easier to keep my position on the padded bench in the back of the tuk-tuk by holding onto the ornate railings on each side of me. Stuart had his own firm hold on the metal rail as we entered a large roundabout. All at once, I saw a car move into our lane.

"Look out, Stu!" I automatically withdrew my right hand as did my friend just before the two vehicles slammed into each other and bounced back into separate lanes. Had we not moved our hands, they would surely have been broken. Thanking quick reflexes, we kept a more watchful eye back to Khao San.


## Drugs In Your Coffee, Sir?
*Thursday, November 24, 1994*

I was nosing around the Khao San street stands close to noon. It was hot and I was killing time. Vendors were always friendly, chatting with me and offering better prices each time I dropped in. I suddenly felt a tap on my shoulder.

"I'll buy you a coffee if I can look at your travel guide." An enthusiastic voice piped up from behind me. I turned to see a short, thin, dark man who looked like a Thai. His accent, however, was British.

"What?" I said back to him.

"I'm planning to travel to the north, but I have no book," he said. "I'd love to treat you to a coffee for the favour of letting me read your book." The request was bright and friendly and I immediately agreed. He suggested that we go to a café just up the street.

"Sure, why not?" I nodded and followed him across the road. Out of nowhere, we were joined by a woman introduced to me as the man's girlfriend. It was then I began to observe how the two acted as we walked. It was not the pace of relaxed travellers having a friendly chat, but one of absolute purpose; quick-paced and driven, with occasional glances backwards to see that I was still with them.

I had paid particular attention to a certain section in my travel book called "Dangers and Annoyances." There was a lot of talk in this chapter about with the issue of intentional druggings. I had also been told of the occasional event of this type by other travellers. Typically, an unwary tourist is quickly befriended by a local con artist. The friendship soon involves the offer of drinks and/or food which contain sleeping drugs, usually a lot of them. Once the victim is fucked up enough, the con artist usually poses as a good friend of the poor chap, openly taking him back "to the hotel." Once there, the tourist is stripped of his passport, money, traveller's cheques and, who knows, perhaps his anal virginity, among other possibilities.

My intuition told me to be cautious. Part of me wanted to turn and disappear into the crowd, but I was also very curious. I decided to play their game for awhile, to see just how far it would go. I tried to appear oblivious, following them through the moving cars as we crossed the road.

We walked into the Hello Restaurant and my "friend" chose a table out on the verandah while his girlfriend went inside to get us some coffee. I set my book within clear reach of the man and waited to see if he would actually pick it up.

"Great place, this," he said.

"Yeah, great," I said, just looking at him. He seemed to avoid my glance by staring at his hands folded in front of him. He started to chat about a lot of stuff that really had nothing to do with travelling. In fact, it sounded as if he had been around Bangkok for quite some time. I sat calmly and pretended to be oblivious to the fact that he was full of shit.

The woman soon appeared with only two cups of coffee. She set them down on the table and told her boyfriend that she suddenly felt sick and wanted to go back to the hotel room. She slowly rubbed her stomach and looked at me with a pitiful expression. The man told her to go home and that he would see her later. She walked out of the restaurant and looked back just once, as she was about to disappear into the crowd. I watched her secretly the whole time, glancing over the man's shoulder as we talked. She seemed surprised to see that I was staring right at her when she glanced back toward our table. Looking nervous, she turned and vanished.

At this point I was sure that this was a dangerous situation and that I must avoid drinking the coffee at all costs.

The man pushed the coffee to my side of the table. "Here, drink up!"

I told him I would get to it but made no move toward the cup. He stirred his own coffee nervously. He seemed agitated by the fact that I was in no hurry to start drinking. Further insistence on his part only increased my suspicion that there was a foreign substance lurking in the cup.

Finally, I could take no more of this shit. I had lost my patience at having my time wasted.

"So, do you actually want to look at my book or not?" I asked. We had already been sitting for five minutes and he hadn't even glanced at it, placed so close to his hands on the table.

"Oh, yes." His interest was suddenly piqued. He picked the book up and began to quickly flip through it, showing only a passing interest in the contents. He soon put the book back down and changed the subject.

I stood up at the table and looked right at him saying, "Nice try, loser. Try to mess with somebody else next time."

"What do you mean?" He feigned shock and confusion.

"You know damn well what I mean." I grabbed the mug and poured the contents into a potted plant next to our table. As the last drops left the cup, I could see remnants of some sediment dripping off the rim. I glared at the little weasel across from me, grabbed my book and made for the exit. I had gone no more than ten paces when I turned around to see where the man was. He was nowhere to be seen. I returned to see if he had made his way to the back of the restaurant, but he was gone.

# CHAPTER 5: CHUMPHON TRAIN

*Friday, November 25, 1994*

I sipped a rich cup of coffee as I waited for my friends at the Hello restaurant, noticing how good the sugar and cream tasted. "The only things that should go in a cup," I thought.

"Yeah, man! Ready to go?" Mel's exhuberant voice caught my attention. I turned to see her standing with Stuart across the street. They had just arrived from their hotel and had already hailed a tuk-tuk. Stuart was busy haggling for a price as Melanie gestured me to join them. I threw some money on the table, signalled the waiter, and carried my baggage to the waiting taxi.

Taking my last glance back down Khao San Road, I saw David the Englishman. He was looking right at me, a smouldering cigarette hanging loosely from his wry smile. His arm held a thumbs-up hand high in the air. He had crawled out from his Pat Phong rat's nest just in time to see us off. I returned the gesture until the tuk-tuk carried us around the corner and out into the traffic circle.

The ride was as wild as I had expected. The cheaper the fare, the faster and more aggressively the drivers seemed to go. Sort of a discount price with a scare-the-shit-out-of-you tax added onto the service. Once we reached the train station, I climbed out of the tuk-tuk, feeling the urge to kiss the solid ground in thanks for arriving safely.

A huge crowd milled about the station as we joined a slow lineup for tickets. The train wouldn't depart for an hour so we waited in a small café next to the ticket booths. Not hungry at the moment, I purchased take-out and set it down next to my guitar case. Once we were finally called to board the train, it took some time to find three seats together. Another twenty minutes passed before the old train groaned out of the station and past the shanty houses lining the tracks. The route took us along a water canal, the scenery quickly becoming monotonous with its palm fronds, brown water, and corrugated tin roofs. Smiling children watched our passing and waved from their tiny homes.

The Thais sitting next to us seemed eager to talk and used us as a private language lab. We also tried our best Thai phrases. I divided my time between engaging in conversation and watching the view as the

train left the outskirts of the city. All the way I could not help noticing the piles of trash and garbage strewn all along the tracks. The
majority of it was paper and plastic packaging courtesy of modern
convenience. Styrofoam seemed to dominate the contents of the litter.

The trip continued into the early evening when the conductor
made his rounds through the train to announce our arrival.

"Chumphon. Chumphon," he droned. Stuart shook Melanie out
of her sleep.

Dark night surrounded us as we climbed down onto the platform.

"Ferry for Koh Tao! Koh Tao!" Two men shouted out into the
crowd. What luck!

Stuart caught their attention. We were greeted and led outside to
a small waiting truck. It had a rugged roll bar in the box so I stood in
the back, hung on tight, and enjoyed the feel of the night wind on my
face as we drove to the dock. The large blue vessel sat silently in the
black water. Many other people were waiting on board. Tickets in
hand, we scrambled onto the vessel to find space. I was throwing my
bags onto the deck when I heard a woman call my name. I looked up
at her and she smiled.

"I was wondering if you would show up," I said. I walked across
the deck and sat down in front of her.

"I wondered the same thing about you," said Catherine. She
smiled and slid over to give me more room beside her. "Nice to see
you again."

Melanie and Stuart, noticing that I was slightly distracted, found
themselves some private space in the corner of the deck.

Catherine had ventured south toward Chumphon over the previous few days.

"I was going to hang around for awhile but I remembered your
offer and decided to take a chance on meeting up with you. I had
almost given up when it got so close to departure," she said.

"Glad you came. If I had known, I would have tried to get here
earlier." I smiled at her and leaned back against the deck wall.

"How long are you staying in Koh Tao?" she asked.

"Not sure..." I hesitated. "I guess I'll know when it's time to leave."

"Then where?" she said.

"Indonesia, eventually." I told her.

"So, why are you here in Asia?"

"A fresh start." I replied.

"Fresh start after what?"

"After separating from a relationship," I said. "I needed to be alone again, to find myself, and my dreams."

"Are you going back to her?" Catherine asked. When she asked the question, I went into deep thought.

Part of me wanted to return home after this journey with a renewed sense of who I was, giving me the power to rebuild my marriage but still retain all that I had rediscovered. Yet it seemed that a stronger part of me wanted to simply turn my back on the relationship and move on.

"I don't really know what is going to happen, Catherine," I said. "For now, I am just taking life one day at a time, trying to learn as much as I can about myself again." She nodded with sympathy.

"What about you? You mentioned your boyfriend is on Koh Tao."

Catherine looked sad as she answered. "We haven't seen each other for a long time. At least a year. I planned to stay here for a month or so but I don't know."

"You don't sound too happy about the idea." I said, speaking honestly.

"It has been so long and I am afraid that things may have changed." I thought she was about to cry.

"Perhaps we both need to take life one day at a time," I said.

"Maybe you're right." She leaned into me, giving me a gentle hug. I held my face against her neck and she smelled sweet.

The boat roared to life and slowly slipped out of the harbour into the darkness. The passenger count seemed large and I wondered if it matched the number of lifejackets onboard. I looked around and eventually, at one end of the deck, found a large set of marked lockers containing the safety equipment.

As the ship headed into open water, I went to the bow and looked out to sea. The waning full moon shone in the night sky. I could make out a few small islands ahead to port. The captain announced that we would not reach Koh Tao until 6:00 AM so I knew the voyage would take us a good distance off the coast. The cloud cover grew and soon shut out the moonlight.

I returned to my place on the deck and made a makeshift bed next to Catherine. As I bedded down, I shivered in the cool air. I dug up my sweatshirt for warmth. Catherine was already asleep beside me. Space was scarce and I had to squeeze myself close to her. Trying my best to not wake her up, of course, woke her up.

"Sorry, I didn't want to disturb you," I whispered.

"It's okay. I am cold, anyway." she said. She snuggled close to me for warmth. As we fell gently into the dark of sleep, Catherine held my hand in hers. "Goodnight," she whispered softly. She leaned over and lightly kissed my cheek.

### "Just sit right down and you'll hear a tale . . . "

I awoke around 2:00 AM to feel the boat tossing on a rough sea. I slowly sat up and noticed that I was not the only one awake. A few people near to me looked pretty green as they stared with concern into the dark water. I glanced down to see Catherine sleeping like a baby next to me. Her calm face made me smile. She looked so relaxed and contented.

Others were getting up because they had to throw up. One little boy about five years old was having a particularly hard time. I thought that he and his parents were German but I wasn't sure. He was fussing a lot and finally his father got him up and took him to the ship's lower deck.

An obnoxious young Dutch girl, seeing them leave their bunk, jumped into their spot. When the two came back, the father complained to this young woman who refused to move. The man and his son finally had to clamber up into an uncomfortable shelf-like bunk just above the woman. I thought she was being quite ignorant as I lay there silently protesting to myself. I wanted to say something in support of the other two but found myself slipping back into sleep. Before long I woke to the sound of the Dutch woman shrieking in disgust.

The young boy was still sick and had puked again. He had thrown up over the edge of the shelf, sending a copious stream of barf cascading onto the woman's head. Horrified, the young woman got up and gave the pair a dirty look before storming off to deal with a face full of vomit. I lay back on the deck and laughed. I had just witnessed a great example of karmic payback: God—1, Dutch Twit—0.

A trip to the toilet was soon on my agenda, not for sickness but for bladder relief. The sea was still rough as I hung onto anything I could find, climbing past people and objects. I reached the bridge and found stairs down to the lower deck. The wooden railing looked like one from a typical country house. This waist-high railing was the only thing between the dark, surging ocean and me. Through the door of the wheelhouse I saw the captain concentrating on his task of getting us through the stormy night. Just as I stepped toward the stairs, the sea threw the ship over the crest of a high wave and I felt myself being thrown forward. At the same time, the vessel rolled slightly to the left. I looked down and saw nothing but black water. Instinct kicked in and I put my arms out to grab hold of something solid. My hands felt the edge of the wooden rail and gripped like a vise. If the rail had been any shorter or if the boat had rolled over any further to the left, I would have been shark bait.

Catherine woke again when I squeezed in beside her. She looked at me with sleepy eyes for only a moment and pulled me close. We both drifted back into sleep.

# CHAPTER 6: KOH TAO, THAILAND

*Saturday, November 26, 1994*

A slight stirring woke me up. Catherine had shifted in her sleep and pulled herself away from my arm which draped over her shoulder. I lay there silent with my eyes open, listening. The tossing sea had grown quiet and the ship's motor was silent. I looked at my wristwatch. 5:00 AM. I sat up and surveyed the darkness. We had reached the island and were now sitting with the anchor down about two hundred metres from shore. Dawn was emerging. With it, silhouettes of coconut palms became apparent against a clear tropical sky. The air was cool and fresh. I breathed deeply.

I stood up, careful not to step on anyone around me, and climbed onto the gunwale of the ship. I sat and dangled my legs over the side. As the ship floated in the water, the sound of waves gently caressed the hull. My thoughts drifted back to the stormy night we had just passed and I was relieved we had reached the island safely.

At 6:00 the ship's motor awoke with a huff. The captain then slowly manoeuvred his vessel into the pier. Catherine finally stirred when the loud motor came back to life. I climbed back down to the deck to gather my things.

"Good morning, welcome to paradise," I said to her as she sat up to stretch.

"Hi," she said, rubbing her eyes.

"You slept through quite a storm last night," I said to her.

"Really?" She had not noticed it at all.

"Yeah, I almost ended up falling into it, too." I told her about my nocturnal trip to the toilet during the worst of the big waves. She listened with eyes wide.

"It's so beautiful." Catherine gazed up the clean sand beach stretching northward, away from the pier. Sunrise was striking the tops of the palm trees and a slight breeze had picked up.

The tiny village of Ban Mae Hat sat against the edge of the beach. The main street ran parallel to the water and a cluster of buildings hugged the shoreline. The great number of scuba diving shops, each with colourful signage, reflected the popularity of this sport. Groups of bungalows spread northwards along the beach and, behind them, thick coconut groves.

Once the crew had tied off, we descended to the boardwalk.

"Where are you staying?" I asked Catherine.

"I think the bungalow is on this beach," she said, checking her map.

I introduced Catherine to Stuart and Melanie as they caught up to us on the beach.

"And where are you staying?" she asked.

"Probably the south end of the island. There is supposed to be a nice quiet bay with a lot of places available." I tried to entice her to come with us, saying, "There are also good diving spots on that side of the island." She smiled at me and turned toward the first row of bungalows.

"Maybe I will run into you again."

A hint of expectation seeped into my thoughts as I watched her turn to leave.

"One day at a time, remember?" She kissed my cheek and walked down the dirt road without looking back. Despite being totally turned on by her, I put my feelings aside, wished her well and turned to join my companions.

"A little busy, were you?" Melanie grinned widely.

"Just a bit distracted, that's all," I laughed. My attraction to Catherine was undoubtedly engraved on my face. Stuart winked and grinned in silence.

The town's main intersection served as a temporary parking lot for small pickup trucks and local businessmen, all jostling for position. As the large crowd of passengers reached the beach, men in the trucks started shouting out bargain prices for space at their bungalows. Many had pictures of their facilities and tried their best to lure customers. Takers climbed into various vehicles and were chauffeured away into the coconut forest.

The three of us ignored the noisy exchange and instead chose breakfast by the water. We preferred to walk the few kilometres in the cool morning air. After eating, we made our way along a dirt track into the forest.

The road meandered through hilly terrain. Lush greenery filled the narrow ravines and coconut groves were plentiful. We walked past what was obviously a coconut processing plant, a massive pile of empty shells lying next to the small building. The road then sloped down to the south end of the island and the beach of Chalok Ban Kao. As we walked out onto the beach on the open bay we were greeted by a sudden downpour of rain.

Melanie shrieked as she scrambled for shelter. She discovered a small, dry porch and pulled our gear under with her. Once all my baggage was stored, I walked back out into the deluge and stood on the sand. Within moments I was completely drenched. Stuart joined me as Melanie looked on. The water was warm and ran in streams off my forehead and down into my mouth.

Without warning the downpour ceased. As if someone had closed a tap, the wall of rain turned to bright sunlight, and the clouds parted in the centre of the bay. I shook the remaining drops of water from my face and hair.

"That feels so good," I said. Stuart agreed, wringing his shirt out onto the sand.

Under a brightened sky, we continued our search for shelter. At one corner of the bay we came across a man sitting in the shelter of his bungalow, quietly watching our approach. When we were near, he came out to greet us.

"My bungalow has free showers, too," he said, chuckling. He had seen us standing in the rain. "I am Klong." He was a thick-set fellow with an infectious grin that held a burning cigarette. He ushered us inside.

"Welcome to Laem-Klong," he said to us. The place was named after himself and his sister, with whom he ran the business. I recognized him as one of the men we had seen at the dock earlier that morning.

"I have two cabins left in the back. Come, I will show you." He led us out the back of the kitchen and up a small hill directly behind. Walking beside me, Klong nudged me gently with his elbow, pointing to the guitar case hanging from my shoulder. "I have a good room for you."

The remaining cabins were tucked away above a tiny bathshed on the lower road which led back to the other side of the island. Standing on tall stilts, the cabin porches fairly hung in the air. They offered plenty of shade.

"Perfect," I said, sighing with contentment.

"Yes, perfect." Klong nudged me again as he handed me a key. He pointed upwards and I looked up at the front wall of my cabin and smiled.

A faded blue guitar hung off the front of the small hut. Many years of sun and rain had faded and cracked the blue paint. Absent of strings, the old instrument hung in quiet exile. My companions approved of the decor.

"Gotta like it," I said, grabbing the key tag and climbing to the porch. I looked out from the small platform and saw the edge of the beach in front of the kitchen area. Further out, the rocky end of the bay, sunlight glared off the water. Tall palm trees filled in the forest area below the cabins. I turned, unlocked the door, and placed my bags inside. The interior of the hut was quite simple: a small shelf covered with the remains of melted candles, an elevated sleeping area with an old mattress, a mosquito net hanging from the ceiling by a string, and one lonely light bulb at the end of a white wire. After laying my bags on the bed, I turned back to the porch to check out my friends' abode next door.

A slight movement on the inside wall above me almost made me jump out of my skin. Looking up, my eyes met those of a giant gecko just over a half-metre in length. I shouted in surprise, causing the lizard to make a slight jerk. After the initial shock, we simply stared at each other. He was a beautiful green colour and covered with bright blue spots. At first I began to protest his presence, but soon discovered that he was not the slightest bit interested in me, nor in my futile attempts to evict him from the premises. I finally accepted my reptilian roommate and left him alone.

The three of us, satisfied with our rooms, returned to the beach-side kitchen and the beautiful view of the water. The bungalow was located in one corner of the large bay. Tables and chairs sat lopsided on the sandy floor of the dining area. The retaining wall at the edge of the building dropped off into the clear water. A long wooden walk-way extended from the beach in front of the entrance out and around the rocky shoreline.

"You can see Big Buddha at the end of the point," Klong said, directing our attention out over the bay. A huge rock formation of giant boulders sat piled at the edge of the sea. One large round rock did, indeed, resemble a head sitting upon stone shoulders.

## Smoke a L'il, Swim a L'il

*Tuesday, November 29, 1994*

Despite the many warnings about dabbling with drugs in Thailand, my new friends were quite determined to purchase pot here on Koh Tao. A friendly local resident had offered it to us as we wandered down the beach on one of our first days there. He told us the island's only law officer lived on the far side and rarely visited this end of the island. It was said that the cop turned a blind eye most of the time. My friends gave the man their business, buying small bags of local smoke, heeding his warning to keep it low key. More hesitant to buy, I happily bought beer for my thirsty friends in exchange for a puff or two.

"Never keep this inside your hut. You should hide it somewhere outside and never smoke it on the beach in the daytime," he said. Thanking him for the advice, they took the prize to their cabin.

Any and all consumption occurred on Melanie and Stuart's front porch. They were both true hemp lords, Melanie being the undisputed queen of joint rollers. Her craft at rolling was uncontested. Huge, perfectly uniform, smooth-burning stogies would always emerge from her grip. Stuart took the skill for granted but I continued to marvel at these little beauties.

I was a little uneasy during the rolling/smoking process, wondering about a potential visitation by the police. I always felt like an armadillo lying on its back, my watchful eye on the road below.

This particular morning, Stuart and I decided to do some snorkelling in the bay. The sun had already heated the sand up considerably. Our feet felt as if they were burning as we walked half the length of the beach. Finding some rocks in waist-deep water, we rested and donned our fins and masks.

Swimming away from the beach over a sandy bottom, darkness loomed ahead of us. As we continued, the water started to deepen and I noticed that the sea floor was covered with sea cucumbers and small stones. There wasn't much colour and everything looked somehow dead. We reached deeper water and I saw coloured coral ahead of us. I steered toward a steep shelf while Stuart, ahead of me in the surf, waved his hand and gestured me to approach.

The gloom began to clear and at once I saw large beds of coral and the movement of many fish. Some of these local residents scurried for cover as we passed overhead. Other fish swirled around us like a rainbow of bright colours. The fan corals, seaweed, and plants drift-ed in the current. Diffused light danced around us, bouncing off everything in sight.

"Unbelievable!" I shouted to Stuart as I stuck my head above the water. A large boulder sat submerged just under the surface. I climbed on top and sat with my head and shoulders above the water. Stu joined me on the resting spot.

"Now this is the life, isn't it?" he exclaimed. "There are so many colours down there that I have lost count."

"If we only had air tanks instead of these." I shook my snorkel in discontent.

"Yeah, I can't wait to go diving," he replied.

"You and me both." I said.

"Oh well, it's better than nothing," Stuart slipped back into the water.

We swam further out into the bay, the shadow of the ocean depths looming ahead. It was then the reef fell away into blackness. A cascading slope dropped into the deep. I paused for a moment, draw-ing my breath. Below us lay a small canyon created by large sub-merged boulders and coral of many sizes, in rich and vibrant colours. A wide variety of fish curiously investigated our presence, swimming all around us without fear.

Stuart and I swam for about an hour, exploring the many caves and fissures. Schools of fish, particularly parrot fish, swirled around us as they fed on the coral. At one point I let myself float quietly. A large school of parrot fish surrounded me and began to feed on the coral just under the surface. I could hear the sound of their sharp, beak-like mouths scraping and scratching at the coral bed.

Big Buddha sat stoic above us at the end of the point. The strange pile of boulders had the distinct shape of a person sitting by the sea. This shape was even more visible from here than from the bungalow. The humungous boulders towered over our heads as we floated in the sea. We then attempted to swim around the point to explore the next bay but soon realized there was a strong tidal current running past the headland. Considering the possibility of rip tides, we decided to stay where we were. Once satisfied with our explorations, we turned back from the ocean depths and swam toward shore.

Suddenly, I stopped dead in the water, signalling to Stuart to do the same. I could see something slowly coming through the murky water, its sleek body glistening in the filtered sunlight. Seeing us, it became curious and headed in our direction.

"Do you see it?" I asked Stuart when he lifted his head above the surface.

"No . . . what?" He had no clue as to what I was talking about.

"We've got company. Look over there, just under the surface."

I pointed to the edge of the beach we were swimming toward. Sinking his mask, Stuart finally saw what I was talking about. His head flew up into the air.

"Is that what I think it is?" Stuart was in urgent need of an answer.

"Yeah, it sure is." I stuck my head under again and watched the creature swim closer as I began to consider a dash for the nearest point of land. The creature loomed closer and began to follow us at a distance, its large eyes watchful of our actions. The long body, large eyes, and jaw of a five-foot shark came into better focus through the dim water. I saw a spot of black on the tip of its sharp dorsal fin. I looked over to Stuart and he stared at me with the same intensity that I was feeling inside.

"I think the best thing to do is to swim toward the beach at a calm, steady pace," I said to my friend.

Stuart agreed, adding, "Let's hope he's had lunch."

As we headed for the beach, the shark continued to follow. Reaching shallower water, it finally lost interest and turned away, disappearing into the ocean. All the same, Stuart and I were running as we climbed out onto the beach.

I later learned that our visitor was a black-tipped reef shark and that a specimen of his size would not normally be dangerous.


## Time for Thinking

It was here during these days on Koh Tao that I began to think a great deal about my life. It seemed to be the first time during my journey that I had a chance to take some time for myself. Before Koh Tao I had busily occupied every moment and had not yet begun to look inside.

I reflected on my relationship, my wife, and my choice to travel solo and felt that much of what I was going through could not be put into words. Overall, I felt melancholy and wondered if I had done the right thing by travelling alone. Aside from the heavy feeling, there was also one of calm. It was a feeling deeper than my own emotions, a contentedness and a trust that the universe was unfolding as it should. I felt a solidness about my own strength and well-being that was becoming stronger as time went on, a feeling I had not experienced since before my relationship with my wife. I was doing exactly what I needed to do for me, not for anyone else.

The biggest mistake I had ever made was to put all the things I felt were important on the back burner and to think that the relationship was all that I needed. I had used the relationship to fill an empty part of myself, only later feeling resentment rear its ugly head. I had depended on our union for strength; I was suffocating in my own neediness. I had become boxed in and felt my only option was to leave. Once again alone, I now had the opportunity to fill the empty space between who I was and who I was to become. At the same time, I had a sense of second-guessing my own intentions. I began to feel strange, being so far from my own world. I had come here to search for answers, but perhaps all the answers were back at home. The rainy days reminded me of my own sadness. Had I made a big mistake in leaving or would the mistake be in returning home?

I realized at that moment I had not thought about Jill at all. Not for a long time. My concentration had been focused on what was going on as I travelled. It was as if she had never existed.

I began feeling guilty for all that had happened between us. I soon remembered that this was not just my creation; both Jill and I had contributed to the demise of our relationship, consciously or unconsciously. I also had a sense of going with the flow, of letting go of what had happened and allowing myself to meet whatever was to be with an open heart.

As I looked out to sea I felt lifted from turmoil. The view reminded me of a bigger picture. The sea, so beautiful, was always changing. A world of events lay unseen beneath the reflection of its surface. It was full of new things all the time. I compared this image to my own situation and allowed the idea of change to exist, trying not to feel overwhelmed. I felt that this was the best way to prepare for whatever the future held for me.

I also took notice of the people of the island, making their living as best they could with what they had. Perhaps this would help me find the answers to my own questions. Observing them, I got the sense of the members of a team working toward a common goal and purpose, never begrudging a task put before them. I saw the inherent equality and the usual added respect for the elders of the family. The teamwork of my relationship, for the most part, had been good, but I recalled moments where my criticism of her created a wall between us. There were always rocks on our road that, as time went on, got bigger and my willingness to deal with them had faded away. This stemmed from a feeling that my partner was trying to change who I was, a feeling that had stuck in the back of my mind for a long time. There was so much of who I was that I had been willing to give up in exchange for the relationship. So many things I would get around to at some later date. To get these things back into my life, and to find those things that made me tick, I felt I had to leave.

I looked out over the bay, watching the tide as it began to shift once again.


## Critters

My resident gecko friend was interesting and extremely useful. Naming him Gary, I learned to appreciate his presence in my hut as a great consumer of pesky insects. During the hot afternoons he would join his friends in a chorus of their own tune—the sound that gives them their name. A repeated croaking sound of the word "gecko" would filter through the trees. Gary was quick to join in with his brothers. The sound would repeat four or five times, the last finishing with an audible drop in tone, then, silence. Each time I heard it I laughed in wonder.

At night, Gary would cling to the outside wall of my hut, next to the small light bulb I left on for him. The light attracted a multitude of insects which Gary would catch with great swiftness. His stomach seemed to be a bottomless pit; he would feed for hours. Joining him on one occasion, at the other end of the porch, was a beautiful praying mantis. It was a brilliant green and about eight centimetres long. I had never seen one before so it was a treat to watch it feed, its praying arms grabbing flying morsels from mid-air. Both creatures were very fast and their prey never stood a chance.

The creatures I encountered here which gave me real chills, however, were met at quieter, more unexpected times. These were the giant spiders.

The biggest spider that I had seen so far in my life was probably a wolf spider, measuring four to five centimetres in diameter including the body and legs. The first time I had to deal with a spider of the typical Thai dimensions was in the best place for a surprise encounter— the shower.

The bath shed down the slope from my hut was a small building with a cement floor surrounded by corrugated steel walls and roof. Inside, there was a concrete cistern of cool water called a *mandi*. A large plastic scoop was used to pour water over your head during a standing shower. After soaping up and shaving, one simply poured more water over the head and body to rinse.

I found myself in the bath shed late one afternoon, just finishing the rinse cycle of my shower and about to dry off. I had hung my towel on a small nail behind the door. Standing in nothing but my sandals, I turned around to reach for my towel. Just before my hand grabbed it, my peripheral vision caught a slight movement, pulling my eyes toward something resting immediately next to the towel I was seeking.

Every cell in my body felt the instant presence of an adrenaline spike as I came face to face with a giant arachnid that could have eaten that typical wolf spider for a snack. The diameter of this spider was a good twelve to fifteen centimetres. I felt my eyeballs grow to about the same size. My cry of surprise shook the metal walls of the small shed. This made the creature cringe slightly and retreat into a small crevice for its own defence.

Once learning of the presence of these residents and where they could be found, any future visits began with careful examinations of all corners of the shed. I found there were more late at night so I used my flashlight to reveal the safest path. These spiders were generally very calm and would sit quietly on the wall, watching me. I even saw a few of them carrying egg-sacks the size of walnuts under their fat abdomens. These ones were more reclusive and apt to disappear more quickly, no doubt in the interest of their future young.

The most disturbing encounter, however, happened in my own bed a few nights after my shower stall incident. The bed in my hut had a mosquito net hanging from the ceiling. Tucking this in around the edge of the mattress before sleep would prevent unwanted guests from disturbing you. I soon learned that one should remain diligent with this practice even during the daytime, to prevent any passers-by from settling in only to be revealed later.

I had seen a few giant cockroaches scurrying over my sheets. Getting used to these, I would sweep them out and usually reset the net. As the time passed and I became more relaxed in this little paradise, I started to get lazy with my net. This particular evening I was about to get a reminder of the importance of the simple chore.

I had gone to bed late and spent some time writing in my journal before turning out my small flashlight.

I had laid my head down for no more than a few minutes when I became aware of a scuffling sound, the sound of something crawling over on a piece of paper near my head. Reaching for my flashlight, I turned it on and sat up in bed to see what was making the noise. Thinking it was only a cockroach, I looked around for the telltale shape among the various items beside me. Lifting my overturned journal revealed another giant spider of a different species. It was more rectangular in shape with grey colouration. Upon my discovery, both the spider and I froze. My first instinct was to slide back toward the opposite side of the enclosed space. When I finally moved, the spider decided to retreat as well. His retreat, however, ended up to be an advance toward me. He had run back toward the net wall and up the inside of the mesh barrier. As the net sloped from all four corners of the bed up to a central point suspended from the ceiling, the spider was soon directly opposite my face. He finally stopped only a short crawl from my nose.

As we sat staring at each other, I stealthily drew my leg out of my sleeping sheet and carefully opened one corner of the net with my foot. Managing to flip the net outward, I created a fairly large opening not too far from where the arachnid sat. To my surprise, the spider immediately responded to my offer of an escape route, bolting out around the edge of the opening, never to be seen again.


## Dive School

When we showed up for the first morning of class, our excitement was evident. The morning dive was underway, divers and guides stuffing their gear into large black duffle bags. Wet suits, inflatable vests or BCDs (Buoyancy Compensation Devices), tanks, fins, and weights were carried down to the beach and into the belly of the large dive boat moored there. Before long the vessel backed away from the shore and sailed out of the bay.

"Hello, welcome to Carabao. I am Wolfgang." The co-owner of the shop greeted Melanie, Stuart, and me, showing us into a small classroom.

Soon a tall muscular man came in with an armload of books and charts. Placing the items on the desk at one end of the room, he introduced himself.

"Hello, I am Carlsberg. Like the beer, you know?" he said.

"Yeah, sure," we said, laughing.

"Ya, good. Actually, I am Carsten. Carlsberg is better. It will remind you of my favourite beer," he said.

"Why do you want us to be reminded of that?" I asked, pretending to be indignant.

"To remind you of the kind you will owe me," he said calmy.

"Owe you?" Melanie asked curiously.

"Ya. One mistake, one beer," he said back to her.

Our laughter drowned out Carlsberg's attempts to carry on with his class. A fourth student walked into the classroom in the middle of the laughing fit. He looked around as if he had come into the wrong place but was soon welcomed by the teacher. Jerry would end up being my dive "buddy" throughout the course.

The first few days of classwork were balanced with afternoon shallow water sessions just off the beach. Carlsberg could do nothing but laugh at us novices, struggling in and out of the surf with all the heavy gear on our backs. Eventually our skills were sufficient and we were ready to explore the ocean.

Over a period of a week and a half our group went through two complete dive courses and made twelve dives. The unforgettable experience of exploring the priceless gift of that underwater world bonded us. Carlsberg was our instructor throughout both courses. We had grown quite fond of him by the end of our stay on the island, despite his constant whining for free alcohol.


### Fierce Fleet
The "shark" boat was an old fishing boat. Long and thin, the bow

stuck sharply out into the water. Painted along the sides of its bow was a tooth-filled mouth that gaped and snarled. It looked forbidding as it sped across the sea. This ship was used for almost all of Carabao's dive trips and the toothy grin became a common sight.

Carabao's other ship was, by far, more popular. It was not until halfway through our two courses that the mighty mothership of all dive boats returned to her harbour. She had been taken to Chumphon for refitting and a new paint job. The news of her imminent arrival had been circulating for almost week now and the rest of us were going mad trying to find out more about her. All we knew was that she had been in service at Carabao for a few years. The day she arrived at the beach, excitement was high. Groups of people boarded several longtail boats to take part in the official re-christening ceremony in the bay.

The great ship sat in the quiet water, her fierce gaping mouth rivalling the shark boat's maw. Her name, painted across the front of the bridge, shone in the setting sun. Just before the final rays of daylight, our small armada gathered in a circle around her as Wolfgang told us the story of the ship's history and her upgrade.

An old fishing boat in service at Carabao for three years, she had finally been converted into the ultimate dive charter boat. Tank racks, compressor, storage space, sundeck, coffee bar, and a new GSP (Global Positioning System) made her the pride of the Carabao fleet. At last, Wolfgang stood up, holding aloft a bottle of champagne.

"I hearby re-christen this vessel *Thai-Tanic*, mothership of the Carabao fleet," he said as the bottle struck the hull. The shattering glass was drowned out by screams of glee from the crowd witnessing the event. Champagne poured over the "mouth" of the ship, one of her painted eyes seemingly staring us down.


## Into the Arms of the Ocean
*Thursday, December 8, 1994*

Shark Island lay offshore around the corner from Chalok Ban Kao. We sat onboard the shark boat, bouncing over the waves toward the chosen spot. For our first ocean dive, we set to work preparing our equipment under the watchful eye of Carlsberg. He in turn prepared to call us on any mistakes and tally up our debt of beer. He managed to rack up only a few points as we worked to avoid any errors. I lost a point when I referred to my fins as flippers, reluctantly promising to pay up later.

The boat slowly approached the rocky outcropping off the south end of the island. A stone wall rose up out of the sea and pierced the blue sky. The rock was light in colour and reflected the sunlight with intense brightness. Dropping anchor in about fifteen metres of water, the captain shut the motor off and helped Carlsberg distribute the gear. As soon as the anchor hit the water I plunged in with mask, fins, and weightbelt.

"Hey, wait for us," shouted Carlsberg. He laughed loudly and tossed my tank and BCD over the side of the ship. Strapping my gear onto my body, I paddled in the waves, waiting for the others to join me. Melanie and Stuart did as I had, their gear being tossed in after them.

Floating under the bow of the shark boat, I held my masked face down into the water. The view to the bottom was clear and fish of all colours swam everywhere. My excitement grew. As a child I had dreamed of being like Jacques Cousteau, exploring the deep and the dark. My breathing was uneasy at first but soon I relaxed and just floated in the sea, looking into this alien world. Some fish ventured closer and I tried to identify certain species. I scanned the surrounding water for any more curious sharks.

I finally looked up to find the rest of the group in the water. We all gathered in a circle and did our pre-dive checks. My "buddy" Jerry had brought his girlfriend along for the ride, although she was not going to dive. She was a slight woman wearing the smallest string bikini I had ever seen. It hung loosely from her thin frame as she leaned over the side of the ship.

"Have a lovely time, dear," she said, slinking over to give Jerry a parting kiss from the ladder. "I'll be waiting for you." She planned to stay on the boat; the skipper was more than happy to be alone with her onboard. She took photographs of us in the water and then proceeded to peel her top off and lie on the deck.

The boat captain's eyes grew large and a strange grin came over his face. His face made me crack up while the look on Carlsberg's had me choking on my snorkel. I noticed the captain gazing at the woman's bare breasts. At the same time, I noticed my own unconscious desire to observe her naked skin. Soon all the men in the group were glancing over at the half-naked woman lying in the sun. Melanie saw us staring and laughed. The woman's tanned, naked breasts had pulled a collective primal trigger in all of the males present, an unconscious biological response.

"Really, must you do that, dear?" Jerry looked embarrassed yet aware that he was powerless in the situation. He joined our circle beside the boat and checked in.

We emptied the air from our vests and began to sink. We were surrounded by bubbles as we were swallowed by the sea. My immediate sensation was of being enveloped in the biggest life force on Earth, a power so huge yet so gentle. We all turned over to face the sea floor and I was entranced. The descent, marked by the equalizing of our ears, was being investigated and monitored by a number of fish in the water.

At one point a beautiful fish, blue and red in colour, floated with me, right in front of my mask. It looked into my eyes and seemed to almost speak to me.

"What are you?" I imagined it asking through the glass. It soon lost interest and drifted away.

One of the first skills we learned was how to use neutral buoyancy. By adding enough air into a BCD, a diver can hang suspended in the ocean, neither ascending or descending. With neutral buoyancy, divers can manoeuvre around and over underwater obstacles by simply breathing. Breathing in causes increased buoyancy, thus causing a diver to ascend. In turn, a strong exhalation increases weight, causing descent. We soon became quite good at this technique and put it to good use.

At one point I almost landed knee-down in a bed of long-spined sea urchins. I was trying to find a place to rest on the bottom and had been carried too far by the current. When I realized where I was about to land, my BCD came in handy as a quick ascent tool. I pulled my knees up high as my vest lifted me up and away from the sharp black spikes.

The currents proved a challenge throughout the dive. I felt myself fighting the drift and soon tired, increasing my air intake. I felt slightly panicked for air. I signalled my "buddy" and Jerry and I dropped to the ocean floor behind the rest of the group.

Jerry used signals to ask me if I wanted to surface. I shook my head, indicating my desire to rest for a moment. I remembered Carlsberg instructing us to do this if we were hyperventilating and in panic. I rested near a large stone for a few moments and slowed my breathing. I was soon ready to rejoin the others. Carlsberg checked in with me and I cleared him with an okay sign. He turned and led us further around the rocky island.

Carlsberg had instructed us to keep a constant watch on our personal air supplies by monitoring the pressure gauges attached to our tanks. When one diver's gauge registered only fifty Bar (fifty units of barometric pressure), we were told to signal our instructor and prepare for resurfacing. As we explored yet another richly coloured coral bed, Jerry got Carlsberg's attention by pointing to his own gauge. Carlsberg nodded and led us out of the coral toward the ship. Carlsberg retraced our path and led us to the ship's anchor, embedded in the sea floor. Here we gathered into a loose circle and checked in for our ascent.

Swirling round in a graceful dance of bodies and bubbles, we slowly drifted upward from the sea bed. I concentrated on a slow exhalation of air, the tiny bubbles rising with me, and felt as if I were being held in the hands of God as I approached the surface. Suddenly I returned to my side of the world. My eyes went blind from the sunlight. I spat out my regulator with a scream of intense joy. What had seemed like only five minutes had been forty-five.

The first thing we heard when we reached the surface was the excited cry of Jerry's girlfriend as she skipped back to the edge of the boat ladder.

"Hello, Jerry," she cried out, waving her hand frantically. She was still topless and had now gotten to the point where her bottom half was just hanging from her hips. Jerry looked up and in his stiff accent said, "Really darling, do put something back on." We all laughed hysterically as Jerry looked on, horrified. These two sounded like a couple I would expect to see at an upper-class English afternoon tea party. In this context, their stiff accents were hilarious.

"Oh, all right." She complied and dressed herself much to the chagrin of the captain who had gotten used to the idea. The rest of us hauled our gear out of the sea and sat back with cold beverages, enjoying the warm afternoon sun.

"There's only one thing wrong," I said to Melanie.

"What's that?" she asked after a moment, sipping on a cold beer.

"That I never did this years ago," I laughed and took a long drink from my can.

## After Dark

*Friday, December 9, 1994*

The afternoon was muggy, with just a bit of cloud overhead. We boarded the shark boat once again, rounded the southern tip of Shark Island, and headed into another small bay just to the north. The slope of the island was steep as it dropped to the ocean. Thick groves of coconut trees covered the shoreline. The sun was just setting and soon we would be in pitch-black darkness.

We started our descent and dropped to a spot on the clear, sandy bottom and formed a circle. Carlsberg told us to turn our torches off. Once we were in darkness, our instructor began to wave his hands around, causing the night-black water to suddenly turn into a swirling mass of strange green light—phosphorescence. Each of us tried it, creating eerie, ghost-like clouds in the water. The phenomenon kept us amused for quite some time. Finally, Carlsberg led us into the black to explore more of the nocturnal world and its strange creatures.

My eyes caught sight of small red lights darting in and out of the crevices of a large boulder. Closer inspection showed them to be the glowing eyes of small shrimp. The red eyes danced nervously and their owners raced to hide when my torch approached their lair.

At one point, a bright beam of light made me look over to Melanie who was trying to get my attention. I swam over to her to see what she had discovered. A small puffer fish had been spooked out of its hiding place and had blown itself up to maximum size. He was trying to make us shiver in our fins but his menacing look was offset by the funny grin on his overstretched face. Keeping guard in front of his home, the fish stared us down until we carried on past him. Looking gratified, the tiny fish slipped back into his hole.

Ting, ting, ting. The sound came from behind me. A diving knife was being tapped on an air tank. This signal is used for distress but also for getting someone's attention to something important. Carlsberg was trying to steady his light on the creature he had found.

As I turned toward the sound, I saw his torch reflecting off something behind the coral about six metres in front of him. Stuart settled in beside him and shone his light in the same direction. By the time the rest of us had arrived, our collective activity had flushed the quarry out from behind the safe confines of the coral bed.

A giant sea turtle drifted up into the spotlights. The creature stared back at us, a gentle grin on its face. The turtle gracefully streaked through the water, propelled by its powerful front flippers. Before long we were left far behind as the turtle made for a quieter neighbourhood and privacy.

One of the strangest creatures I met was a type of stone crab. It was very alien-looking, with one claw much bigger than the other and a misshapen shell with the texture of a stone fish. It showed no fear as it watched me intently. I showed it to Carlsberg and he looked at me with questioning eyes, shrugging his shoulders. After the dive, he claimed that it must have been a sea monster or something *sama-sama* (a local euphemism otherwise translated as "Same same, but different . . .").


## Tunnels

I followed Carlsberg over the top of Green Rock, a huge algae-shrouded boulder which marked our starting point. The current was strong so we dropped to the bottom to avoid tiring ourselves. Wearing gloves to prevent cuts from coral, I followed head-first into an amazing labyrinth of tunnels and small caves. I could see air bubbles from my regulator scrambling wildly around and out of the confines of the narrow passages. Taking care not to scrape our equipment on the coral walls around us, we continued through the meandering caves. At one point we paused one at a time to gaze in at a huge grouper trapped in the rear of a small cavern. Emerging out the other side, we found Carlsberg, waving at us to look at what he had found. We saw the last few glimpses of a banded sea snake darting away through the coral.

Our return to the ship was met with excited cries from the crew. A small fin whale had been sighted just two hundred metres off the bow, heading north. We searched from the deck and could see it blowing, now about a half kilometre away. The captain thought to follow it but the whale quickly disappeared.

"Imagine looking out from a cave to see the eye of a whale staring back at you," I said to Stuart.

"Well, just as long as that whale wasn't hungry," replied my friend.

## Chumphon Pinnacle
*Sunday, December 11, 1994*

Chumphon Pinnacle is a submerged mountain whose peak is eighteen metres below the surface of the ocean. Carabao's mothership, *Thai-Tanic*, would carry us to the dive site, almost an hour off the southwest coast of Koh Tao.

The dive shop buzzed with excitement. Today was to be the great ship's maiden voyage with students and recreational divers. Five separate groups of divers, including our class, were preparing to dive on the Pinnacle. Wolfgang, the proud co-owner, was leading one of the teams on today's expedition. Five tenderboat loads of divers were taxied out to the ship in the harbour.

*Thai-Tanic* sat quietly in the water, gentle waves lapping under her hull. The early morning sun was already warm. The captain coaxed the engine noisily awake and a black cloud of smoke blew over us. We let out a great cry as we climbed aboard.

We first prepared our gear and stowed it safely on the lower deck. The aroma of hot coffee drifting from the galley had us all holding out our mugs. On the upper sundeck, maps of the dive site circulated, giving the divers a preview of the area we were about to explore.

*Thai-Tanic* left Koh Tao behind and churned out into deeper ocean. I watched the waves being cut in half by the bow.

The goal on this expedition was to follow GPS (Global Positioning System) coordinates to a position slightly to one side of the Chumphon Pinnacle. Then, using a long rope as a guide line, we would descend to the peak's summit and over the other side to an ultimate depth of forty metres. Our group was to break off to perform various exercises before rejoining the others. I studied picture books, trying to memorize various species I might see, including sharks. The only shark features that seemed to stick in my mind were dorsal fins and teeth. Both nervousness and excitement hampered my ability to concentrate.

Being the maiden voyage of the *Thai-Tanic*, we had been joking about impending disaster out on the water, icebergs obviously erased from the list of possible hazards. Wolfgang was the only person who saw no humour in our predictions.

Soon enough, a mechanical breakdown afflicted the vessel. A short, bobbing delay soon ended when the generator was repaired, allowing us to continue across the sea. However, bad luck did not intend to let us off so easily.

The only way to accurately find our dive site was to follow the guidance of the GSP locator. About ten minutes before we reached the site, the battery for the computerized device decided to die. I laughed at the fact that the crew hadn't thought to bring another power supply along for backup. A few hot words were exchanged between the crew and Wolfgang as an attempt was made to rectify the problem. We had lost our way a full hour off the coast of Koh Tao.

Luckily, another ship was sailing out to the same dive site that morning. It caught up to us and slowed to render assistance. Quick communication between the two vessels soon had us in convoy formation and back on course.

When the vessels cut their engines I glanced over the railing into the dark water below. I followed the other divers off the top deck to the stern. There, we strapped our gear to our backs and one by one jumped into the sea.

As I stepped off the back of the ship, I felt some nervousness from not being able to see any land on the horizon. Inflating my vest to full capacity, I bobbed about in the swells. Almost immediately I noticed that I was drifting away from the ship. I kept the slight current at bay by kicking my fins to bring me alongside the ship's hull.

After a long moment I dipped my face down into the water. At once I felt panic and my breathing raced out of control. I quickly traded my regulator for my snorkel to save my air supply from being drained before leaving the surface. I tried to relax but at first found it impossible.

Looking down into the ocean, I could see nothing but my feet and fins silently dangling in the mouth of a blackness and depth I could not comprehend. My heart continued to race and my stomach felt like it was about to empty itself. I lifted my mask and joined the check-in circle.

After a quick rendezvous we sank below the surface. I fell in behind Carlsberg as he followed the lead line. Guided by the rope, I began to fall downwards as a skydiver would—arms and legs spread out to my sides. It felt amazing as I fell into nothing, into the black deep. It was surreal.

Blackness confronted me. What could I see? I felt as if my eyes' ability to focus was failing when just up ahead I could see a ghostly shape of...something. Suddenly the rocky spire of the Chumphon Pinnacle appeared before me. Many fish soon swam into view. Swirling around the contours of the underwater mountain, groupers and parrot fish encircled us, as did beautiful butterfly fish.

Reaching the top of the spire, Carlsberg turned to check on our progress. He looked up at me "skydiving" down toward him. I saw him laughing, massive clouds of bubbles emerging from his regulator.

Joining him at the top of the Pinnacle, we signalled that all was okay and prepared to continue the descent. Carlsberg turned and disappeared head-first over the wall. I felt my stomach pitch as I followed, falling into nothing once again. We soon passed thirty metres as I glanced at my depth gauge. The drop had been very rapid and I realized how, in a very short time, easily one could pass the maximum depth of forty metres.

During our descent two moray eels stuck their big heads out from the coral to see who had just fallen into their territory. They grimaced as they slithered out from their protective caves. The abundance of other fish was astounding and the schools were much bigger than I had seen on previous dives.

We landed on a sandy slope next to the side of the mountain. Coming to rest at thirty-seven metres, we performed a test for effects of nitrogen narcosis. While aboard the *Thai-Tanic*, we had performed two tasks timed by stopwatch: tying a bowline knot and performing a simple math equation. The test would determine if our ability to do these tasks was affected by deep diving. As we settled into a tight circle on the sand, I looked up and could not see the surface. A pale-green dome of light was the only reminder of the distant daylight.

Being the first person to perform the tests, I felt no effect. Stuart was next, followed by Melanie. As Melanie was doing her test, I started to notice a feeling of light-headedness, as if I had just consumed a few beers. I found myself chuckling to myself, bubbles sputtering out of my regulator. Jerry had his turn and the feeling became more apparent. I signalled Carlsberg, waving my index finger in a circle close to my temple, indicating that I felt a bit loopy. He nodded and instructed us to begin a slow ascent to shallower water. Rising only a few metres, I felt the dizziness disappear almost immediately.

We rose slowly, following the contours of the rock wall. Eventually the underside of the ocean's surface came into view. Light returned to our vision as schools of fish swarmed around us. Every so often we met other groups of divers as we explored the rocky shelves.

Suddenly there was a flurry of excitement from one of the other parties near us. The divemaster who was leading this group suddenly stopped and began signalling furiously to his students. He pointed with one hand while holding the other, fingers flat and vertical, above his head. We had been told earlier that this signal meant only one thing: shark. Cautiously, we followed Carlsberg over to his hiding place amongst the thick beds of coral. Carlsberg motioned us to stay put for a moment while he went ahead to investigate. Peering slowly over the edge of a short rock wall, he soon signalled us to approach.

We joined him and peered over the shelf, sighting a five-metre leopard shark lying on the sandy bottom, its sharp dorsal fin standing straight up from its back, black eyes staring. With its leopard-like spots, it blended well into the surrounding terrain and was hardly noticeable. After a few minutes we left the shark to its rest and swam back to the face of the mountain.

As we slowly rose upward, more creatures, including moray eels, noted our passing with slight protest. Most intriguing were the beds of black sea urchins. Apart from long sharp spines, they have round, coloured bumps on their shells that appear to be eyes or sensors. They became aware of my presence as I swam by, aligning their spines with my position.

It was a brilliant spectacle of colour and movement. Light diffused through the water, reflecting off everything. I felt comfortable and yet out of place all at once. Floating, perhaps, like a child in the womb, I drifted in the void. I felt a connection to all things around me in the warm current. In contrast to the physical sensations, my mind raced with thoughts of home. Why did I leave Jill? Where was I to go? The future felt as dark as the void behind and below me. All I wanted was to let her go, to set her free from where our relationship had taken us. My feelings of resentment were unfair but were very real. It was not fair for either of us to live this way. I prayed for her well-being and breathed deeply once again. Cleansed by the sea, the water washed away the stress in my body and thought. An image of Jill drifted with me and I felt the sadness tighten my gut. What could I have done differently? I exhaled and let her image fall away into the depths.

The exhaled breath of all the divers created huge clouds of air bubbles which slowly rose to the surface. As the atmospheric pressure decreased, I noticed that the bubbles expanded in size. Forming perfect domes with flat bottoms, they grew until they burst apart into smaller bubbles before continuing upward.

With a last glimpse at my air gauge, I made as slow an ascent as I possibly could. Injecting a very small amount of air into my vest, I drifted slowly toward the surface, trying to remain absolutely conscious of everything around me. My breathing, all the small air bubbles scurrying around and across my body, the wetness of the sea, the warmth of the water, light scattering over my face and body, and all the small fish floating with us just out of range, coming along as if to say farewell.

A shroud of air bubbles soon consumed me and lifted me into the sunlight. I surfaced just under the bow of the ship. I felt transformed as I emerged from the alien world.

"You are all very good divers," Carlsberg said that evening. "It's really too bad."

"Why is it too bad?" I asked him curiously.

Carlsberg mused, "Well, I've been getting rather thirsty lately . . ."

## Full Moon

*Saturday, December 17, 1994*

I sat by the sand at Ban Mae Hat, in a pub at the edge of the beach. The Safety Stop bar was attached to one of the village's main dive shops, a structure which allowed customers to walk in from the road behind and emerge onto sand, but not before passing the bartender in the corner.

There had been a lot of excited talk about the upcoming full moon celebration. In order to prevent another mass exodus to the beach party at Hat Rin, the owners of the Safety Stop planned an open party with fresh food cooked right on the beach along with cheap beverages. A number of musicians planned a jam session to coincide with the event and had placed posters all over the island a week previously. I had walked over from Laem-Klong in the late afternoon to meet some of the players. A Japanese fellow named Sam introduced himself and added my name to his list of performers. He informed me that all musicians would get a free seafood dinner in exchange for performing. I got acquainted with the other players and settled in as the sun dropped over the far side of the island and dusk settled over the sea.

People began to show up for the party just after sunset. By the time my friends had shown up, the music and food were in full flow. Gathered in a large arc around a group of blankets used as a stage area, the crowd was entertained as each musician took to the stage with small sets of songs. I got up to perform and played for close to half an hour. After I finished, I sat back and enjoyed the sound of a young woman singing bluesy ballads. At one point, I felt a tap on my shoulder. I turned my head and greeted Stuart and Melanie who sat down beside me.

"Sounds good," Stuart said to me.

"Yeah, there's been a good variety of music so far. Everything from country to blues, rock, and folk," I replied, watching the performance.

"Have you played yet?" Melanie asked.

"Yeah, I just finished a short time ago," I replied, shifting my position. "Are you hungry? I was just going to get some dinner." I stood and handed my guitar to a young man who wished to borrow it for his upcoming set.

Soon the crowded beach erupted with a collective cheer as many began to point out over the dark water. The face of the moon slowly lifted itself out of the ocean, a huge orange disk semi-obscured by small banks of cloud. Their eerie silhouettes, blown by the wind, danced on the lunar sphere. Before long the full moon hung complete above the shining water. I could see the pale moonlight on the tall trees.

The music continued and was eventually drowned out by the noise of the crowd's loud, drunken conversations. Despite the din, other musicians performed for whomever cared to listen. Individual performances slowly digressed into a collective blues jam that soon became endless. I finally sat out after what seemed to be the fourteen billionth twelve-bar phrase.

As the evening grew old, people migrated further up the beach toward the sound of a loud techno-dance party that was heating up at the north end of the shallow bay. My friends felt the urge to join the exodus.

"Do you want to join us?" said Melanie.

"Sounds good to me," I said. I was tiring of the repetitive blues jam. I thanked Sam and the others, reclaimed my guitar, and trotted up the waterline behind my companions.

The distant flicker of tiki torches guided us as we started out into the night. The moon was bright, the light's reflection off the water like a blinding beacon. Ahead, the constant throbbing of pop dance music was pumping out into the night. As we got closer we could see people dancing to the music, the rest sitting at tables or on the sand.

My two friends were huge dance fans and immediately went to the dance area on the sand and stayed there for the rest of the evening. I decided to sit in the sand closer to the water and watch the action. With pounding bass coming from the loud speakers, it was hard to enjoy the tranquil scene in front of the crowded beach party. Waves flickered with moonlight and a light wind came in off the water. The brightly lit beach ended north of us at a rocky headland and just off the point a small island sat basking in the glow of moonlight. Unfortunately, this noisy soundtrack did not do justice to the view.

It was nearly 2:00 AM when I finally reached my tolerance limit. The noise pollution was driving me to find a quieter place to rest. I felt the desire to return to my little hut across the island. I stood and made my way through the crowd of bodies on the sand. By now quite a few people were paired off, making out or, in some cases, making love on their blankets.

Seeing these loving couples together brought feelings of loneliness from deep within me. I needed to be alone. In part, the restlessness was aided by the incessant pounding of the music. I noticed my friends settling down on the beach beside a small group of trees. Stuart and Melanie had brought blankets and extra clothing with them, obviously planning to spend the night. I continued my course through the maze of blankets.

Passing one couple, I recognized the woman to be Catherine. She was hugging her boyfriend, her head hanging over his shoulder when our eyes connected. She glanced up at me and, for an instant, smiled into my eyes. She looked happy in the arms of her lover and in that moment I wanted so much to be that man. I vaguely recalled the warm sensation of being held in Catherine's arms aboard the ferry from Chumphon. My stomach tightened slightly and the cool night air made me shiver. I blew her a kiss, detoured around her blanket and turned away down the beach.

## Ferry to Thong Sala
*Tuesday, December 20, 1994*
We watched the port of Mae Hat slowly grow distant as we sailed around the headland. Familiar dive sites came into view as we sped over the water: Green Rock and the tunnels, Shark Island and the rest. Finally, as the ship rounded the south end of the island, we caught a last glimpse of Chalok Ban Kao and the Big Buddha. Looking closer, I saw the *Thai-Tanic*, quietly waiting for yet another voyage to begin. I watched her for a long time, her contours growing smaller as we sailed away.

I closed my eyes for a moment and dreamed of diving into a deep ocean. I could feel the surreal sensation of falling . . . falling. The ocean in my dream was bottomless. I felt I was falling . . . further inside myself. I fell into the black unknown, away from everything familiar down into . . . what? My eyes opened at the sound of laughter; some people next to me were sharing a joke. I looked over the sea, recalling my time here and feeling intense gratitude for all I had experienced.

The sun was warm on the open ocean and soon the outline of Koh Pha-Ngan drew clear and crisp. Koh Tao now looked smaller than ever, the distance veiling it in a blue haze.

# CHAPTER 7: KOH PHA-NGAN, THAILAND

## Hat Rin
*Tuesday, December 20, 1994*

The pace of life on Koh Pha-Ngan was quite upbeat compared to that of Koh Tao. Nowhere was this more evident than at the dock upon arrival. Many people approached us offering places to stay, complete with photos of bungalows and facilities.

"Let's get a bite to eat first," said Stuart, already heading for a small café at the side of the street. Shuffling through the gauntlet of vendors, I rested my gear against a wooden table and ordered a small snack.

"Where are you supposed to meet your friends?" I asked Stuart.

"I'm not quite sure yet," Stuart replied. He pulled out a large map of the island and began to run his fingers over the paper. "How did they spell the name of the place, Melanie?"

Melanie rummaged around her bag, finally revealing a tattered letter stuck inside one of their guidebooks. After a moment, she responded. "What's written here is H-a-t T-h-i-a-n."

Stuart scanned the map for a few moments. "Well, here's a place called Hat Thian, up on the east coast of the island."

The map showed a tiny bay of the same name, north of Hat Rin, on the east side of Pha-Ngan. I felt uneasy about staying in or near Rin beach because of its reputation as a huge party town. I wanted to find a quiet place by the ocean where I wouldn't be disturbed by loud music. Still, I decided to join them on the trip to Rin beach, just to check out the scene.

We flagged down a taxi driver and negotiated a price to the other side of the island. Piling into the back, we sat on the long padded benches built along the sides of the covered truckbed. At least they looked comfortable.

Being a passenger in one of these small taxis was an experience that would begin as an enjoyable trip and end up a nightmare. It wasn't as bad as my memory of riding in a tuk-tuk, but nonetheless scary enough. The first round of sharp corners that sent me and others flying into the middle of the truck box soon had us concentrating on developing improved passenger skills.

Now, it's not just the skill of these drivers that causes riding to be a scary proposition. The tropical rains cause deep crevices of washout in certain areas, making the road extremely treacherous. Many blind corners hide surprises like this. At one point we got to see the aftermath of a roll-over. A small vehicle had dropped its front wheel into a hole in the road, causing it to flip onto its roof. Thankfully, nobody was injured. All the passengers had bailed out in time, just as the truck began to go upside down. The driver stood in shock next to his overturned workhorse. His eyes, as big as plates, surveyed the damage to his fenders.

We reached Hat Rin after about twenty minutes. The last half of the ride was calm and smooth, allowing me to regain a soft seat. The south side of this narrow peninsula was covered with small houses and seemed to be a residential area. The north side possessed a beautiful, curved beach and an abundance of tourist bungalows.

Hat Rin was a zoo. I could tell from the start that I wasn't going to be here long. Buildings were crammed tightly together with no breathing room. The distance from one porch to another wasn't more than a metre or so. You could probably reach into someone else's window without much effort at all. The Thai owners were certainly cashing in on every piece of their turf. It was stifling.

The main square was full of shops and food stalls. The scents of spicy food drifted in the hot air. Bands of roving, mangy canines hulked in dusty corners, whimpering for scraps. I kept my distance. There were large open sores on their bodies. The chance of brushing into one with my leg was too gross to think about. The animals scuffled about like nervous shadows.

Crowds milled around small pubs. With elaborate discotheques and easy availability of illicit drugs, in all shapes and forms, the scene here was one of all-out partying all the time.

"This is a little too rowdy for me," I said to my friends. I needed sleep at some point. "I'm going up to the other side of the island, north of Thong Sala." I had read about nice quiet bays and great beaches.

"We just have to find our friends first," said Stuart as he again pulled out his map. A trip to Hat Thian would involve a lengthy drive over the centre of the island or, more likely, a very choppy longtail boat ride.

"Why the hell would they go all the way up there?" Melanie was frustrated.

"It's pretty remote, isn't it?" I looked at the map of the coast.

"It's fucking removed," laughed Melanie.

The day was getting long and it would be too late to travel there before the sun dropped. Mel and Stu agreed to spend a night here and begin their search in the morning.

"I think I'm going to get out of here. This place is way too busy for me," I said.

"I know what you mean," Stuart said. "Why don't you leave a note for us at the post and we can get in touch with you later on?"

"Sure, sounds like a good idea. I'll be settling in for a couple of days so I'll leave a message for you by the weekend."

"See you later, John," said Melanie. She leaned over and kissed me on the cheek.

"Good luck, mate, we'll see you soon," Stuart shook my hand firmly.

I left my friends to their search and wandered back toward the centre of Hat Rin in search of a taxi to Thong Sala. It would only be a few days before our paths would cross again.


### Silver Beach

My choice of transport was vast as many vehicles were returning to the ferry for more customers. I rode all the way to Thong Sala alone in an empty pickup. Open roll bars offered me lots to hang onto while I braced myself through the rough section of the main road.

A switch of drivers in town took only minutes. I had read about the beach of Hat Yao, on the northwest coast of Pha-Ngan. By all accounts, it had plenty of quiet space and was not too far from town.

"Hat Yao?" I asked one taxi driver.

"No, over there," the man said. He pointed to a small black Toyota truck parked across the street. I saw the driver start to pull away.

"Hat Yao?!" I shouted as I bolted across the road toward him.

"Yes," the driver said. He stopped and waited for me to climb into the back. I squeezed in with a group of locals heading home with their bags of groceries. We bumped along as I balanced my luggage in my lap.

Another wild twenty-minute ride ensued. This time a meandering maze of dirt roads snaked along a flat coastline. Finally the road rose up onto a coastal headland. At the top of the hill a huge gate marked the entrance to a private mansion. From here, the road sloped down toward a beautiful beach with clear water and wide, white sand.

The truck came to a stop just past the gates of the large house at the bend in the road. By this time, I was the only passenger left in the van.

"Why are you stopping?" I asked the driver.

"You want Hat Yao?" he asked.

"Yeah, but I paid for a ride to Hat Yao, not a view of it," I said.

"Here Hat Yao." My driver was not driving me down the hill.

He refused to take me any further toward the beach, despite my loud protests, and I was left with a half-kilometre stretch to finish off on foot. Half cursing and half laughing, I stood briefly staring at the cloud of dust now hanging in place of my ride.

I left the dusty path and walked along the tide line, strolling ankle-deep in the waves. It was late afternoon and a great number of people were gathering to watch the sunset. I still had about twenty minutes of light left to find a place to stay. A lot of places were full but I could see an unassuming place with small cabins set back from the beach. A small sign for Silver Beach Bungalow marked the thin trail to the owner's house. I walked down the path to a covered dining area.

"Hello?" I said loudly. "Hello?"

It was not long before a beautiful and very pregnant young woman appeared in the doorway. She led me down to the beach to a small hut identical to the one on Koh Tao, minus the stilts. I gladly accepted the small cabin as my own.

The young woman quietly placed a sheet on the mattress and left me to settle in. After a few things were put in place, I walked down to the beach to watch the sun go down.

I lay on the sand as the sun dropped toward the edge of the sea. I looked at my watch and it was just before 6:00 PM. Darkness would soon come.

I pulled out my guitar and played for awhile as the small clouds turned various shades of red and purple. It wasn't long before the owner came out to the beach. I heard him walking toward me, down the path from the house. As he came up behind me, I turned to meet him.

"I am Sit. Welcome to Silver Beach," he said. "You play good. I like music, too."

"Thanks, nice view." I invited Sit to join me on the sand.

I had heard him making the rounds, introducing himself and welcoming his guests. He had followed the sound of my guitar to my hiding place.

He sat on the beach with his fingers busy in a small plastic bag. Holding out his hand, Sit offered me a bit of tobacco rolled up in a small leaf. I had to keep a grip on the leaf as I held it. Otherwise, it would have fallen apart. I am not a smoker, but so as not to offend my host, I accepted the small stogie. It was a gesture of friendship. Sit set a match to the end of my cigarette and the acrid smoke curled up around my face. My head was soon reeling from the effects of the nicotine.

"Good, no?" asked my host.

"Yeah (cough), great," I sputtered. Sit grinned and chuckled.

"You are English?" He was trying to guess my accent.

"No, I am from Canada. A city called Vancouver."

"Yes, many Canadians come here," Sit commented.

"You live in a beautiful place," I told him as the sun finally fell over the edge of the world, immersing us in twilight. "How long have you been here, Sit?"

"I was born here. We have had the bungalow for six years. I work with my mother and my wife," he said.

"Your wife is very pregnant."

"Yes, baby is coming soon. It will come in one month."

"Are you excited?" I asked.

"Yes, but very nervous, too," he said, digging at the sand with a small stick.

We talked for quite some time. Sit was curious about where I had been so far and what I did back in Canada. He finally asked me to play some more music. I strummed out some songs as the darkness grew thicker. Sit even knew a few of the songs that I was playing, so he sang along, an impromptu jam session on the edge of the evening tide.

"Are you hungry?" Sit asked finally. "Let's go to the kitchen."

"Yeah, sounds good." I was more than hungry—I was famished.

I pulled out my little light and led us both up the tiny path to the kitchen. Set in front of their own house, the bungalow kitchen sat in a grassy courtyard among the beach huts. Tables and benches sat in the front 'room' of the structure, under a large roof with open sides. I pulled up a seat at one of the tables but Sit gestured me to follow him into the back.

He led me into the kitchen. The aroma of cooking spices was intoxicating. I came into the room as he joined his wife, Nang, who was preparing food at a small counter.

My host pulled a small chair out of the corner and placed it by the central table, bidding me to sit. Nang finished preparing my dinner as well as their own and they asked me to stay and eat with them. Accepting their hospitality, I joined them at the central table. I felt at home with these people. I was amazed at how friendly most Thais were to strangers arriving on their doorsteps.

After dinner Nang brewed cups of coffee with sweet milk and set them down on the table for us. Without a word she went back to more chores outside the back of the hut.

Sit told me about the special opening night of a small club just through the coconut grove, behind the main road. The pub was built by a local who made all his cash through dope sales. It just so happened that I had arrived on the day of the official grand opening. The party had started at noon and was sure to last long into the night.

Getting some last-minute directions from Sit, I headed off into the darkness in search of the new pub. As I walked away from the bungalow, the ambient noise soon faded and the buzz of cicadas and all the other creatures of the night surrounded me. The sound I was really waiting for, however, was the sound of coconuts falling from the trees.

I had been informed on Koh Tao that the highest cause of death on many tropical islands, by far, was getting hit by a stray coconut tumbling out of the palm tree canopy. I was given explicit direction by Klong and some others to always walk on the roads, especially at night. They said that in the daytime you can still get away with straying off a path, if you can see clearly and get out of the way by spotting the incoming nut. I was also warned to double check where I was sitting on a beach and to make sure that there were no overhanging trees above my blanket.

I could hear the occasional nut drop to the earth as I walked in the dark. I soon shut off the flashlight as the moon lit the road well.

When coconuts fall the first thing you hear is a slight rustle of palm leaves as they break away and then the solid thud of the husky nuts hitting the ground. By the deep thud they make on the ground, I could tell that they would deliver a deadly crack on the head.

I could hear the noise of the pub in the forest ahead of me. I followed the road until I came to a fork. Turning right, I was blinded by a huge lamp whose beam was set to illuminate the trail to the club. I could see many people milling around the building. Half-blinded by the intensity of the light, I stumbled along the dirt road until it curved and led me up to the front of the pub. I came face to face with the owner who greeted all his guests with a free beer.

"Hello, welcome." The man nestled an ice cold bottle into my grasp.

I accepted the cool beverage and wandered into the crowded space. I recognized a few of the travellers from Silver Beach among the people and asked if I could join their table.

The beer flowed as fast as the jokes as we celebrated with the owner into the night. He spent the evening in a drunken state, telling everyone how much he loved them for coming to his new place. We laughed whenever he left our table, stumbling off to the next group of patrons.

During the evening some of the tourists brought out huge smouldering joints, passing them around the tables. The sight of pot made me a little nervous, causing me to take a good look around. I had been told the police were tricky and to be careful here on Koh Pha-Ngan. I felt that Hat Rin must have had higher numbers of police than here at Hat Yao; however, I did not want to find out when they did their trip to this part of the island. A fine of twenty-five hundred dollars US kept my sense of practicality alive and I decided once again, that it was probably better to avoid purchase. For now, I indulged in a few short, nervous puffs before passing the joint on to the next waiting hand. Off in the corner was a pool table being used by a few local pool sharks. A video machine was showing an action movie while a stereo system pumped out good, loud tunes. The pub definitely had something for everyone.

Feeling the end of a long day catching up to me, I decided to leave the party a bit early, much to the protests of the staggering host. I thanked him profusely as I made my way to the exit. He didn't remain upset for long as more customers came in as I was leaving. His gloomy expression was suddenly all smiles as he greeted the newcomers.

Led by the beacon on the roof, I followed the path to where the beam could reach no further and disappeared into the dark forest of trees back to Silver Beach. I was once again lost in the sounds of insects and falling coconuts.


## Aussie

*Thursday, December 22, 1994*

Silver Beach was host to a variety of interesting characters during my stay on Koh Pha-Ngan. Some reclusive guests appeared only whenever hunger brought them to Nang's kitchen. Others were a load of laughs and some were plain outrageous. One of the most memorable people was from "down under."

Randy was an Australian redneck. He had been working in London for about a year and was on the way home to Sydney. Taking up residence in the hut right next door to mine, he didn't take long to seek out my company. Randy's capacity for alcohol and drugs was unmatched. Every time I saw him he was ready to smoke up or go to a pub. Actually, he spent most of his days on a rented motorbike, exploring every dirt road he could find.

His redneck streak showed up not only in the way he partied, but also in his treatment of local animals. There were a couple of mangy dogs running around the place and occasionally they would wander a little too close to Randy's hut. Here, on the island, these animals gladly waited for you to approach them because maybe, just maybe, they might get a treat of some food or something. All Randy did was walk up and put the boots to them.

We had been on the sand drinking a cool beer and I noticed that one of the mangy beasts had returned and managed to sneak into Randy's hut without him noticing.

"I think you have another visitor, Randy."

"What, that fucking dog again?" he steamed. I could see the fury well up in his face as he stood up and walked up the small staircase onto his porch.

"Uh-oh," I cringed at the thought of what was to happen next.

I had only seen animals fly through the air in cartoons, at least until now. The still air was filled with the pitiful sounds of the ugly creature being hit hard, its painful yelps coming through the window of the hut. The next thing I saw was the dog exiting out the door without contacting the ground, until he landed in a cloud of dust and expelled air a good five metres beyond the steps. Coming out of the doorway, Randy examined the sight of his handiwork.

"I got a pretty good kick in there," he said proudly. "Felt a bit like a soccer ball." Despite his mean streak, Randy seemed to be popular with women. One extremely horny Australian woman had discovered him after the first few days of his stay. I didn't see much of him after that. They spent the better part of the days in his hut, making love most of the time. One day I was having a meal after snorkelling off the reef and he wandered into the kitchen to have a coffee.

"You look like a mess."

"No fucking wonder," he explained. "She shagged me silly all night and again this morning. She's gone to town for the day. I've finally got a chance to give my balls a rest. You know, I really don't know how much more I can take."

"It sounds the shits. Do you want me to take over for you?" I said to him, laughing. "Seems like she's going to wear you out."

"She's sure trying to." He said this as he was eying another woman who was walking by in the distance along the beach.

"So, where's your 'Sheila'?" he asked me when he finally unlocked his eyes from her ass.

"Well, my luck is not as good as yours. I am really quite shy when it comes to meeting women," I explained.

"That doesn't matter, mate. You just have to have the right lines."

"That has never worked for me."

"I know a line that will work with any woman you want to meet," Randy went on.

"Okay, lay it on me." I awaited the lesson.

"Just say, 'Fuck me if I'm wrong but do I know you?'"


## Reunion

While exploring the Hat Yao area, I discovered a road leading off through the forest. It started at the north end of the beach, next to a rocky outcropping upon which sat another bungalow complex called

Bayview. From here the track led to the next large bay along the coastline, at the top corner of the island. The day I first walked down the dusty road I found a small sign marking a place called Hat Tian. Another arrow-shaped piece of wood was nailed askew on the same tree. The moment I read the sign, I had a vision of Melanie and Stuart searching in vain for their friends on the entirely wrong coast of the island, sitting out on a lonely beach, cursing their friends for choosing such a meeting place.

Actually, their friends had chosen pretty decent digs after all. I walked down to check it out and saw a scene similar to Silver Beach, except that Hat Tian was a lone bungalow, without the ambient noise of other guest houses. When I first saw the place, I thought to move here for the rest of my stay but chose to remain at Silver Beach. On my next trip to town I dropped a note for my two friends in Thong Sala's postal outlet. My brief greeting also included the news of Hat Tian's existence on my side of the island. Trusting they'd get the message, I waited for a response.

I was hanging in my hammock one cloudy afternoon, reading a book from the kitchen's library. I had gotten so used to the passing of people along the beach that I did not notice the couple approaching from the beach entrance beside me.

"There you are," Melanie said as she shook the ropes by my head.

"Hey, easy on the furniture, will ya?" I grabbed her arm, laughing and pulling her into a tight hug, my arm around her neck.

"Looks like a good find, John," said Stuart as he inspected the premises, nodding.

"Not as good as what your friends found," I reminded him. He shook his head and laughed.

"The day we got your note, we ran into them in town," he said. "We just moved up here today. We've been just east of Hat Rin since we saw you last."

I apologized for ditching them so soon after arriving at Rin beach. They wished they had joined me in my hasty exodus—it was an absolutely chaotic scene with lots of people wasted pretty much all the time. The trouble was the partying kept going until the wee hours of the morning, along with the constant throb of techno-music.

"We at least moved out of earshot of it for awhile," said Melanie. "Our second choice was similar but not as crazy as the main beach."

"Well, I am glad you finally made it to the sensible side of the island," I said jokingly.

"Yeah, too bad it took so long to get Stuart out of the bar," Melanie nudged Stu with an elbow and a smile.

"Come on, if it's a sunny day . . . of course I'm going to have a few, aren't I?" he jibed.

"We should get together. Maybe I'll come up to your place for a meal one of these nights," I said to them. We planned a rendezvous for a future night before they finally wandered back up the beach to their home.

"I'll bring the biggest stereo I can find," I said to them as they parted.

That short visit really cheered me as I read the rest of the afternoon away. These two really loved life and knew how to have fun. Their playfulness inspired me. Their zest for life rubbed off on everyone around them and I yearned for a similar connection in my own life.

It was to be the last few days that I would spend with these companions I had travelled with for so long. Their friends had been away in Malaysia and had returned to rendezvous before the whole group headed south again to explore the Cameron Highlands, an area of rich tropical forests in the central Malay mountains. From there, they would move on to Australia.


## The Green Light of Sunset
*Sunday, December 25, 1994*

Nang was in the kitchen when I entered the back door, was busy preparing food, and at first did not see me. I knocked lightly on the door to announce my presence.

"Good morning, Nang."

"Hello, John," she said politely.

I walked to where she stood beside the table. I gently took her hand and placed a large bundle of incense into her palm.

"Merry Christmas," I said to her. "This is for your family. I have enjoyed staying with you and your family here on the island." She beamed with delight when she received the gift. A few other guests had given gifts to Nang and Sit throughout the day, as gestures of gratitude for their hard work and for their willingness to take strangers into their home. She set the incense with the other items on a small shelf.

"Thank you," she said, hugging me. "You coming later for dinner at beach?" Her English was basic but she managed well.

"Dinner?"

"We make dinner for guests tonight. You come."

"Okay, sounds great," I said. I walked to the ice box and took out a few pieces of fruit before closing the lid. I pulled a small logbook out from under the front counter and added the list of food to the tab to be paid at the end of my stay. It was always amazing to me that the Thais had such a level of implicit trust for the travellers staying with them. Sticking the small notebook back into its place, I put my lunch in my pack and made for the door.

"See you, Nang," I waved and turned through the doorway.

Taking the trail toward Hat Tian, I broke away and pursued one of the smaller trails leading into the forest. The cool, moist air enveloped me as I entered the shady groves of trees. Coconut trees along the side of the trail had been felled, making the hiking a little less hazardous.

It wasn't long before the trail became quite steep. I clambered up the slope and reached a small plateau where at once I heard the sound of water ahead of me. I followed the meandering path as it dipped and rolled over rugged terrain. Finally, the trees opened up along the edge of a small stream. Lush greenery shone along the bank, humidity dripping from leaves, and the water bubbled and swirled around small boulders as it slipped by me.

I continued on until the hill turned straight up and became a small cliff in front of me. I could go no further. I looked up to see where the stream emerged from the rocks above me, creating a beautiful waterfall. The misty veil of water fell noisily onto the rocks by the foot of the trail. Finding a dry place for my belongings and my clothes, I soon stood naked under the rushing stream. I basked in the refreshingly cool water, rinsing the sweat of the climb from my skin.

I strung my hammock between two trees and let the breeze dry my body. It felt good to be exposed and open to nature, my pale skin a sharp contrast to the green shadows. I breathed deeply and listened to the rich sounds around me; the water splashing on the rocks, the wind gently whistling through the trees. At times I could hear a few unknown creatures moving through the branches. I realized they were geckos when I heard their comical croaking. The insects were numerous but they never really seemed to bother me that much. The wind felt good on my damp skin. I soon grew cool and reached for my clothes.

As I ate my lunch of bananas and mangoes, I thought there was no place I would have rather been on this Christmas Day. This close connection with nature was so peaceful. I could feel it soaking through my skin.

Yet, at the same time, I felt restless. My thoughts kept distracting my attempts to enjoy this scene by the water. I felt I was searching for some place to go, instead of just being where I was. I sat with my racing mind, trying to allow myself to explore the reason for my uneasiness.

A desire to understand the nature of the changes I was experiencing on my journey overtook me as I processed thoughts and feelings. So many wonderful things had been put before me yet I felt somehow removed from them. Any lessons I had learned seemed intangible. I felt I needed something concrete to prove that I had changed as a person. I felt I was still the man I was when I arrived here. What had I learned? What could I use to take me to the next step of self-discovery? I sat silently in my confusion and prayed. I asked for a sign, for a catalyst to bring me to another level of understanding.

The afternoon slipped away. I finally untied my hanging seat, gathered my stuff into my pack, and scrambled down the embankment to the flatter stretch of trail further down the waterway. By the time I reached the ocean the sun was nearing the horizon. Ahead, I could see a fire flickering on the beach in front of Silver Beach. A small crowd of people had started to gather. A gentle breeze carried the acrid smoke from the fire past me and on down the seaside. I looked back to see a trail of blue haze hanging out over the bay. I began to collect chunks of wood, arriving at the fireside with an armload of driftwood fuel.

Watching the sunset seemed to be a popular activity among many of the travellers I had met. Many had turned it into a ritual at the end of each day. They would cease whatever it was they were doing, pour themselves a cool drink, and head to the edge of the sea to view the spectacle of colour.

Sit was busy getting a nice hot bed of coals prepared for the evening meal of squid and fish.

"Need any help, Sit?" I asked my host.

"No, Mr. John. I am okay," he replied. He insisted that I just relax and join the others on the beach.

Among the people here were, of course, Australians, a few more Canadians, a guy from Israel, and a small group of Swiss. They had all gathered in groups by the edge of the water and were watching as the sun neared the sea. I strolled among them to find a place to sit. I noticed a young woman sitting on her own off to one side of the crowd. I made my way to the open space beside her on the beach.

"Mind if I join you?" I asked.

"Not at all," she said in a thick Australian accent. "My name's Libby."

I had seen Libby at Silver Beach for a day or so. A strong swimmer, she spent most of her time taking long tours out to the edge of the reef. I would see her walking out of the water, her body sleek and buff in her short wetsuit.

"Nice to meet you," I said, introducing myself. "Looks like a good front row seat."

"Yeah, it sure is," she said. "Waiting for the green light is my favorite part of the day."

"Waiting for the what?" I asked, puzzled.

"The green light of sunset," she said. "Have you ever seen it?"

"No, I haven't. What is it?" I asked.

"It's a rich rush of green colour that flashes in the sky at the instant the sun drops over the horizon. If you look carefully, you'll see it."

I was intrigued. I had always seen the rich bands of colours in the twilight sky, including a rich green hue. But I had never seen it flash. We waited for the sun to dip until there was only a small, bright piece of it left reaching out with its rays, as if to fight gravity itself. I saw the sun disappear and immediately noticed a brief flash of pale green light. It was a flash like that of a distant lighthouse, just on the horizon. When the green burst faded the light from the sky behind flooded in to replace the beams of sunlight. An even paler layer of green light emerged, creating the first of several spectral bands which filled the sky from the horizon to the first few visible stars.

"That is amazing," I said to Libby. "I can't believe I've never seen this before."

Libby made a slight murmur but her eyes never moved from

where they were fixed. She was absorbed in the moment and continued to stare at the evening sky.

"The change in colour is so amazing," she finally said to me.

The word 'change' stuck in my head. I remembered my afternoon at the waterfall and my need for clarity of mind. The uneasiness and fear had felt like a wall pushing me back into myself. My anxiety around acceptance of change had made me unable to move forward. I was resisting stepping into unknown territory and the struggle was exhausting me. Then I asked myself what I could do to change my view. I closed my eyes and breathed deeply and consciously allowed myself to be where I was in that moment. The moment I gave up resisting, I felt a deep calm inside. I felt the heavy feeling in my chest start to dissolve.

I looked back out over the bay to the shimmering clouds above the horizon. The pale green light had deepened and more rich colour bands could be seen growing with the twilight. It was a transformation. A metamorphosis. Like a chameleon, the sky and the day were growing new skin. Like them, I felt the changing as well, like the tides. I thought about Jill and how we had drifted apart and all that had come to pass. But this time I let go of my attachment to my fears of being alone and being faced with the unknown. My body relaxed as I let go of my guilt, fear, and regret. I accepted that I was safe and that I could do whatever I needed to survive. I had to let myself trust in faith and fate. I sat in that moment and gave thanks for an answer to my prayer, with the sound of the wind and the buzz of the insects in my ears.

Now my challenge was to use my energies for growth rather than self-judgement. I had a vision of things left to be accomplished. I also envisioned an end that was too near. I had allowed so much time to pass without focusing energies and talents, without making my life more alive. I had become someone else other than me. I now knew that I was free to choose for myself. It was a beginning . . . a start to reclaiming the magic of creation.

"Hey," a voice said to me. Pulling myself out of my thoughts, I looked up to see Libby. I had not noticed her standing in front of me.

"Are you coming?" she asked. She turned and walked toward the fire where the others now stood. Sit was shouting for us to come and have our Christmas feast.

I lagged behind for a few moments as the sky grew quite dark. I inhaled the cool evening air and smiled to myself. Finally, I stood and walked to the firepit.

Sit joyfully placed a plate of rich food into my hands. "Merry Christmas, Mr. John."


## A Day in the Life of Silver Beach
*Tuesday, December 27, 1994*

Sit ran the sputtering engine for a few minutes as we set out the fishing tools. He had stuck a wide-brimmed flowered hat on his head to protect himself from the sun and stood proudly at the helm of his tiny ship. When the engine had warmed, he turned the craft out into the deep water, straight out from the beach. Soon the tiny boat was bobbing along the tops of large offshore swells. After a few more minutes the captain cut his engine and we sat floating in the middle of what, according to Sit, was prime fishing territory.

"You take this one," instructed Sit. He handed me a jig line hanging from a small stick. A number of small hooks were tied along its length.

"Where's the bait?" I asked.

"No need. The fish just bite at the flash of metal," he said.

Working off the stern, I bobbed the line up and down quickly in the water. I got my first bites almost immediately.

"Hey, they're biting already." I pulled the jig line up to find three tiny, yellow fish hanging from the transparent string, fighting furiously to return to the sea.

"They are hungry today, like me," Sit said as he reached out to grab hold of the fishing line. He removed one of the tiny fish and impaled it on a larger hook. The metal tip pierced in and through the back of the bait fish. He instructed me to put the rest of the tiny bait into a small basket at my feet. He turned and threw the main line over the side.

For a good hour we sat in the bobbing waves with not one large fish to show for our efforts. A few bites had us excited for awhile but all of the fish seemed to escape. We moved our vessel to other spots to try our luck but we were definitely not having a good day. Our morale was fading fast. I could see it in Sit's face. Fishing to him was not just a sporting thing you did with your buddies on a Saturday afternoon while drinking a few beers. It was his livelihood, his way of feeding his mother, his wife, and soon, his child.

There were a number of other ships out on the sea. A few of the boats had lines of fish traps that they were tending. We soon saw the men on one particular boat pull a wire trap full of huge fish to the surface. They must have emptied twenty or twenty-five good-sized fish into their hold. Sit watched them with particular interest. Three hours had passed and still no big fish had come our way. We were both frustrated as we sat and watched everyone else haul in their catch.

"Hey, leave some for us," Sit cried out at one point, smiling back at me from the helm. At last Sit started the engine and took us further out to sea. He managed to intercept the boat that we had been observing earlier. It turned out that the captain was a good friend of his. They exchanged greetings as we pulled along side the ship. A short conversation in Thai resulted in Sit asking his friend if he could spare a few of the large fish. I could hear the humour in the voices of all the men, probably ribbing Sit for not being able to catch his own.

The captain soon threw a small pile of big fish into the bottom of our boat. Sit's face lit up with glee and a huge smile took over his face.

"Okay Mr. John, we go home now. Fishing is easy today," he said. We both laughed uproariously, agreeing to tell Nang how we had caught these fish on our own.

Around 11:00 the heat of the tropical sun was intense so I took refuge in the shady confines of my hammock. The hottest times of the day would find me in such a place, away from the searing heat. I enjoyed this time whether I was reading or writing in my journal.

Thong Sala had an outdoor Muay Thai arena that held large bouts on weekends. To get the word out about the attraction, small pick-up trucks equipped with huge loud speakers and billboard signs would cruise the island, broadcasting to all the bungalows along the coast.

I had just set my journal down on the porch rail and closed my eyes for a short nap when I heard an engine whining in the distance. Thinking it was one of the usual town taxis, I took no notice until my ears were pierced with the sound of a bull horn.

"Muay Thai, Muay Thai, Muay Thai, Thaaaaaaaaai Boxing!!" The crackling voice spewed out of the metal speaker cones, grating my eardrums like sandpaper. I was reminded of my frustration with the Dickie Dee ice cream trucks that invade North American neighbourhoods every summer with their silly little songs that repeat forever. This music had always driven me mad. I had joked many times about having fantasies of putting a few bullets through their speaker cones to stop the obnoxious sound. Here, I was ready to pitch a few coconuts at the truck by the time the driver finally left. Unfortunately, he returned a short time later as he made his way back south to Thong Sala. Always louder than they needed to be, the pulsating announcements got the better of most of us, including the locals. Once the noisy vehicle had gone, peace and quiet returned to the beach.

Hat Yao had its own massage therapist. A tiny old man carrying nothing but a shoulder bag and a small bamboo mat, he would cruise the sand looking for prospective clientele. I had seen him many times, but just in passing. I had heard from others who had been patrons of his service and they had nothing but good things to say. A friend to everyone who lived on the beach, he could be seen visiting families who had bungalows along the strip of sand in between sessions. This particular day, he had come for a visit with Sit and Nang when I went to pick up a cool drink from the kitchen. He offered his services and I asked him his price for a normal bodywork session.

"One hundred *baht*," he said to me. Six dollars. I couldn't afford not to.

The old man took me down to the edge of the sea and selected a shady spot to set his mat down. He began his work without uttering a single word.

A steady breeze, strong hands, and the heat of the day soon had me fast asleep. In fact, my masseuse had to wake me a few times to tell me to change positions on the mat. The last time I woke I checked my watch and an hour had raced by like five minutes. I gladly paid him the fee and sent him on his way. Today was a busy day for him. He hadn't gotten very far when a woman who had seen him work on me stopped him as he walked along the shoreline. Once again he set to work in his outdoor spa.

The beach was also frequented by a few local food vendors. Thankfully, their sales pitches did not blast me out of my hammock as the bull horns had done. Their incessant manner, however, would sometimes have me ready to toss them into the surf.

The one vendor who sticks out in my memory was the lady who sold cakes and cookies. She lived somewhere on Hat Yao and was a common face along the seaside. Her wares were freshly baked, usually still warm. I had patronized her on occasion so whenever she was strolling by Silver Beach she would detour up and around my cabin, just in case I might need another snack. She sold many varieties of cake but I had never really understood how wide that variety was . . . until today.

I heard her coming closer, the chant of her sales pitch drifting in with the breeze. I glanced down the beach to see her familiar large sun hat, and metal tins tucked tightly under her arm. She stopped every once in awhile to talk to friends and then slowly made her way closer to my neighbourhood.

I wasn't in the mood for any snacks, or so I thought, as I had just finished lunch following my massage. I had gone back to my hammock to wait out the rest of the day's hottest rays. When she came upon me I was attempting to doze awhile.

"Chocolate cake," she said as she strolled by. Not looking up, I simply said "No" and made a light wave of my hand, indicating I wasn't interested.

"Pumpkin cake . . . carrot cake . . . vanilla cake . . . banana cake . . . ganga cake . . ."

The last two words rolled over my synapses and I went from wishing that she would go for a swim to wondering why she hadn't come sooner. She had made a few funny muffins as part of her daily baking and was now trying to unload them as quickly as she could.

I had never had the chance to try one of these treats because she was often sold out by the time she reached my part of the beach.

"Let me have one of those," I said to her. Selecting a green-spotted muffin from her tin box, I laid a few coins in her hand.

"Try to eat quickly," she told me. "Police don't like those ones." She looked around as if she were watching for hidden law enforcement.

"No sweat," I told her as I stuffed the morsel into my mouth. It was pretty damn dry for a freshly baked cake but I enjoyed it all the same. Happy at yet another sale, the woman thanked me and headed back onto the beach and the next bungalow.

I felt a slight buzz from the cake, but it actually induced more sleep and I found myself waking up from a "nap" some three hours later. It was late afternoon and the temperature much cooler. I forced myself to exit the hanging bed. Packing my wallet and flashlight into my waist pouch, I made my way over to Hat Tian for my appointed rendezvous with Stuart and Melanie for dinner and a few drinks.

## Special Shake

"Sorry I'm late," I said as I patted Stuart on the shoulder. He was sitting with a small group of people in a secluded corner. "I had a slight delay." My misadventure with the marijuana muffin remained in my thoughts as I found myself a space on the bench.

"Are you good and hungry?" asked Melanie. I simply gave her a smile and took hold of a paper menu from the pile on the table. She could not imagine how hungry I was. After our meal we sat around in conversation. Carlsberg bottles littered the tabletop and the kitchen was kept busy with further orders of snacks. One of our group finally got the attention of the owner and waved him over to the table.

"Can I order a special shake?" he asked. The owners eyes lit up and a wry smile came over his face. Nodding as he turned, he re-entered the kitchen to prepare the order.

"What is a special shake?" I asked the person who had just made the request.

"It's great," he said. "The owner makes it from a special recipe. It is a drink made of chocolate milk, nuts, spices, and lots of marijuana all whipped up in a blender."

Stuart and I looked at each other and started to chuckle. I think we both knew at the same time that we had to have one just for the experience of it.

The owner returned to our table a few minutes later with a rich-looking shake in a tall glass. It was so thick that the straw stood straight up in the tumbler.

"Two more please," I indicated that my friend and I wanted one of his treats.

He smiled again and returned to his refuge in the back of the bungalow.

"How is it?" Stuart asked his friend. The young man did not say a word as his mouth was busy drawing the concoction up the feeding tube. He simply raised his hand and made an okay gesture.

Stuart glanced over to me, "I think that means he likes it."

Not too long after that, the owner emerged from the kitchen holding two tall glasses. A few patrons who had obviously had one of these before followed his progress to see who had made the order. He slowly walked over to our table, careful not to spill any onto the sand floor. Placing the drinks in front of us, he looked me in the eye and smiled.

"Have a good day," he said.

The shake tasted rich and delicious. It was hard not to take it up into the straw as fast as I could. Stuart was having the same problem. Back at the counter, the owner would occasionally glance over to see how we were enjoying his recipe. Stuart and I gave him the two thumbs up sign and he laughed with delight.

Daylight began to fail around us and tiki torches were lit to hold back the blackness. By the time 9:00 rolled around I was feeling quite groggy from the shake. It had acted more like a sleeping pill in a glass; I struggled to keep my eyes open at the table. Finally giving in to the call of my hammock, I bade good evening to my friends.

With my trusty flashlight in hand, I made my way out to the dirt path which led up a steep hill to the main road. In the daylight there is an amazing view of the sea and small islands in the distance. At night the view is the cosmos, brilliantly gleaming without the interference of urban lights. I stood in the middle of the road as the half-moon dimly cast shadows around me. I tipped my head back and gazed into the night sky.

I was blanketed in stars. Here in the vicinity of the equator, the night panorama was unfamiliar to me. I recognized a few constellations and enjoyed the sight of ones I had never seen. I don't remember seeing the Big Dipper during my entire trip but Orion made its familiar pattern in the night sky. I looked on and on. It was as if I could see into the night forever. I stood in awe of the view for what seemed like hours.

I finally turned to make my way home, keeping to the road and listening for the familiar sound of dropping coconuts.

Reaching my hut by the beach, I quickly readied myself for sleep. I felt fatigue overtaking me. After climbing into my hanging bed and lighting a plethora of mosquito coils along the porch rail, I was soon fast asleep.

At 2:00 in the morning I woke up. I wasn't sure why—I just woke up. My eyes opened to see a dark figure looming over me. I could see it was a man by the size of his torso. The length of his hair helped me recognize that it was Randy. He was asking me something; he wanted to give me something.

I snapped out of my sleep and sat up in my hammock. Randy had perched himself on the railing while slowly taking a puff on the mouth of a giant bamboo bong that someone had found on the premises. It had become known as the house bong, as guests would take turns pulling it from its hiding place in the crook of an old palm tree, under a piece of withered leaf fibre, replacing it when they were done just in case the police came by.

Randy had filled the bowl with a generous pile of spice and passed the smouldering mound over to me where I sat.

"Here, have some," he said.

I graciously turned his offer down, relating my earlier encounter with the sacred herb.


## Hat Rin: Acid and Sunrise
*Friday, December 30, 1994*

It was the middle of the afternoon when I heard a loud roar outside my hut. It was the sound of a motorcycle being revved up more than it needed to be. I had been writing in my journal and quite enjoying my quiet time. The odour of bike exhaust was now filling my hut and I wanted this racket to end. I finally stuck my head out of the door to protest, only to see the smiling face of Randy staring back at me.

"How you goin', mate?" he asked, laughing.

"I was great until you showed up with that thing."

"I'm going to Hat Rin," he told me. "There's a big rave party tonight. Do you want to come along?"

Ever since I had come to the islands, the idea of going to a major party spot had been the last choice for me. This time, however, I decided to take him up on the offer.

"How are you getting there?" I asked.

Randy twisted his wrist one more time and another loud roar and cloud of blue smoke screamed from the dirtbike. "Hop on, Johnny boy. All you have to do is hold on tight."

I thought twice about the transport, especially driven by this mad party fiend.

"Promise you won't kill us both?" I asked him. I had seen so many tourists in Thong Sala covered with scabs, recovering from crashes suffered from riding the island's rough, uneven roads.

"Just don't let go," he said back with a grin.

"What time does the party begin?" I was curious as to how long the night might be.

"Midnight. I figure if we go early and get something to eat, we can get a place in the pub and sleep until the party starts and go all night," he said.

"Wait a minute," I was confused. "Sleep? In the bar?"

"Yeah, sure. I did it last week, no problem," he went on. "Lots of people do it. The place never fills up until after midnight anyway. The owners don't really care because they are sure to get plenty of paying business after we wake up. That way we can be sure to get a table and we can last the night." I laughed at the strange reservation system.

"Sure, I'll tag along," I said. "Just let me get my stuff together." I threw a blanket and small kit into my pack. With just enough money to tide me over, I entrusted my passport and papers to Sit who happily tucked them away in a safe place.

The bike ride was wild and rough and I struggled to hang onto the tiny seat. Fortunately, Randy was an experienced driver and, despite the rugged terrain, managed to make it as comfortable as possible, although sometimes I wondered. Lack of a helmet also gave me good incentive to grip on for dear life, the thought of hard ground increasing my gripping power ten-fold.

Arriving in Thong Sala, we stocked up on beer and water. We packed it on my back and were soon travelling down the more treacherous road to Hat Rin. Washouts along the track gave Randy a test of his skill as he weaved around the bad spots in the dirt road. My skill as a passenger was also challenged. Loaded down with beverages, my body would shift back and forth on each and every corner, throwing the bike slightly off balance each time. That, mixed with the passing truck taxis careening in the other direction, had us hoping we would not end up in the deep, bramble-filled ditch off the right side of the road.

The ride soon levelled out as the road flattened and we entered Hat Rin. The congested little community sat stuffed onto the edge of the sand, surrounding a small bay. The beach itself stretched out to the northwest for quite a distance.

We pulled into the central square where I had arrived with Mel and Stu on my last quick visit. There were many bungalows literally built on top of each other. A central street bordered these accommodations and from here the town spiralled up and around a high hill. At the top of the hill was our ultimate destination—the Half Moon pub.

"I'll be back," said Randy. "I've got to find a place to park the bike for the night. I've got some friends just up the hill. I'll dump it off and come back and join you." He restarted the beast and roared out of the square, riding a slalom course through a group of dogs nearby.

Randy returned and we both stocked up on food to go and made for nearby Hat Rin beach. Finding a suitable place on the sand, we dined ravenously. During our meal a few dogs began to wander a little too close, hoping to win a free meal ticket from one of us.

"Bastards," cursed Randy. He began with shouting to keep the animals at bay but they were soon back and closer this time, whining and drooling saliva onto the sand.

Randy finally stood and met his first guest with a good solid kick to the head. The creature yelped in pain and retreated, but only for a moment. Unfortunately, the dog decided to test Randy's sympathy a second time. This time, Randy's boot struck twice in quick succession. The mangy creature rolled in pain on the sand. I was upset at the way he was treating the animals.

"You don't like these dogs much, do you?" I chose the words with care.

"Can't stand the bastards," he replied, disgusted. I left it at that. After eating, we remained on the edge of the bay, enjoying a few beers before heading to the hill-top nightclub.

"Are your friends going to join us, Randy?" I asked him.

"Hope so," he said. "If I can get them off their asses." He laughed. They were friends he had worked with in England. Heading to Australia as well, they were here for only a few days.

"Let's go and see if we can't encourage them," Randy told me, getting to his feet.

We walked to his friends' bungalow and tried to talk them into going with us. They had plans to go to the party but not until much later. It was now 10:30. We also learned from them that the pub didn't really get going until around 2:00 in the morning. We stuck with our plan and went on without them.

We wound our way along the path to the club sitting on the very top of the hill. When we entered, music was pumping and a few people were dancing but the place was rather empty. I noticed a few couples already fast asleep under tables. We set up a small camp in one corner, under a short-legged table by one of the side windows. Surprisingly, I was actually able to sleep, even though the music was loud.

I awoke at 2:00 to the throbbing sound of techno pop, vibrating the floorboards I lay on. The smell of booze and cigarette smoke hit me with a nauseating punch. Then I remembered that I had actually made the decision to come here. Sitting up, I noticed that Randy was already up dancing with some girl he had discovered. Seeing that I was the last remaining sleeper in the room, I pulled myself together and ordered a refreshment before the owner had me turfed out.

"Good morning," Randy said as he returned to the table. "Care for some of this?" He held out his hand to reveal two small pieces of paper imprinted with colourful designs. I recognized them to be blotter acid, LSD. He had found a dealer in the club who sold it to him as he danced. I declined. Happily staying with beer, I told my friend to cut loose for the evening.

So as not to let it go to waste, he calmly tossed both pieces into his mouth and drank an entire bottle of beer to wash them down.

"Nice knowing you, Randy," I said to him, shocked.

I had a great time dancing with lovely women and laughing at the escapades of my spaced-out pal.

I managed to stay in the club for quite awhile before my tolerance for the sound ran out. Not being a huge fan of modern dance/club music, I soon felt as if the continuous beat and rhythm would wear a hole through my head. I really wanted to leave and go somewhere nice and quiet. I checked my watch. It was 5:15 AM.

"I have to head out, bud. This music is making me ill." I had reached my limit. He looked up at me and said something incoherent and scattered. He seemed to look right through me and then began to laugh uncontrollably. I laughed back, stood up and waved good-bye.

"Take care of yourself, mate." I laughed sympathetically at my friend's wasted condition, turned, and made for the door.

I walked down the path toward town, aided by dim lights by the fence. People were still coming up the road to the club. It was now 5:30 AM and the rave was in full swing. Taking only a few minutes, I arrived on the strip of sand where Randy and I had eaten our dinner earlier that evening. A few people remained in a nearby club but the main throng had either headed up to where I had just come from or had retired for another day. A few employees were raking up the mess of the evening's revelry into neat piles in front of the beach clubs.

Pulling my beach towel from my bag, I found a suitable resting place on the sand. It was cool by the water so I donned my sweatshirt. My head pounding, I lay down on the sand and looked at the sky, trying to shake the effects of the noise pollution I had endured for so long. My body shook for some time as I slowly began to relax. The stars were gleaming although the first hint of dawn was creeping into the early morning, a noticeable dome of light over the ocean horizon. My eyes closed and I drifted off into slumber.

Suddenly I was rudely woken by the sound of a ferocious dog fight right next to me. I sat up to see a number of mangy, slobbering dogs hovering over my blanket. Perhaps they thought I had expired and I was a free meal to be had. The fight was between the two dogs closest to me and I figured that they were arguing as to who got to bite me first. My quick movement startled all of the animals. My surprised shout got the attention of the remaining beasts and they began to back away from my sleeping space. Warily winding their way down the sandy waterfront, they soon left to pursue other sources of food.

Thankful for not being eaten, I sat up to see what time it was— 6:00. The sun was almost kissing the lip of the world. A few diligent bar employees were still working. Watching them, I saw a sight that made me cringe.

As dawn was breaking, each club along the beach had a person who was busy digging a huge hole in the beach. Into these holes went the various piles of garbage that they had spent so much time collecting, a fresh layer of sand on the top to disguise the existence of the stuff. The rest of the work was, apparently, left for the tide to wash away.


### New Year's
*Saturday, December 31, 1994*

The new year of 1995 had come at last. Celebrations were happening all along Hat Yao bay and, as a gesture of good will to his guests, Sit had yet another dinner feast set on the beach. This time, however, we all pitched in on the preparation of food and the barbecue site by the water.

During the set-up we were disturbed by the horrible cries of a large pig that had been tied to a stake beside the Gypsy Bar. It was now meeting its end as the main entrée for the club's dinner. Whoever took on the job should have had more experience because this poor animal had a long, slow, and painful death. The cries for help lasted too long for me to feel comfortable. Myself and others like me were ready to go and get the job done, just to put the poor bastard out of its misery. Ready to make our move, the air finally fell silent and the hair on our necks soon lay flat once again.

Another seafood feast was enjoyed by all of Sit's guests and we sat, singing and laughing by the ocean, until just before midnight. Handing out cool Carlsbergs for our efforts and help, Nang and Sit proposed a toast to health and prosperity.

When the midnight hour arrived we all shouted the countdown into the night air. The sounds echoed through the still palm trees and over the silent waters of the bay. Our revelry continued with our own fireworks display. Most of us had collected various kinds of rockets and bombs from stores in town in preparation for this night.

The fire was stoked up and we lit up the beach front for well over an hour. With all the guests taking turns setting off bombs, roman candles, and the inevitable flying bees that had become my personal favourite.

One guy had a whole row of stuff set up. He'd sneak in from the back to light a lot of fuses quickly, making it resemble a real fireworks display. The rest of us set off rockets, candles, and bees anywhere and everywhere. Huge ceramic balls, coming in all sizes, with nothing but a wick on top, were quite popular. They produced a shower of fiery sparks and a shrill whine that continued for some time, depending on the size. Someone had purchased one of the large ones and I swear it went on for two to three minutes in an unrelenting plume of fire. The rowdy mayhem carried on until late into the night. Many of us stayed near the fire, keeping warm as it slowly burned down to nothing but coals.

The next day was slow as not too many people were up early. Having not consumed that much alcohol, I was up and about in the earlier hours. Nang was up as well, not because of having enough sleep but because of a lack of it.

"Sit missing," she told me. She was very distressed. She had been searching everywhere for him but with no luck. After searching their own place thoroughly, Nang had just come back from asking her neighbours whether her husband had ended up on their doorstep.

"Don't worry, Nang. I am sure he is not far." I tried to reassure her that he was perfectly all right and would return soon. I sat with her as I ate my breakfast to keep her company. She was grateful for my help even though she was still uncomfortable at Sit's absence.

"It not like him," she told me. "He never go with not telling me."

I again reassured her that perhaps he had gone for a drink with friends and would be back. Still worried, Nang went back to her work, hopeful that I was right.

Mid-afternoon heralded Sit's return. Much to the relief of Nang, he had resurfaced after a night of rowdiness with his cousin in Thong Sala. Apparently he had a few drinks on the beach with us and then decided to go off with his relative to tie one on.

When I heard he had returned I went in to the kitchen to find him slowly eating soup and extremely hung over.

"Not drinking again for awhile, Mr. John," he said, in obvious pain. Not one to drink much anyway, Sit rested there, nursing his swollen head. Meanwhile, Nang let him know how she felt in an angry tone.


## Farewell

It was during the next few days that people started to leave Pha-Ngan. It seemed that each evening another familiar face climbed into the back of the truck taxi and left for the ferries in Thong Sala. I, too, was planning my departure. I had bought a ticket to Penang, Malaysia a few days earlier. I was sad to be leaving Koh Pha-Ngan. I had made many friends and I would miss them all, especially my hosts.

During my last few days, I had a final visit with Melanie and Stuart at their Hat Tian cabin.

"We have been through a lot together in the last two months," I said as we sat and reflected on the adventures we all had shared. "I am going to miss you two."

"Same for us, mate," said Stuart. "It's been a slice." They were leaving for Malaysia in just a few days.

"Just stay clear of the drugs down there," I warned, thinking of the harsh penalties that surpassed even Thailand's enforcement.

Melanie laughed. "Oh God, there's lots of good drugs in Malaysia."

"Well, then just don't get caught," I said. We all embraced one final time.

"Just don't forget my postcard from Yemen," I said, walking toward the trail home.

"Yeah, man!" shouted Melanie, her smile burning into my memory.

My last evening on Pha-Ngan was with Sit and Nang. Once I had packed all of my things, I sat in the kitchen with my gracious hosts and enjoyed a last meal before the Thong Sala taxi made its rounds.

"Not much longer until the baby comes," I said to them. "I hope that all goes well with you and your new family."

"Thank you, Mr. John," said Sit. "Maybe you can come back to see us again one day."

"I would love to come back to see you. It has been a privilege to stay with you."

Soon, I heard the Toyota taxi's engine winding closer and closer to the rear of Silver Beach. Taking my cue, I bid my friends farewell. Sit saw me out to the truck, lifting my bag into the covered box. Climbing in, I turned to shake his hand. His was the last face I would remember of Pha-Ngan.

Over my three weeks here I got to know Sit and Nang quite well and found them to be some of the most beautiful people I have ever met. So giving and so friendly to strangers. Their life was very simple, but I could feel how good it was through their eyes. There was nothing like the smile on a Thai's face to remind me to think twice of things I thought to be problems.

"Chok dee (good luck)!" he shouted as the truck carried me away into the night.

# CHAPTER 8: MALAYSIA

## Penang
*Saturday, January 7, 1995*

I rolled over, sticking my face into the frame of the tiny porthole close to my head. Careful not to wake the young woman still sleeping beside me, I stared out into the dim light of morning. The ferry boat was pulling into the cluttered harbour of Surat Thani in southern Thailand. The myriad docks were plugged with ships of many shapes and sizes, mainly fishing boats. A few people moved about the decks of some vessels, preparing to sail into the cool morning air. I quietly opened the latch and swung the brass window frame inward. A small breath of air rushed in and brushed against my face. With it, the sounds of a few sea birds drifted inside the stuffy confines of the ferry.

The cool air made my body shiver. I was soaked with perspiration from sleeping on the blue vinyl mattress under my sleeping sheet. The crowded room smelled of bodies and sweat, the fresh air drifting in through the window giving me some reprieve from the stale air. Muffled coughs came from various areas of the floor as other people began to wake up.

Once docked, the ferry's engine died with a shudder. Many passengers rushed for the exit, creating a massive people-jam at the small doorways. I slowly gathered my possessions and waited patiently for the crowd to dissipate. I quenched my thirst with some water, slung my pack and guitar over my back and made my way to the gangway behind the other passengers.

Marching off the end of the wooden gangway, I entered a large compound full of vehicles. The crowd kicked up a sizeable cloud of dust amid the mass of small trucks and vans. Shouting by the local Thais drifted over the crowd of passengers as they tried to draw clients their way. This southern Thai city is a major centre for transport to all areas of the country. I wandered through the crowds and vans, my ears attentive for the place name I wanted.

"Penang!" I heard the call as I walked to one end of the busy compound.

"Yeah," I responded to the cries of a tiny man wearing a worn cap on his head.

"This way, please." He guided me over to yet another cramped, vinyl-benched pick-up truck.

"Oh, God," I said to myself. Surely I wouldn't have to travel all the way to Malaysia in one of these? Reluctantly, I threw my baggage into the back of the box and climbed inside. As I entered the truck box, I noticed an attractive woman facing me on the opposite bench.

"Good morning," she said to me. I settled onto the hard seat across from her. My first thought was that her accent was decidedly Canadian.

"Hi, I'm John," I said.

"Lisa," she said plainly. She was tall and blond, with a healthy figure. She wore shorts, a halter top, and sandals. I felt myself being turned on by her as I checked my watch—6:00 AM. It seemed that my ever-active libido refused to get any sleep at all.

"So, where in Canada are you from?" I asked with a smile.

"Langley," she responded. "How did you know I was from Canada?"

"We sound like we're neighbours, especially since I'm from Vancouver."

"Very good," she said, laughing.

"Let me try again," I said to her. "Do you know anyone from Langley by the name of Holcroft?" One of my workmates, from Langley, came to mind.

"Yeah, Larry Holcroft," she said to me, taken aback by the coincidence.

I simply stared at her in disbelief. It turned out that the Larry she knew was the son of the man I worked with in Vancouver. She had worked with Larry Jr. a few years previous. Recalling this story some months later, both Larry Sr. and I were amazed at how small the world we live in really is.

"If you get any better at this, I am going to have to leave," she said in jest.

"Don't worry," I said to her. "I'm already freaking myself out." We both laughed.

We were the only passengers in the back of the truck when it finally rattled out of the dusty compound and onto the road.

"Do you think we'll get to ride to Penang in a bigger bus?" asked Lisa, trying to get comfortable.

"I was wondering the same thing myself," I said.

"I sure hope so—my ass is sore already," she complained.

We soon got the answer to our question as the small truck dumped us off at a travel agency office that turned out to be a bus depot. Several other people were waiting for their transport to arrive. Lisa and I bought steaming hot coffee and sat on the curb by the office.

"How long are you going to stay in Penang?" I asked her.

"Just for a few days. I have to get my visa renewed so I can head back to Krabi," she said. Krabi is a beautiful seaside area near Phuket, on the west coast of the country. "You like it so much that you want to stay longer?"

"No, actually I am working up there," she replied.

"What are you doing?" I became curious.

"I'm an actress and I have been hired for television commercials that are filmed there."

I was intrigued. "Is there a lot of work in that field?"

"If you have the right look there is," she said as she tugged on a lock of her blonde hair. "However, there can be long delays between some jobs. It just depends how much time you have and how long you are willing to wait around." By her attractive looks, I could see why the Thai producers would want to work with her.

"What a great way to make money for travelling, though," I said.

"Yeah, it sure is," she agreed, smiling. "I also did pantomime work in Japan for a few months before coming to Thailand."

"In clubs or theatres?" I asked.

"No, just on the street as a busker," she said. "You can make a hell of a lot of money there."

"So, how about you?" she asked me.

"Travelling south, eventually to Indonesia before returning home." I said.

"The solo trek?" she asked.

"Yeah. Just taking some time to myself for awhile."

"Time to clear your head," she said, nodding thoughtfully. "I can relate to that."

"I have been travelling with other people but I still feel I am on a solo journey. I will also be meeting friends from Canada along the way. One meeting is in Kuala Lumpur and the other in Semarang, Java," I told her.

After the short delay, a Mazda MPV pulled up in front of the tiny office. Lisa and I placed our bags in the back of the van and grabbed the front bench seats inside the vehicle. There were ten passengers altogether. Once we were aboard, the driver popped the clutch and the van jerked its way out into the morning traffic of Surat Thani and onto the highway heading south.

Lisa dozed on my shoulder as the van sped its way down the highway. Unfortunately, I could not sleep due to my nervousness about the driver's skill. As we wove in and out of slower and oncoming traffic, I lost count of the close calls that made me hold my breath.

It wasn't long before I could see signs and billboards heralding the proximity of the Malaysian border, namely the large yellow ones that display a giant skull and crossbones and the warning: Death to Drug Traffickers. My thoughts went back to Melanie's comments back at Hat Tian regarding drug use in Malaysia. I chuckled at the memory. My laughter woke Lisa up.

"What's so funny?" she asked sleepily. I told Lisa the story of my drug-crazed friends.

"They are crazy to even think about it." She closed her eyes again and shifted in her seat. The frequency of the warning signs increased and, by midday, we had reached the Thai-Malay border.

Even though I did not possess any illicit substances, I still felt a bit nervous, the image of the skull and crossbones etched in my mind, as the van pulled into the border compound. We stopped at the north end of a long building and were told by the driver that we would have to get out of the vehicle, collect our baggage, and walk through the border individually.

"You didn't pack any extra 'things' did you?" joked Lisa. I didn't laugh.

To detect any illegal substance, the Malay border guards employed the noses of canines. With the vast numbers of tourists going over the border by bus each day, a search of each and every person would have been impossible.

I looked into the building ahead and saw that the long corridor was sided with high metal fencing. It looked to be about fifty metres from one end to the other. I knew damn well that behind these fences the dogs waited. The highly trained hounds had been trained to start barking the moment they smelled any type of drug being carried through.

I approached the narrow entrance behind the other passengers. A Thai border guard signalled me to put my passport in his waiting hands. Placing an exit stamp on an empty page, he handed my papers back and motioned me toward the caged walkway. Praying that some scumbag had not slipped anything into my pack when I wasn't looking, I nervously walked the length of the gauntlet. I could see no dogs but that did not mean that they weren't there, ready to give the word to the boss. At the other end stood Malaysian border guards, cold looks on their faces. There they cleared us past the desk with the bang of a stamp.

Another two hours passed before Butterworth, the city on the mainland side of the island of Penang, slowly emerged over the horizon. There was frequent ferry service between Butterworth and Georgetown, Penang's main city. Recently, a solid bridge to the mainland had been built. Because of the slow bumper to bumper traffic, however, the driver chose the ferry route instead. When asked, our driver told us that the ferry was still the faster of the two methods to cross the water. We joined the busy queue and crept forward until we finally parked on the deck of the flatbed ferry. Soon afterward, the vessel left the dock and gently approached the island in the distance. I glanced at my watch and saw that it was 5:30 PM. The twelve-hour journey had taken its toll. I felt spent and exhausted from the cramped conditions of the minivan. As if to welcome us, the sun emerged from behind the grey clouds and danced upon the water of the bay.

### Roommates

"Do you want to share a place to stay?" Lisa asked me as we unloaded our bags from the back of the van. The driver had parked in a central square off one of Georgetown's main streets.

"Sounds good," I said. "Do you have any ideas?"

Lisa had been reading her guidebook while we took the ferry across the small seaway. "There are quite a few places in this immediate area, so I think we shouldn't have too much of a problem."

In fact, it didn't take long at all. Almost across the street a large hotel with a well-tended courtyard opened onto the main street in front of us. A small café could be seen from the street, tables and chairs dispersed amongst the greenery. The air in the shady confines cooled us as we entered the courtyard. It felt good after the hot stuffy van ride. We carried on past the restaurant and made our way inside the lobby.

An old man greeted us at the desk and we asked him if there was room.

"Only four-bed rooms left today," he told us.

We stuck our heads into the lodging and saw that it was clean enough for our liking. Despite the extra space, the price was still decent so Lisa and I agreed to take the room.

Just as we were paying for the room, two men came up to the desk, asking about accommodation. They seemed friendly enough and, after a short chat, Lisa and I decided to share our room with them, to make it even more economical. Settling into our space, we became further acquainted with our new roommates.

Tim and Jason were quite a pair. Old friends for years, they had joined each other for some travelling in the area. Lisa was surprised to find out that Jason was also heading to Krabi to work as an actor in film and commercials. It seemed to be a booming business.

"I was in Bangkok for awhile, working on a number of commercials for different brands of booze," Jason told us. "I just finished a two-week set of shoots for Chivas Regal."

"Sounds tough," I quipped.

"Yeah, mostly on my liver," he retorted.

He went on to tell us that during the shooting he had made outrageous sums of cash, as well as having unlimited access to the whiskey tap. Needless to say, he needed a break from his good fortune.

"Are they going to pay for your rehabilitation, too?" I asked him, laughing.

"Nah, this bloke lives for it, mate," said his friend with a grin. Tim had come over from England and was looking to do something more than working for his dad in a London carpet shop. He fit the perfect image of an English soccer hoodlum. His rowdy energy was full on all the time. He also possessed a sense of humour that cooled the rough image to hilarity, despite his glistening bald head.

The two friends badgered each other endlessly and had both Lisa and me laughing so much that it hurt to move.

Hunger overtook us and we made our way out into the Penang

evening to search for food and drink. The smell of exhaust, dust, cigarette smoke, and cooking food permeated our senses as we wandered through the old town.

After a filling meal of *roti janai* (bread and a thin lentil dipping sauce), roast mutton, and rice, we stopped in at a number of bars, including a place called the Coconut Bar. It was the only pub that we found which hired a live act, one guy and his guitar. This local man was a very talented player who sang tunes by the Beatles, the Stones, and other classic bands.

During one of the man's breaks, I approached him at the table where he sat with a woman who seemed to be his wife or girlfriend, and a few other people. I introduced myself and he pulled out a chair and asked me to sit.

"My name is Clarence," he said in a friendly voice.

"I really like the songs you are playing," I told him. "I was wondering if I could come down with my guitar one night and sit in with you for a few tunes. I have been wanting to jam with someone for a long time."

"Hey, that sounds great," he said enthusiastically. His toothy smile widened. "If you want, you can play a whole set of songs. I think it would be good to mix it up a bit. Just come down when you like and we can get set up together."

Thanking him for the opportunity, I rejoined my friends. The four of us remained until closing time before returning to our hotel.


## Drug Quest
*Sunday, January 8, 1995*

I followed my book's map and made my way down to a small seaside park where I found a shady spot along the high seawall. I perched myself there for the rest of the afternoon. The light breeze kept me cool and had me dozing off at regular intervals, my fatigue from the late night before slowly wearing off.

Sunday afternoon soon became early evening. As I made my way down the street to the hotel, familiar voices cried out my name from far behind me. I turned to find Tim and Jason jogging to catch up to me.

"Where have you been, you little wanker?" joked Tim. "Sleeping all day, were you?"

"I guess I'm just not as immune to alcohol as you two are," I replied. "Where did you go today?"

"Ended up at the market over town. It was good fun," Jason said. "Met lots of nice women, too."

"Yeah," continued Tim. "You should have come along. We would have set you up with a nice little tart."

"I'm in no shape for any little tart today, unless she's a nurse," I said. My friends laughed.

When we reached the hotel room, we found Lisa fast asleep. Being the subtle men that they were, both Jason and Tim crept close to Lisa's pillow and started to whisper in her ears at the same time. Whatever they said to her seemed to have its effect. Lisa sat up with a start, glaring at each one in a sleepy daze.

"You never stop, do you?" I told the pair.

"Never stop until you get what you want," said Tim.

"Yeah? Well you won't be getting any of that from me," said Lisa. She fell back onto her mattress, pulling the covers up over her head. The two companions snickered with mischievous delight.

"Do you want to join us for some dinner, Lisa?" I asked her.

"Not now, I'm too bagged." Her muffled voice filtered through the blanket.

"Aww . . . don't want to play?" Tim was persistent. A pillow hit him square in the face.

I dragged the two hoodlums out of the room so that Lisa could have some peace and quiet. We wandered back out into the darkening streets in search of dinner.

After dinner we wandered into a small bar and enjoyed yet another round of beer. As we sat and chatted, I noticed my companions getting noticeably restless, especially Tim.

"I could use some good dope right now," he finally said. Jason agreed with his friend. The pair had been talking about a potential purchase for a day or so already.

"Why?" I asked.

"Because it's Malaysia," replied Tim.

"What about the penalties?" The law was so strict here: stiff fines, jail terms, and death by execution were on the list of consequences for dabbling in drugs.

"That's exactly why we want to do it." Tim smiled as he spoke.

"Yeah," agreed Jason. "Kind of like a 'fuck you' to the system."

"If you get caught, you'll be the only ones who get fucked," I told them.

"We just won't get caught," said Tim confidently. "Besides, I really want to get high."

"Are you sure you don't want to join us?" asked Jason. When he asked me this, his facial expression etched itself into my memory: a classic grin of boyish mischief with an open invitation to join in on the fun.

"No thanks," I graciously declined. "I prefer a cold beer over cold steel bars anytime."

They planned to begin their search for illicit substances down by the public square where I had spent the better part of the afternoon. I tried once again to dissuade them from the attempt but they were bound and determined to pull off the stunt.

The two adventurers soon got up the nerve to make their move and we left the small pub. I escorted them as far as the gate of our hotel and then turned to wish them well on their quest.

"Gook luck, you guys, and watch your asses. I can't afford to bail you out of the slammer." I couldn't believe that they were actually going to do this. I stood in the gateway and watched as they headed into the night.

"Just be ready to open the door for us later," said Jason. They disappeared into the darkness and I wondered if I would ever see them again.

At around 2:00 AM I woke to the sound of knocking on the front door out in the lobby. Had our brothers returned, stoned and unscathed? I stuck my head out of our room to see their familiar faces, leering through the glass doors at the end of the common room. They looked like frantic fish trying to escape an aquarium.

"You didn't bring any cops along, did you?" I whispered through the crack between the doors.

"Just open the fucking door, you wanker. We're freezing," Tim pleaded. I glanced down at the latch and noticed that the door had a padlock on the inside. I had to find the key.

The hotel had a night watchman who possessed a key, slung around his neck on a string. The problem was that he was now fast asleep on a small bed in the rear office. His snoring reverberated off the walls as I entered the small room in an attempt to wake him up. My first thought was to pull the string from around his neck. I changed my mind for fear that he would come to, swinging madly. He was a pretty big guy and I did not want to take the chance. Instead, I tried to shake him from his slumber.

"Hey, buddy. Wake up." I shook his shoulder in vain. He didn't even budge. I tried again, this time more forcefully. No luck. He was dead to the world. All the while the two left out in the cold were frantically knocking on the glass. Unfortunately, they could not see the difficulty I was having with the keep. I finally grabbed hold of the end of the mattress, giving it a few sharp yanks. At last the old man stirred and sat upright, squinting at me. I gestured that some guests needed entry and he sleepily but happily made his way to the door. My friends came in from the cold, shivering, and sat on a couch just inside the doors.

"Thanks, mate." Tim gave the doorman a thumbs-up to thank him for opening up. The man nodded sleepily, turned, and walked back to his bed. The three of us sat on the couch together as I heard their tale. We spoke quietly so as to not wake any of our neighbours in the hotel.

"We ran into a rickshaw driver who wanted to sell us some grass, but he first had to go fetch the stuff," said Tim. "He told us to meet him by the park in an hour and so we hung out in a local bar in the meantime. When the guy showed up he handed us a really skinny joint and charged us almost twenty-five dollars."

"You paid twenty-five dollars for a joint?" I asked in shock.

"Yeah, well . . . ," Jason shrugged. "Anyway, we paid him and then he took off really quickly." He went on with his story.

"Then we wanted to get rid of the evidence in case the rickshaw driver was working with the cops, taking off to tell them where we were. So we climbed down off the seawall in front of the public square to the rocks and walked along a thin strip of sand next to the waterline. We found a large drainage culvert coming out of the wall. We ducked into it and smoked our prize."

"It wasn't a sewage drain, I hope," I said to him with a grin.

Tim piped up, "At least it would have covered up the smell of the grass."

"Nice image," I said. "Up to your knees in shit holding a joint that just broke your wallet."

"Luckily for us, the smoke drifted away on a stiff lateral breeze,"

Jason continued. "Then we heard people above us and became paranoid that they might be cops or something. We hid in the culvert for about an hour, until we were sure the coast was clear. We ended up freezing in there with these thin clothes on." He tugged on his shorts and T-shirt, his body still shivering. "We came back here through as many dark alleyways as we could, making sure not to be seen by anyone."

"So, for all of that paranoia, hiding, and freezing of your asses to get a buzz from a pin-joint, was it worth it?" I asked.

"Every penny, mate!" Tim replied.

"The adrenaline rush was pretty good, too," added Jason. Safe at home, the rowdy lads had pulled it off and made it back safely to play another day.

### Bed Bugs
*Monday, January 9, 1995*

"Oh, shit!" Lisa sounded like she was going to be sick. I glanced over to her bed and she was sitting up, staring and scratching at her arms and legs.

"What's up, Lisa?"

"I think I got attacked by bed bugs last night." She slowly got up and walked over to my bed and sat on the edge. She wore only a bra and shorts. I could see that her entire body was covered with small red marks. I reached over to my first aid kit and pulled out a small bottle of calamine lotion and handed it to her.

"Thanks," she said, taking the medicine. "God, I feel like I'm going to go nuts from this itching."

Jason lifted up her mattress and discovered a huge nest of, let's just say, many insects. They hung in ugly clumps along the bedrail, red and swollen with Lisa's blood.

"Whoa . . . " he said, disgusted. He immediately went and told the landlord, who came in to assess the problem. He left the room and returned with a rag soaked in diesel fuel. He wiped the bugs out of the bed frame and had a new mattress and sheets brought in to replace the original. Now soaked with fuel, Lisa's bed smelled like a loading dock.

Meanwhile, I helped Lisa by putting calamine lotion on her back. When I first looked at her, I couldn't believe my eyes. Every spot on her back had at least one bite, red and slightly swollen. The lotion quickly started working and soon she sat more or less comfortably, her body painted like a white leopard.

"Thanks, John," she said. She got dressed in a loose-fitting pair of sweats and T-shirt.

The first thing I did when Lisa stood up from the edge of my bed was check my own skin for any evidence of bites. Then I stood up and lifted my own mattress to see if there were any insects lurking underneath. In fact, we all did. Unfortunately for Lisa, hers was the only bed stricken with the vermin.

"Looks like you're the only one, sister," I said sympathetically.

"Just my luck," she said, the lotion drying in caked blotches on her skin.

## News from Home

The market along the waterfront was busy. Rich smells of foods cut through the air almost as soon as we turned the corner into the park area. The market was set among groves of tall trees along the seawall. The shady areas created an oasis from the intense heat of the day. Vending carts of all sizes were clumped together in one central area. Smoke and scent rose up like a mist into the bright sunny afternoon.

We joined in the crowd, strolling through the maze of stands and stalls. Making stops at the various booths, I managed to collect a wide variety of small snacks, including fried bananas, curried chicken, fresh pineapple, mangos, and a huge cup full of guava juice. My companions were busy doing the same.

Lisa shouted to me from a small patch of grass that she had found among the shady trees near the seawall. I joined her with my payload and placed myself on the ground beside her.

"Mmmm . . . " She peered inquisitively at the things I held in my hands. "Looks good," she said as she nabbed a fried banana slice from the pile and stuffed it in her mouth.

"Yeah, you bet it is." I was already savouring the rich curry spice sauce and chicken. The burning yet sweet spice had me reaching for a mouthful of cooling juice. "I can't believe how rich these flavours are." We were joined by Jason and Tim once they had made their choice of food.

Curious locals would walk by us staring not only at us but at the fact we were relishing their local cuisine. One young girl approached me and pointed to my lunch, "Good? You like?" I smiled back at her.

After our feast, we lay on the grass and relaxed in the shade. It wasn't unlike what everyone else was doing as the heat of the day burned down on the dry stones of the seawall.

As I lay on the ground, I suddenly felt compelled to phone home. Over the past few days I had been thinking about calling Jill, to reconnect. Part of me had been avoiding the idea altogether, yet my gut instinct told me I needed to speak with her. The nagging feeling continued as I tried to enjoy my rest under the trees. At last, I decided to break my silence with her.

"I've got to call home," I told Lisa. "Are you guys going to be around for awhile?"

"Yeah, we'll be here," she said. "Good luck with the call." I had shared my story with Lisa on the bus from Thailand.

I left my friends and found myself a quiet spot at the edge of the park. I wanted to take a few moments to collect my thoughts before making the call. It had been so long since I had heard her voice and I wondered what I would say to her. More importantly, what would she say to me? Jill and the life I had left behind seemed a world away. It all felt so foreign to me after only eight weeks away.

My resistance was huge. Part of me wanted to return to the shady spot with my friends and forget the whole thing. I knew at that moment that the resistance was my unwillingness to take responsibility for my actions. I wanted to hide from my own feelings of regret and guilt. Yet, at the same time, the fact that I felt strongly about striking out on my own for a period of time was too important to deny. I did feel guilty for leaving on my own but knew that I had to in order to gain my own strength. I could feel myself drifting away from her and, at the same time, wanting to be closer. Wanting to be closer so much it felt like need.

After a few minutes of thinking, I fished through my waist pouch for a small list of phone numbers stashed with my passport and traveller's cheques. Checking the time, I realized that it would be early morning in Canada. I would be catching her just as she was getting up to start a new day.

"Maybe I should wait . . . " I began to feel the excuses percolate into my imagination. At last I walked over to one of the pay telephones by the roadway and lifted the receiver to my ear. I slowly punched a combination of buttons which linked me to a Canada Direct operator. I recited the numbers to her and waited patiently for the rings at the other end. As I held the receiver, my arm was ready to snap the handle back into the cradle. "You've got to do this . . . "

The phone rang a few times before I heard a click as the receiver was picked up. I held my breath while I waited for Jill to answer.

Our conversation began with small talk as we told each other what we had been doing in our separate lives. She had been busy preparing for a musical event in Vancouver with a friend and had seemed to enjoy it. With the informalities out of the way, we finally got to the deeper issues of our relationship.

"So, how do you feel about us and where we're going, John?" Jill's voice told me that she needed a straight answer.

I hesitated. My voice stuck in my throat as my mind reeled and fought madly for words to say. I was in turmoil. Part of me wanted to be with her forever, and the other part of me had, perhaps, left her long ago. The few moments of silence on the phone line seemed like an eternity as Jill waited for an answer. My dry mouth finally opened and I spoke.

"I . . . don't know, Jill. I just don't know . . . "

The remainder of the conversation was painful and brief as Jill expressed her anger and her hurt over to what I had said or, rather, what I hadn't said. She also told me that the moment I had shared my own uncertainty, for her, the relationship was over. There were a few final words and then a static click and . . . silence.

My thoughts swam and I felt lost in time as I stood by the pay phone box, using it as a brace. The conversation faded in my memory and I could only see my hand putting the receiver down, as if in a movie.

I lost it. I stood and let out some of my pent-up emotion in technicolour as local Malays within ear shot froze in their tracks, their eyes fixed on me. Their mouths hung open and I left them standing there with a few clear memories of an extremely uptight tourist. I felt drunk as I made my way to the spot where my friends were still sitting, drinking cool beer.

"You look like you've seen a ghost," said Lisa. "What's up? You look sick." I sat in silence for a few moments, not knowing just what to say to her.

I can't remember what I said to my friends. My mouth was on its own; my mind was somewhere else. I spoke to them briefly and then stumbled away to find a place to sit alone on the edge of the seawall. I sat staring out over the water, tears running down my face.

Jason soon came over and joined me on the rock wall. "Are you all right?" he asked.

"I don't know," I said to him. I strained to talk. My mouth was bone dry and water did not seem to help at all. "It's hard to know what I am right now."

"I know what you are going through, mate," Jason said. "The best thing you can do is keep going, with your head up and know that you've got friends around you. Just let the experience make you a better and stronger person."

In my present state, it was hard to hear these words from Jason. I did not want to believe any of it and a big part of me just wanted to tell him to fuck right off. But I soon regained my composure. I felt the support from Jason and drew strength from him.

"Remember, you are not the only one going through this, either," he reminded me.

I thought back to the moment when I had seen the green light of sunset. The concept of "change" I had contemplated was now staring me in the face. I had done what I needed to do, leaving to regain my own strength. Jill, in turn, had done what was necessary, closing the door through which I had departed. How was I to deny this natural course of events? Yet, inside, my resistance was real. My stomach boiled and sweat flowed from my brow. After a time, Jason had me focus my feelings on the road ahead. The only way I could make a difference for myself now was to step forward, into the future. Retracing the past would not allow me to accept the end of my relationship. It was over and I had no choice but to move on.

Jason sat with me for over an hour and I felt supported by his presence and his advice. I thanked him sincerely for his help. As a result of his words, I felt more prepared to handle the changes facing me and felt I could gain strength in the remaining time I had in Asia.

## Club Gig

Jason and I rejoined Lisa and Tim in the shade of the trees. I raised a toast to my companions for their support and their friendship.

"I love all you guys. I really appreciate being able to share this stuff with you. It helps a lot to talk about it," I told my friends.

Tim handed me another beer, "It's a lot easier just to get drunk and forget about it, too." His sense of humour always made me laugh, even when I was feeling shitty. We spent the rest of the afternoon enjoying the atmosphere and even more delicious food from the vendors.

"Hey, I want to show you the culvert where we hid out last night. Come on," Tim urged us to follow him. Walking along the stone wall, we found a small staircase with rusted railings leading down onto the rocks below. The tide was almost out, allowing us to walk on the rocks as they had done the night before. Tim proudly led us to a wide cement pipe jutting out of the wall. A small trickle of dirty water dribbled onto the sand.

"Let's look around for the roach," joked Jason.

"Didn't get your money's worth last night?" I laughed. Following the shoreline we walked below the seawall until we reached a restricted dock area surrounded by fences. One remaining staircase led us back topside.

It was early evening when we walked back through the town, admiring the beautiful architecture and recognizing the streets of our own neighbourhood. There were huge ditches, almost two metres wide and occasionally spanned by flat cement slabs, along the streets. Down in the bottom of the ditches, huge rats loomed in the damp and dark corners. Some looked as big as cats. Grotesque teeth protruded from not so friendly faces; slimy tails dragged through the filth.

I felt good and wanted to blow off some steam. I would be leaving for Sumatra in the morning and wanted to say farewell to my mates.

"Come down to the Coconut Bar with me tonight," I told them. "I got an invitation to sit in with the guy we saw on Saturday. It should be fun."

"As long as you're buying beer, I'll go anywhere," joked Tim. I promised to bribe him.

Coconut Bar was busy by the time we got there. Clarence was in the middle of his first set of songs. He saw me walk in with my guitar slung over my shoulder and gave me a huge smile as he sang. I waved back and took a seat with the others at a corner table. At the beginning of a short break, Clarence came over and sat with us.

"Hey, how are you doing?" He shook my hand with a firm grip. "So, you want to play some music, do you?"

"Yeah, if it's still all right with you." I said, hopeful.

"Sure, it is fine with me. Just let me check with the boss." He walked over to a man sitting near the bar and I could see the man looking in my direction as Clarence spoke to him. Soon, Clarence waved me over to meet the owner of the club. Without much emotion in his voice, the owner spoke directly to me.

"You can play for one hour." He turned and disappeared into his office.

I had a great time performing and managed a good response from the audience. Unplugging my guitar from the small P.A. system when I was finished, I looked up to see a waiter standing behind me. He set two cold bottles of beer down on the bar as payment. I looked past the waiter to see the boss waving at me as if to say thank you. I waved back and saw him give Clarence a glance, signalling him to get back to work. During my set he had taken advantage of the time to go off and hang with his gal and consume a raft of beer. By the time he came back on, he was noticeably impaired but cut right back into the music without a hitch.

I returned to the table where my friends waited, cheering my efforts. Setting my guitar back into its bag behind my seat, I returned to the side of the stage to collect my drinks. Walking back to the group, I handed one of the frosted bottles to Tim. His eyes lit up with delight.

"I knew I was going to buy you a beer, buddy," I told him. "But I didn't think I'd have to give you half my paycheque."

# CHAPTER 9: SUMATRA

## Hydrofoil
*Tuesday, January 10, 1995*

Waking early, even before my alarm brought me into consciousness, I silently slipped into my clothes and woke my friends to say farewell.

"Take care, John." Lisa sat up in her bed and gave me a hug and kiss on the cheek. "Good luck and call me when you get back to Canada. I'll be home in July."

"You bet I will, Lisa," I said.

"Keep looking up," Jason told me from his bed in the corner. I walked over to shake his hand.

"Thanks again for all the help yesterday," I told him.

"Anytime, mate. Just hope you don't need that kind of help too often," he said.

"No doubt," I agreed.

I sneaked past Tim's bed. "Take care, Tim."

"Mmm," was his only response. His beer-induced slumber seemed to be too much for him.

I handed my key to the front desk man and signed out. Making my way into the morning, I breathed the cool fresh air.

My rush to leave early soon met, unfortunately, with a long delay. The conditions at sea were rough and stormy. The ship was running late, pending a change in the weather. After a two-hour wait, crew members finally allowed passengers to board. Choosing a window seat, I dug out my travel guide in search of accommodation in Medan.

The huge hydrofoil made its way out of the harbour bound for open sea. The vessel was old but comfortable though the seats were a bit cramped. The crew tried to make up for the lack of comfort by playing cheesy martial arts films and music videos. There was a snack bar with things like chocolate bars, pop, juice, and sandwiches, none of which I wanted to trust in my stomach.

The ship finally reached the open water and the powerful engines lifted her up onto the wings under the hull. For a brief moment the thrust pushed me back into my seat. The sky was clear above us but the sea was heavy and black to the horizon. Soon sheets of rain began to blanket the front windows of the ship. There were times when a constant river of water pounded down from the sky. At one point it almost looked as if we were submerging into the ocean and my stomach pitched. All the while there was still nothing but a black, smouldering sea outside the window. It was to be a six-hour journey over huge swells and through walls of rain. Eventually, in the distance, I began to see a horizon. The dark, black island of Sumatra.

The word 'Sumatra' conjures up tales of deep, dark jungles, ancient tribes, and strange secrets. The elusive orangutan, the rafflesia (a one-metre-wide flower that smells of rotting meat, fertilized by flies instead of bees), deadly snakes, rivers that rise without warning, the colourful Batak people of the Lake Toba region. As a kid I had always imagined Sumatra to be a dark, mysterious place. I stared out the window and watched the coastline get slowly closer, looking blacker all the time. The water matched the colour of the shore. My childhood dream of seeing it was about to become reality.

The ship soon neared the coastline and entered the port of Belawan, about twenty kilometres from Medan. The sky loomed grey as the crew tied up to the pier. The rain continued as I emerged from the ship and climbed onto the dock with the other passengers.

As we entered the outskirts of the city, the bus rumbled over the rough road. My hands tried to hold my book steady so I could study the city map. I noticed a few other travellers doing the same thing.

"Do you know of any good places to stay?" I asked a young couple sitting in front of me.

"Not really," the young woman replied in a thick English accent. "However, there seem to be quite a few places near to where we are being dropped in the city."

"I was noticing the same thing myself," I said. "Why don't we look for a place together. That way if we end up having to share a cab or something, it will be cheaper."

Our search was shorter than expected as we found a hostel stuffed between two larger buildings just a block and a half from where we were dropped. The sign was hidden beneath the boughs of a small palm tree rising above a white cement wall. Luckily, we showed up in time to get the last available beds. Just after we arrived some other tourists from the same boat came in but were turned away.

Dinnertime conversation revolved around destinations. There was talk of Bukit Lawang, the small town near an orangutan rehabilitation centre. Others spoke of Banda Aceh, a city at the northern tip of the island, where Muslim tradition was very strong, and about the people and the area of Lake Toba. There was a great deal to see in the north of Sumatra but from the things I had heard and read, getting around here by road transport was a literal pain in the ass. Road systems were unpredictable, as were the vehicles that negotiated the rough terrain. Bus trips were long enough without delays like washouts or accidents. Places like Bukittinggi were a grueling twenty-three-hour ride away from here.

My thoughts hung on the idea of seeing the orangutans in Bukit Lawang. I also really wanted to check out Toba's musical inhabitants. I had read that music was a huge part of the region's life and there were a lot of players there. I chose to split my remaining time on the island between these two destinations.

After a few drinks I headed to my dorm room. The hostel did not do the co-ed thing, so the men were segregated from the women, except in the private rooms. The dorms slept about ten people. Some of the other men were still awake in conversation when I returned to the room. We finally attempted to get some sleep but the constant howling and barking of a dog just outside the window prevented this. The creature was pathetic. One of the others became frustrated and wanted to throw something hard at the wretched beast but the open window was too high to reach. So we all lay awake, listening to the pitiful wailing.

## Medan
*Wednesday, January 11, 1995*
My nose was not to be spared in Medan. Overall, I think it was the most polluted place, next to Bangkok, that I encountered in Asia. I used my bandanna to wipe my eyes if they started to run from the dirt in the air. I sometimes wondered how people here did not go blind from the foul air. Hot wind, in gusts, would carry clouds of dirt and exhaust into my face. The worst places of all were, of course, the intersections—just when you needed to see what you were stepping in front of.

The main culprit was the *becak* (pronounced 'bechak'). Outlawed on the island of Java because of its polluting nature, it is a weird metamorphosis of motorcycle and rickshaw with a simple motor that spews out the foulest clouds I have ever seen. There were so many of these smoke-spewing wrecks that I sought to escape the foul air. They just kept coming around the corners, puffing out more smoke and burning oil. I could taste it on my tongue. There were a few times when I gagged on the "flavour" in my throat. During the hottest part of the day, I managed to find refuge in a modern shopping mall near the centre of the city.

On my way back to my hostel, I did some exploring in the back streets where I could breathe a little easier. I found a music store with a number of guitars hanging in the front window. I walked inside to find the owner in the middle of a jam session with a customer who was checking out a new electronic keyboard. They were sitting side by side near the back of the store, each playing a small synth/piano. The music was great. I listened to them play for a few minutes, tapping my feet. When they finished, the owner turned to greet me.

"Hello, you play, too?" he asked me. Stepping back from the piano bench, he urged me to sit.

"No, I don't play keys. I play guitar," I told him.

"Okay, good." He walked over to the wall and pulled a new Fender acoustic from its hanging cradle and handed it to me. After bringing me a chair and a guitar pick, he sat back on the bench and looked over at his first customer, who did not seem to mind the interruption at all.

"One, two, three, four . . . " The music started again and I happily joined in. Luckily, the guitar I was playing was in tune. The song we were playing was a funky blues number with a great feel. These guys were happening. We continued through a few more songs until the other customer began speaking to the owner in the local language. I got the feeling that a sale had been made. I hung the guitar back on its hook and thanked the man for his invitation to play.

"You want to buy this guitar today?" he asked me. "You play good."

"Thanks, I have one already," I replied. "I am just looking today."

"Sure, no problem," he smiled. He did not seem upset by the fact that I wasn't planning to buy anything from him. I wandered through his shop, looking at more instruments as other customers came in. Finally, I waved to him and exited the store.

I returned to the hostel and washed the scum off my skin and cleansed my nose, black from smoke. Sleep came quickly as I dreamt of orangutans.

# CHAPTER 10: BUKIT LAWANG

## Rambutans and Dust

*Thursday, January 12, 1995*

A cloud of dirt blew into my face as I stood at the edge of the roadway across from the large compound that was one of the city's main bus stations. I had just climbed out of the rear end of another truck taxi crammed with local Sumatrans. The journey from the hostel was a crazy ride through the Medan morning rush-hour. I was slowly adjusting to the lack of driving skills, or rather lack of care for skills, in Indonesia.

"Bukit Lawang!" A short, stout man was shouting out at the top of his lungs into the crowds of passengers. The bus he stood beside wasn't much prettier than the one I had ridden from the port two days ago. Rust was the most attractive of its features. Clouds of blue smoke spewed from its tail pipe.

I squeezed through the crush of people to the open door of the bus. I was motioned to give up my bag to one of the handlers on the roof.

"Sorry, I'll keep my bags with me. Thanks, anyway." I waved them off, preferring to stay close to my gear. It was small enough that it wouldn't take up too much room anyway.

I sat watching the mayhem of passengers and hustlers criss-crossing the compound. During the wait, fruit vendors carrying loads of fresh produce walked below the bus windows.

"Hey!" I shouted to an old woman near my window. "Over here, please." The woman rushed to the side of our bus and looked up at me with a toothless grin, hoping for a sale. She began speaking to me in Bahasa, the local language. I hung my hand out of the window. In my fingers I held a five hundred rupiah note (the equivalent of forty cents). She snapped up the paper note with glee and handed me a giant bunch of ripe rambutans. I had only seen this fruit on local stands and it had intrigued me. Red, with long hair-like skin, it tore open easily to reveal a translucent fruit similar to a lychee nut. The flavour was sweet yet bland, something like a watery grape. There were so many rambutans on the branches in my lap I had to give some to fellow passengers.

The bus made its way through the busy city and left the solid pavement of the "highway." As we climbed into the mountain range parallel to the coastline, the types of vegetation and trees changed rapidly. Beautiful green hills and coconut groves bordered the road and murky streams flowed under narrow bridges. All the while, dust from the road floated gently through the bus, sucked in through the open windows. Passing through small villages, I caught glimpses of locals going about their morning business. For the most part the journey was fairly smooth but there were some stretches of potholes that my kidneys didn't particularly enjoy.

"Shit, learn how to drive, buddy," I heard a woman ahead of me say. She sounded Canadian.

"If he learned how to drive he'd be out of a job, I think," I responded. The woman and her male companion turned and laughed.

"You may be right," said the man, grinning. He had a thick blond beard and a curly head of hair. The couple seemed familiar for some reason. I couldn't quite place them but, after a moment, I remembered.

"You two were on Koh Pha-Ngan in Thailand, weren't you?" I asked. "I thought I saw you two hanging out in Thong Sala when I was there."

"Yeah, we were on the island for a couple of weeks," he said. "I'm Peter and this is my girlfriend Veronica." The woman was attractive with an engaging smile.

"Are you from Canada, too?" I asked.

"Yeah, from Nelson," said Peter. "You?"

"Jasper originally, but I live in Vancouver now," I replied. "Where are you headed?"

"Bukit Lawang then Lake Toba," said Veronica.

"Same here," I said to her. "Then I am off to Singapore, Java, and Bali."

"We just came from there," she told me. "I can't wait to head north to Thailand." There was a hint of sarcasm in her voice.

"What don't you like about Indonesia?" I asked.

"There are a lot of things that I like about it. It's just the constant hustling over the last couple of months that has been driving me nuts." Her limit had been reached.

"Yeah, I can see that," I agreed that it could be a challenge to deal with.

"But this should be just the right place to get away from that," said

Peter on a positive note. "I can't wait to see the orangutans. Plus, the hiking is supposed to be great." He sat staring out at the countryside.

The air flowing in through the windows began to cool from the increased altitude and we were starting to see many signs for the orangutan rehabilitation station near Bukit Lawang. The centre, started in the early seventies, was similar to other facilities on the island of Borneo. Its mission was to help train the primates to fend for themselves on their natural food sources and to stop depending on humans for their survival.

"Isn't there a woman from Vancouver who does this work on Borneo?" I asked my new friends.

"Yeah, I think so," said Peter. "I believe she's also a professor at Simon Fraser University, and even raised her child with the orangutans."

Soon the bus passed the entrance to Bukit Lawang, situated on the border of Gunung Leuser National Park. We had reached our destination. Pulling into the village, the bus creaked to a stop in the main square and we stepped off into the dirt.

Heading up the trail which bordered the swift-flowing river, we saw a number of bungalows literally hanging over the water above the steep banks. Most bungalows were on the opposite side of the river, reached by small suspension bridges.

"There's the one I was been reading about," said Peter, checking his list. "Yusman." The bungalow had two levels and was open to the river. It looked as good as any other one we could see.

"Looks decent enough," I said to Peter and Veronica as I headed for the bridge. They nodded at each other and followed me to the small staircase leading to the crossing.

Checking for space, we were offered plenty as a large group had just left that morning. While I signed in, the hotel staff took great interest in the guitar over my shoulder. Once we got into our rooms I unpacked some things for the coming days and soon felt the urge to explore the village.

"Do you want to go for a hike upriver?"

"You bet," Peter replied. "Just let me unpack a few things first." Veronica decided to stay behind and have a nap. I closed up my tiny room and sat in the kitchen area watching the river as I waited for Peter to get ready.

The sound of the water was refreshing and I suddenly realized that it was the first natural sound that I had experienced in a good number of days. The noise of cars and people, the smell of *becaks*, was now a good distance downstream. The air was clean and fresh here. The impenetrable green of the thick forests that grew up behind our hostel looked silent and cool, the vines and heavy growth in a tangled mess.

Bukit Lawang itself was small but had enough rooms to support a sizeable population. It welcomed not only tourists but the huge week-end masses of Medanites who travelled into the cool mountains to enjoy some time by the river. There were picnics, loud revelry, and a very popular sport here on the river—inner tubing! Every store and business along the trail had enormous piles of tire tubes that one could rent for cruising the rapids of the river. I watched kids floating by as I waited. It looked like fun.

Peter and I started the trek upstream and noticed just how many bungalows this little village actually had. Small hotels hung off the side of the riverbanks, perched on the large rocks at the water's edge. Small hostels lined the path of the river. Passing a grassy open field, we looked up to see a huge building built into the hilltop. A gigantic sign posted out front proudly announced the location of the village disco bar—Farina 53.

"That looks like a nice quiet place to stay," I said to Peter as I glanced up at huge Peavey P.A. speakers sticking out from under palm fronds.

He laughed and said, "Do you think I should go and wake up Veronica and tell her we found a better place?"

"Nice knowing you," I said.

From here the trail grew steep, the river meandering lazily around the end of the knoll. The heat of the day was quelled by the thick shade.

The trail narrowed and descended to the river's edge through a small grove of trees. There the channel narrowed, creating a small stretch of turbulent water. Above this was a silent pool of beautiful green water. A small boat sat in the water and in it, an old man waited for passengers. When he saw us emerge from the thick forest trail he stood up, balancing himself with his long wooden staff.

"Come. Please," he urged us to board his small craft.

We climbed in and he slowly pushed us across the pool to the opposite shore. From there we hiked up a hill to the park office. A sign on the door of the building told us that the facility was closed until the next day's feeding time.

Peter and I set off on a small hike through some of the trails which led into the forest behind the centre. The air was so fresh and green, the ground cover damp with humidity. It was such a fresh change from a face full of highway dust. We were sure that we could hear sounds of creatures all around us, yet we never saw anything. We were surely being watched quite closely. We could hear the birds and occasionally caught glimpses of them darting through the branches. Even grey squirrels could be seen and heard in the high tree tops. Finding shady rest stops, we sat and listened to the sounds all around us.

## Durian

Retracing our steps, we returned to the river and found the old boat-man waiting patiently by the river. Upon reaching the far shore we thanked the boatman and made our way into the forest trail leading back downstream. We followed the smells of cooking and arrived at a bungalow next to a construction zone.

"Let's grab a drink," said Peter. He was already walking in the door-way.

"Good idea." The hike had parched my throat.

A group of locals joined us at our table, asking us where we were from. I had a strange look from one guy who came up to me and gently pulled on a bit of my red hair.

"Mmm . . . looks like orangutan," he said, a mischievous grin coming over his face.

"No. Oranguman," I replied, smiling.

Two glasses of fresh mango juice were placed in front of us and the locals cooed with approval.

"You like tropical fruit?" one man asked.

"Yes. Delicious," said Peter, sipping with his straw.

"You like durian?" asked another.

I had seen and smelled durian but had never had the courage to taste it. I preferred to ignore it whenever I walked through a food market. As we sat at our table, I noticed that the familiar smell of this fruit permeated the entire restaurant. The local people were becoming adamant that we try the taste treat.

"What do you think, John?" asked Peter. "Should we go for it?" He had avoided the taste as well.

"I like adventure but . . . " I was reluctant. Even the thought of it made my stomach queasy.

"Come on," encouraged Peter. "We're here, so we have to try it at least once."

"Have to, huh?" I reluctantly nodded in agreement as Peter got the attention of the waiter. As soon as we ordered the fruit from the man, a small crowd of spectators gathered to see our reaction to the fruit.

Making sure that we got to experience the entire essence of durian, the owner was kind enough to present the whole, uncut monster at our table. He also placed a large kitchen knife next to the fruit.

"It looks like a morning star," I said to Peter as I inspected the spiky shell which resembled the deadly medieval weapon. I had seen the fruit for sale in Vancouver's Chinatown and knew of its smelly reputation.

We inspected the outside of the strange fruit, trying to find a way to crack it open. The waiter stood by, silently watching us. Obviously, we were being tested to see if we could do it ourselves. The waiting spectators began to grow impatient. Finally, the owner came over with his sharp knife to help us enjoy the culinary delight. Slowly, he inserted the sharp knife into a narrow crease at one end of the fruit.

The durian opened almost as if it was hinged. With strong fingers, the man cracked the fruit open to expose the meat inside. But before I could see the inside with my own eyes, my head was knocked back by a rising plume of stench. I reeled.

"I think we are going to regret this." Peter's facial expressions mirrored mine.

Broken into large sections, the durian possesses large, round seeds covered by a pale, jelly-like meat. Peter tried it first. Using the knife, he sliced into a large piece of the meat wrapped around one of the large seeds.

"Here goes." He gave me one last look before taking his first taste. An expression of what I could only describe as shock took over his composure as he chewed the smelly mess. After a few moments he turned to me with a disgusted look on his face.

"What are you waiting for?" Peter stared back at me. "You're next, buddy."

Hesitating and taking one last look back to see if Peter's condition had changed, I stuffed a sizeable amount of fruit into my mouth and began to chew. It was my very first experience with any substance whose taste seemed to take on a life of its own. Coming alive, the horrid flavour seemed to grow arms and legs, wrapping around my tongue with no intention of departing any time soon.

"More juice!" I cried out to the owner who had already started to laugh at the two of us. He returned with another set of glasses. No matter how much I drank to wash it down, the taste hung on, tenaciously. All the while our expressions were giving the locals a wonderful laugh.

Peter was just as disgusted. "That has got to be the worst thing I have ever eaten in my life."

"And I'm so glad you ordered it." I glared at him. We broke up laughing.

"Good, huh?" One of the locals moved closer to our table and poked at the jelly inside the shell.

"Not a chance." Peter gagged as he drank his juice in an attempt to wash away the taste. He pushed the rest of the fruit into the centre of the table.

"You don't want?" asked one of the men beside us.

"Go for it," I told him. The man and his friends slid in close, happy to finish it off. The durian is a favourite among many Asians and was sucked back into the mouths of these "vultures" like a Dairy Queen milkshake in the hands of Dennis the Menace. Those who had filled their faces tried to convince us to buy another. Nothing they could say would make us endure yet another of these "events" anytime soon. Smiling and laughing at our good sportsmanship, the local men sent us on our way and hoped to see us again.

The day was darkening as we walked the rolling trail downstream. We were getting hungry.

"We should have saved durian for dessert tonight," Peter said, laughing.

Soon, Yusman hostel came into our view. Our legs, tired from the walk and the heat, carried us across the tiny bridge. Stopping in the middle, I listened to the sound of the water flowing under my feet. It was the naturalness of the sound that had me hypnotized for a moment. The sound of industry and human population was far from here and I was wrapped in the sound of the Earth. The cool air filled my lungs. It was so good to inhale, not worrying about what might be getting in.


## Breakfast with Primates

*Friday, January 13, 1995*

Peter, Veronica, and I stood in silence waiting for the red apes to show themselves. We waited along with a large group of other tourists in front of the wooden platform that had been set up in the dense forest grove above the information centre. Thick mist rolled through the trees as the sun broke through the canopy. The long streaks of light brushed our faces and we felt the warmth on our skin.

We had all risen early for our hike upstream toward the station. The walk up the trail seemed easier with the cooler temperature. Upon reaching the top of the last hill, the men working on the reconstruction job recognized Peter and me and laughed as they greeted us.

"Durian for breakfast?" asked one of the men who had joined the feeding frenzy the day before. He announced our presence to the owner of the bungalow who stepped out to greet us with a wave.

We trudged on into the thick tangle of trees leading to the river. Greeted by the same old man in his tiny boat, we gathered on the far shore and walked up to the information centre. A sizeable crowd had gathered as people waited for the guides to lead the way to the feeding platform, located just inside the park boundary.

A brief lecture on the apes was given and all the people in attendance who thought it would be a novel idea to feed the orangutans with the fruit they had in their pockets were told to leave it behind. I was reminded of incidents where tourists ran into trouble while feeding wild animals in my native Jasper National Park.

After all the stray food was dealt with, the guides led the large group single file along the forest trail. The path took us up onto the ridge running parallel to the river. The previous few days of rain had turned it into a muddy track. An abundance of vines and fencing gave us something to hold onto. Hard breathing accompanied the clambering until we finally reached a small plateau. The tall trees had been thinned out to create a natural amphitheatre. A wooden fence stopped our advance and, just past the edge of the barrier, a wooden platform sat between a few smaller trees. Stairs led up to the small deck. One of the guides carried a bucket of food up the stairs and set it down on the platform.

"The food mixture is a boring concoction of bananas and coconut milk," the other guide told to us as his partner set a large pile of bananas beside the bucket of slop. When asked what he meant by "boring," he went on.

"The idea behind the boring menu is so that the animals become just that—bored! Getting sick of your usual food supply would inspire you to go out and get your own food." There was a collective murmur of agreement from the crowd.

One of the wardens grabbed a stick and knocked on the platform, signalling the presence of food. A couple of minutes worth of banging was rewarded with the distant sound of something climbing through the trees. The man with the stick continued his noise-making while the snapping and creaking of branches got steadily louder behind us. The first real noise was that of a baby orangutan, crying high in a tree, abandoned by its mother. While screaming, he or she was breaking off small branches and throwing them down on top of the crowd.

"Look!" said Veronica, excitedly. She grabbed Peter's arm and pointed above us. Cautiously slipping into view was a female ape. She kept her distance from us as the silence of the forest was filled with excited whispering and the clicking of cameras.

The ape crept around the back of the feeding platform and for a moment we could not see her. She finally came to rest, calmly swinging on a long vine and watching us with seeming indifference. Above us, her noisy baby crept closer and began to throw more broken branches and leaves down on top of us. The chattering continued as people dodged the incoming missiles and laughed. The baby could now be seen high in the branches of the canopy, frantically fussing about.

Turning to watch the mother again, we saw another mother-offspring pair emerge from the silence of the forest. The first baby ape's distracting noise had given this mother the chance to approach undetected. She and her baby were silent as she approached the platform. Stopping for a bit of food, the mother rested, her baby gripped tightly to her side. The first mother joined the two apes on the deck. Soon the mother-baby pair left the platform and came straight over to the fence where we stood. Walking down the fence line as if to inspect us, she slowly passed all of the tourists waiting to see her. Her little baby hung shyly under her armpit, its small hands gripping Mom's red hair and its eyes surveying the strangers.

"I wonder what she'll think when she has a close look at me?" I said to my friends. I had always been curious whether an orangutan would have a strange reaction to a human with red hair. Whether the ape would see me just as another human, a funny looking orangutan, or another ape encroaching on territory, I calmly waited for the verdict from Mom as she came nearer.

"Careful, John," said Veronica. "She might just take you home with her. Instant family." She chuckled.

"That's all right," I said to her. "I haven't had a date in awhile, any-way."

The ape got closer and soon stood in front of me on the wooden fence. The result was only a quick glance from her as she slowly climbed onto a tree and swung from the vines. She stopped just long enough for me to capture a photo. The apes returned to feed alongside the wardens who were sitting quietly on the platform.

About fifteen minutes after they had arrived, the apes vanished into the dense brush. Some of the tourists were a bit choked and started to complain about the short sighting.

"The fact that they have gone so soon is actually what we are aim-ing for," the guide told the disgruntled visitors. "The less time the apes actually spent at the feeding stations, if at all, means that they are truly fending for themselves in the wild forest."

At the bottom of the gully leading out to the river I noticed that they had a few orangutans, mostly youngsters, in cages. These were the young of adults killed when their home range was logged by humans. Poaching had also been a problem but, with a lot more awareness, peo-ple watched out for illegal killings and the incidents had dropped in fre-quency the last few years. Staring out from their tiny prisons, the faces of the creatures looked sad and it was hard to look at them as they watched us walking by.

## Friday the 13th and the Power of Water

The afternoon was warm as I remained in the shade of the porch in front of my room. Here, on the upper level of the hostel, I had a good vantage point above the rushing river. I hung lazily in my hammock and listened to the sounds of nature. It was so nice not to have the constant roar of engines and the obnoxious honking of horns blasting in my ears. Peter came out of his room after a short sleep and joined me, pulling up a small chair.

"Awesome place, isn't it?" he said to me.

"Yeah, I was just enjoying the sounds of everything that's not made by humans," I said.

"After Medan, anything is a nice change."

We heard the sounds of children playing below us in the river. Splashing and cavorting in the swift water, they were having the time of their lives. The sounds got even louder as more kids arrived at the rocky bank across from the Yusman hostel. As we watched the kids' attention was diverted upstream as more of their friends joined them. They were arriving on inner tubes carried by the swift current, howling with laughter as the rapids tossed them around in the stream, some being dumped off into the water.

Peter and I glanced at each other at almost the same time and slowly nodded our heads.

"Let's go!" rang out in unison. Laughing out loud, I was already climbing out of my hammock and changing into my shorts as Peter returned to his room to invite Veronica along for the fun. I left the hostel ahead of the other two and spoke to a man in one of the local shops who rented tubes to visitors. Picking out three tubes with the least number of patches on them, I waited for my friends by the bridge. Soon they emerged from Yusman wearing bathing suits and sandals.

"How much was the rental?" asked Peter.

"Don't worry about it," I said. "I think it was a dollar per tube."

"Gotta like that," Peter replied. "Let's go." He picked up his small raft and started to hike upstream. Veronica and I quickly joined him.

We waded into the river where the rapids began to rush down through the forest, just across from the park office. I could see that there was a good mix of small rapids and gentle floating stretches. Reaching the deepest part of the stream, we jumped onto the tubes and put ourselves in the hands of the river.

The cool water whisked us downstream. The shadows swept over us as we drifted into the quieter corners of the river's path. The occasional sleeper (a tree growing along the bank whose foundation had been washed away) was leaning over the river, its branches dragging in the water. Veronica drifted around the end of one such tree while I floated under part of the trunk. The branches were high enough to give me clearance but Peter was travelling a little too close to the bank when he passed under the branches of the tree. One of the larger branches caught him and sent him on an unscheduled dip in the cool water. I grabbed hold of his inner tube as the current began to carry it away. Swimming to catch up, Peter remounted his tiny raft.

By now Veronica had gained distance on us and disappeared around the bend in the river. Not knowing what was coming next, we paddled our way into the swifter stream and tried to avoid the quiet eddies off to the side.

Suddenly, from around the corner we heard Veronica start to scream, "Whooooaah! Holy sh . . ." was all we heard. Neither Peter nor I knew whether we should laugh at the sound of her wailing or try to paddle faster to get to where she was. All we could do was ride the current. We suddenly felt the water gain speed as we reached the bend in the river. Here the land dropped away fairly quickly and created a large set of surging rapids. The standing waves in the middle of the river bobbed us up and down. The waves turned me around backwards and I couldn't manage to steer myself around before being thrown around the final corner.

Twisting my neck, I could now see what had made Veronica so vocal. The rapids now grew steeper, to an angle of about thirty degrees as the water tumbled off a wide ledge and over a pile of boulders, ending in a huge still pool. Veronica stood at the edge of the pool looking like a wet rat after pulling herself out of the drink.

"Go down the middle!" she shouted. "Otherwise there are too many rocks."

"Great," I thought. As if I could choose my trajectory right now, anyway. Still floating backwards, I looked up to see Peter being funneled into the rapids behind me. His eyes got wider as he stared at the path in front of us.

"Holy shit, I hope that waterfall doesn't have a keeper," he shouted to me. A keeper is a strong undertow that can hold you underwater indefinitely.

"Thanks, I needed that." Just as I said this, my tube lurched off the edge of the rocky shelf and cascaded toward the pool below.

Thankfully, the centre channel had enough water rushing through it that it was nothing more that a bouncy, wet tumble over the submerged rocks into the wide pond. Tightly gripping the inner tube, I was carried into the calmer waters, away from the rapid cascade.

"Yeehah!" I screamed from the adrenaline rush and also for the fact that I had emerged unscathed. The sound of my voice reverberated off the trees. With relief, I rolled off the tube and fell into the pool of cool water.

Now it was Peter's turn to take the ride. I waited and watched, mostly to see if he was going to need help if he bailed off the tube on the descent. It wasn't long before I saw his curly-haired head appear above the edge of the lip as he approached the point of no return.

"Hang on, Peter! It's a wild ride!" I shouted to him just before he tipped over the edge.

"Yaaaaaah!" He plunged down the slope, turning backwards as I had done. He lost hold of his tube near the bottom of the cascade and fell into the churning water with a huge splash. The current wasn't strong enough to create a keeper and he soon popped up to the surface, shaking the water from his head.

"All right! That was excellent!" he shouted with delight. He grabbed his tube and swam over to the shore to check on Veronica. "How are you, honey? You okay?"

"I am now but that thing scared the shit out of me," she said, glancing back at the surging channel.

"I think I might just have to do that again," I said. I was still paddling around in the fresh, deep water. "As long as you hit it in the same place again I don't see any problems with getting banged up on the rocks. There is a lot of water coming over that ledge."

"No shit," said Veronica, laughing.

Dripping wet, we trudged back up the long trail and again entered the water, this time with more confidence, knowing what was coming. We all ended up doing the course a few times. Veronica quit after about four trips but Peter and I were still right into it and continued until the daylight was almost gone. I lost count of how many times we did the run. I remember the last trip with the utmost clarity, for it was the one that gave me the biggest scare.

On my final approach to Yusman, I was alone. Peter and I had become separated. The previous attempts at getting around one large boulder close to our hostel had been successful. Until now, I had used my Teva sandals to cushion the pressure of the water, push myself around the end, and continue on under the suspension bridge. But this time I found myself on the wrong side of the stream. My course would have me reaching the rock in the middle instead of closer to the tip.

Both my feet were planted firmly against the stone and it was then I knew I was in trouble. The resulting water pressure backed up against my tube, popping it out from under my ass.

"Oh, shit!" I thought to myself. Predictably, the water sucked me under just as I took a deep breath—I was going to need it. Trying not to panic, my only thought was to protect my head from hitting the rocks and to relax until I could reach the surface for air. Tumbling in the water with no control, I held my arms in front of my face and head. It seemed forever that I rolled helplessly over the unseen boulders. The current had me in its grip and I was going to have to get air soon.

Once I had been washed through the succession of waves, I felt the water become shallow and I soon found contact with the riverbed. Concentrating on remaining calm, I grabbed onto whatever I could to prevent myself from being drawn into the deeper water. I could feel the current slowing and I pulled myself closer to the bank, found my footing, and burst up through the surface, breathing deeply.

My tube had been rescued by a kid who had seen me go under. He was swimming in the stream when I came around the last corner. When I finally surfaced I came out of the water about five metres from where he was standing. Looking back to the rapids, I counted the time it took the water to reach my position on the river's edge. I counted a good fifteen seconds and figured that I had been underwater at least that long. Breathing hard for the first few moments, I sat on a rock and thanked my good sense for keeping me calm.

Peter soon came into view with trouble of his own. He had come around the last corner without a hitch but, when he tried to get out of the river, he got caught in the faster current. Flowing down to the corner, the stream then went through a large metal grate. The grate covered a culvert used to divert the river under the town square and into the valley beyond. The water here was murky and the downward pull of the water by the metal bars would be powerful. Peter fought his way all the way down the stream until he managed to struggle to the bank just above the culvert.

"That was brutal. I thought I wasn't coming out of that." He was dog-tired from the fight against the stream.

"You just missed a show, too." I went on to tell him about what had just happened to me.

Peter was shaking his head as he waded out of the water when his attention suddenly turned to the river. He was looking at something in front of him in the water. Thinking he had seen a fish, I joined him to investigate.

"What is it?" I asked, looking at the spot where he was staring.

There, in the stream, was a human turd, floating where the water would carry it. It was floating just near to where the young boy had been. Realizing then that the kid hadn't been swimming when I happened by, we soon lost the desire to take any more trips down the river. Handing in the rental, I returned to the hostel and used almost an entire bar of soap in the shower.

## Guitar Strings for Sale

Shopping in Indonesia was cheap. It was always possible to get reasonable deals on items displayed in store windows. Because a great deal of the population here in Bukit Lawang played music, guitar strings were sold in almost every store for a dime a dozen. I decided to give them a performance test after stocking up on several sets for only a few dollars.

Opening one of the packages, I could see that the text was German. Feeling thinner than other strings I had used before, the idea of German quality was enough to sell me on the idea, I merrily carried on with the task of putting the strings on my guitar.

The fresh set of strings gave a cool, crisp sound and definition. However, after I had played my third song, I began to notice that the strings were beginning to come apart just over the frets. Pressure from pushing them down on the fretboard was breaking up the cheap metal wrapping of these obviously poor strings. A few days of playing would result in separate loose sections of the coiled string wrap sitting loosely on the centre core, in between the frets. All the strings would buzz and clatter as they were played. I could even slide the pieces from side to side along the string. With only one good set of strings from home left in my bag, I used up all of these crappy sets in the meantime.

It was such a joke to play with these strings as the sound was always accompanied by the low buzzing of the ragged pieces. There were a few old guitars hanging around in the closets of Yusman which had strings in similar condition. Now that mine sounded like all the rest of the instruments in the village, I noticed a marked decrease in the number of requests from people who wanted to play my instrument.

Despite the shitty sound, the quest to jam continued and I was impressed by some of the players. The young men who ran Yusman wanted to play music any chance they could get. Almost every night turned into a lengthy session of playing and singing.

The most requested song in Asia seemed to be "Hotel California." I got pretty sick of hearing it (and playing it) but the locals loved it. There were even a few local songwriters who would proudly bring out their own original songs as well.

One particular song was played a lot and became the anthem of the Yusman Hostel. A poignant description of the village's role in the world and a piece of musical genius:

**Jungle Trek (Sung to the melody of "Jingle Bells" )**
Jungle trek, jungle trek in Bukit Lawang
See the monkeys, see the birds, see orangutan—oh!
Jungle trek, jungle trek in Bukit Lawang
See the monkeys, see the birds, see orangutan.
Walking together, in Bukit Lawang
Talking together, in Bukit Lawang
Walking together, talking together
Drinking together, in Bukit Lawang
Etc., etc., etc.

**Raging River**
On one of my last days in Bukit Lawang, I joined Peter and Veronica on a jungle trek up the river. They had arranged a day-trip with one of the guides who booked his clients through the information centre by the feeding station. When they asked me to join them, I gladly accepted the invitation.

"What time did the guide tell you to meet him?" I asked Peter through the door to their room.

"A little after 9:00." Peter's muffled voice carried through the bamboo divide.

I checked the time. It was already 8:45. "We're running a bit late. Are you ready yet?"

I knocked on the outside of the door.

"Yeah, sorry." The door came open at that moment and the couple emerged, packs slung over their shoulders.

"We kinda . . . slept in," Veronica said, smiling coyly and blushing at the same time.

"Slept in, huh?" I said with a grin. Peter tried to keep a straight face without much luck.

The morning was muggy as we crossed the river and walked the familiar path upstream. The sun had disappeared behind a layer of clouds and the humidity hung on my skin like a heavy cloak.

"We might get some rain after all," suggested Peter.

"Good possibility." I was glad I had my rain gear in tow.

Entering the information centre just after 9:00, we were greeted by the guide who was patiently waiting at the centre's main desk. The man was young, probably no more than twenty. He recognized Peter and beckoned our group to come over to his counter. When we approached his seat, he was talking with a European man and his young son, about ten years old.

"Good morning," he greeted us happily.

"Hi," said Peter. "Sorry about being late."

"It's okay. We have more coming today, anyway." The two others had just signed up for the trek with us. We were introduced to the man, Gerhart and his son, Stephan, from Germany. Their English was not very good but we still managed to communicate.

"Welcome," the guide addressed our group. "My name is Dani. Today we will hike up the river above the centre to enjoy a jungle walk. For the morning we will hike up into the jungle along the river. Later in the afternoon we will come down the river by tubing." He handed each of us a deflated inner tube which we placed in our packs. He carried a portable foot pump, flashlight, first aid kit, a length of rope, and a bag of food.

Following the trail which went up the hill to the feeding platform, Dani led us to a fork in the trail and off in an unfamiliar direction, heading north from the station. The lush greenery wrapped around us as we plunged into the thick jungle. Dampness coated everything as our bare legs brushed against the wet leaves and branches. The trail widened slightly and the slope was steep as we began to climb a short set of switchbacks up into the forest.

Eventually the trail levelled out and we found ourselves hiking at the edge of a forest plateau. To the right the land dropped away steeply to the edge of the river. Every so often glimpses of water could be seen through the trees below. On the left the forest was one thick mat of green, twisted together with vines and leaves. Moisture-laden branches hung over the trail and we were soon reaching for our raincoats to keep dry from dew as we brushed past.

"Do you think we will see animals, Dani?" asked Peter.

"Only if they want us to see them," replied the guide. "Sometimes we see orangutan but most of the time they stay hidden. They are very shy."

I tried to watch for movements in the canopy but saw nothing. We trudged on through the dimly lit trail. The sun tried to pierce the thick treetops, creating only an occasional spotlight on the floor of the dense forest. Clouds returned and soon a light drizzling rain filtered through the roof of leaves. By now we were soaked from the constant contact with wet foliage. After awhile I began to feel a slight tightness on the side of my lower right leg. Thinking I had perhaps scratched myself on a thorn or sharp branch, I reached down to rub the spot with my hand. When I swiped my hand across my skin, my fingers encountered a slimy mass. A huge leech almost eight centimetres long was hanging off my leg.

Gently grabbing the creature just behind the head, I pinched it slightly until it detached itself from my skin. A slight red spot was revealed as I peeled the head from my leg. Flicking the leech away into the bush, I looked for more intruders on my bare limbs. As I looked, I could see a number of them on my rain coat and my pack. A few more hung discreetly on my other leg, just behind my knee. "Shit," I thought, "these things are everywhere."

My fellow hikers were having similar problems with the vile things. Peter and Veronica were busy examining each other for the presence of the creatures, plucking them off each other. Stephan, the young boy, was having a hard time at first. Being shorter than the rest of us, his first encounter with a leech was when one managed to hook onto the side of his face as he brushed past a low branch.

"Aaii, Papa!!" he cried out to his Dad who stopped to help him. His father calmly showed him how to take the thing off with a gentle pinch. He soon toughened up and stopped complaining and was soon able to carefully pluck the little devils off with his own fingers.

The leeches seemed to be everywhere on the trail. We began to notice how they emerged from the trees and bushes, hanging off the ends of leaves, squirming and wriggling their ugly heads in the attempt to catch a ride on a potential passing host. We continued on until the trail widened slightly and the problem of contacting the gripping mouths of these vile creatures was much reduced. Stopping every so often, we would inspect each other, stripping the black, slimy leeches from coats or skin.

At one point Dani was slightly ahead of the rest of the group. He stopped near a swampy section of the trail and waited for us to catch up. When I walked up to him and stood beside him, I suddenly noticed a most foul odour.

"What is that smell?" It was enough to make me want to vomit.

"Oh, my God, what is that?" added Veronica as she and the others stopped beside me. All the faces in the group were twisting up with disgust.

"Rafflesia," explained Dani.

"So that's what it smells like," said Peter. "I'm glad I was not in a rush to find it."

Dani left us to scout through the forest to find the plant while we waited, wondering how this could ever be the smell of a flower.

The rafflesia is the world's biggest flower. It grows to one metre in diameter and resembles a large orchid. Its bright red colour would be enough to attract insects but it is the smell, which imitates the odour of rotting meat, that attracts flies to its moist core for fertilization. Since it is the national flower of Sumatra, Dani was proud to be able to show one off to his guests.

"Here. Come," he said to us from just off the trail. We made our way through the tangle of vegetation and joined him beside a large, damp hollow. In the bottom sat the flower in all its glory. The huge leaves folded back from the centre and were covered with what looked like small warts. The centre of the flower was like a bulbous sack with a rough opening in the middle. Inside the opening we could see a liquid, oozing from glands inside the plant. This moisture was busily being lapped up by multitudes of flies gorging on the mess.

"That is one smelly flower." I backed away from the hollow.

"Definitely not one to give on a first date," replied Peter, laughing.

Clouds of flies swirled around us as they passed to and from the hollow. Soon we had all had enough of the odour and returned to the trail.

"Of all the flowers you could have for a national flower, you guys choose that one," said Veronica.

"Maybe smelly but still beautiful," replied Dani, proudly. He turned ahead of us and led on into the forest.

With young Stephan tagging along, our progress was slowed and it took us longer than expected to reach the turn-around point. After a few hours we finally reached a wide open bank along the river. Dani indicated this would be our lunch stop and we gladly rested by the water. The clouds had thinned and the rain had ceased for now.

Dani handed out a lunch of sandwiches, fruit, and juice to each of us and we ate hungrily. It was early afternoon and we were starving.

"We are running late," Dani said. A tone of concern was in his voice as he looked into the sky. Even though the rain had stopped, the clouds were starting to build once again. "We should be halfway back by now. I think we should get into the river as soon as we can. We might get some more rain today."

Pulling his foot pump out of his bag, Dani asked us for the inner tubes he had given us earlier. We ate the rest of our food while he busily inflated our transport. Periodically, he looked up into the clouds with a look of intensity.

"Why so concerned?" asked Veronica.

"If it rains, the river can get very big and fast. Not so good for us," Dani answered honestly.

"Wouldn't it be better to just hike back out instead?" Veronica continued her inquiry.

"The river is much quicker. If we start now, we shouldn't have a problem." Dani sounded confident.

We packed our belongings and waded into the river, each of us gripping our rubber tubes. Lying in my inner tube, I set my pack in my lap to keep it as dry as possible. With Dani in the lead, the group gave itself to the current of the river as the clouds overhead grew thicker. The river bottom was a gentle slope and we did not encounter too many rapids that posed much of a challenge.

About half an hour passed by and we were making good time down the river. Stephan and his father were enjoying themselves; the young boy squealed with delight while splashing his dad who floated next to him. The rest of us drifted along, close to our guide who still watched the skies with a wary eye.

It wasn't long before the sky opened up, delivering a rain storm the likes of which I had never seen before. It was as if we were standing under the world's largest tap. A wall of water fell from the sky and, in a moment, we were soaked to the skin. The sound of the rain falling into the river was deafening.

"We must get out of the river soon," said Dani, greatly disappointed in the change of weather. He looked ahead of our position and noticed a small cove on the far side of the river. "We must go there."

"But it's on the other side of the river from the trail," I said to him. Looking over to the opposite bank I saw nothing but rocky bluffs, above which sat our morning's path. "Can't we float down further to a better slope? We might be able to hike up to the trail."

"Good idea but no time. We have to get out now!" He sounded adamant. Even as he said the words, I felt the river start to surge. Even the sound of the river began to change from gentle babbling to a louder rumbling as rocks along the banks were slowly being submerged. Further upstream the rain had been falling for some time before the storm had reached us. The upper tributaries had become swollen much earlier and now the flooding waters were just reaching our position. Dani guided the group to the edge of the river and into the small cove he had found, gesturing us to get out of the current as fast as possible. We reached the bank and pulled ourselves and our inner tubes onto the shore.

"Get up to higher ground," he said as he led us up the slope of the riverbank to a bluff about ten metres above the edge of the river. "Sorry, I know we are on the wrong side, but we are safe here."

I looked into the river and could actually see it rising up its banks. The water had changed from a clear stream to a murky, surging torrent. It roared like thunder through the forest below us. As it grew, the flood ran into normally dry places, creating strange new waterways. As a result, the quiet little cove below us now possessed a huge, sucking rapid. I watched, mesmerized, as large items like whole trees floated by our safe haven on the bluff.

"So, what now, Dani?" asked Peter.

"We just have to wait," Dani said. "Nothing to do but wait."

"How long?" Peter asked, cinching up his rainjacket.

"The rain comes fast but should stop soon," our guide explained. "When it does, the river will go down again and we can get back to the other side."

Dani's prediction turned out to be a long wait. The rain continued to pummel the treetops and the swollen river raged on as daylight faded. We sat on the riverbank of the river looking like drowned rats waiting for a ship to arrive. The young boy fussed and cried, his father trying to console him. Almost an hour later the rain ceased but the river's flow did not subside. The flood upstream was still at full strength and it would be some time before the excess water had passed through the small valley. Impatiently, we sat and watched the day turn to dusk. Another half-hour passed. Finally, the river dropped back to its original size, although it was still very murky. Small branches from trees and vegetation still floated by on the current.

"Now we can go," Dani said to the group.

"Is it safe to tube now, Dani?" I asked.

"I think we have to hike," he said to me. "We can float down for a short way and I know of a place to hike back to the trail. It is not far."

"Why can't we go by the river?" asked Peter.

"Too dark now," Dani replied. Pulling his large flashlight from his bag, he turned it on and off to check that the batteries had not been soaked by the rain. "Sorry, but it will be safer to hike."

Dani led us down to the riverbank and into the river. With flashlight in hand, he floated ahead of us as the darkness grew thicker. My companions and I used our own torches as we followed our leader down the stream. The German had not packed such equipment, so we made sure that he and his son were between us and the leader in front. After another twenty minutes on the water, we followed Dani as he scoured the riverbank with the beam from his torch. He was searching for a familiar marker.

"What are you looking for?" Peter asked.

"A big rock . . . there!" he said, excitedly. Light from his torch landed on the side of a humungous boulder in the river. A wide sand bar ran along the bank.

"Go here," he said to us as he held the beam of light in position. Splashing noisely, we waded onto the sand bar with Dani arriving last. "Everybody okay?"

"Sure, but where the hell are we now?" asked Veronica.

"Good fishing spot," he replied reassuringly. "There is a trail just behind you that goes up to our trail from this morning." We turned and focused our lights on a muddy track which led up through the wet forest.

"What about these things?" I indicated the cumbersome tubes we would now have to carry through the bush.

"Leave them here, I will come back to get them another day," said the guide. He was picking up on the fact that his charges weren't too happy by this point in the journey. Dani collected all of the tubes and, using the rope he carried, tied them to a tree by the riverbank before leading us up into the forest.

We climbed the slippery slope and we finally emerged out of the overgrown track onto the main trail back to the village. Keeping in a tight group, we aided each other along with the light from our torches and stumbled through the night.

By 8:00 we finally began to see lights ahead of us. With a feeling of relief, we walked down and past the information centre. Two other guides were waiting. They were relieved to see that we had arrived safely. When their comrade had not returned with his group on time, they had remained at the centre. By now, they had considered organizing a search party to look for us.

Without even saying good-bye to the guide, we left him and walked to the river. Soaked to the skin, we ignored the boatman's crossing, vacant by now anyway and walked through the stream and down the river trail to Yusman. There we peeled off the wet clothing stuck to our skin, changed, and returned to the kitchen, shivering as we pulled chairs up to a table.

"Can we get something to eat?" asked Peter, sounding exhausted.

"Sure," said the friendly young waiter. "What would you like?"

"Anything above body temperature," I said, rubbing my head with a dry towel.

# CHAPTER 11: LAKE TOBA

## Rubber Trees and Dents

*Monday, January 16, 1995*

*"I'll meet you in Lake Toba. Am planning to be on the Tuk-Tuk peninsula at a bungalow named Samosir—the same name as the island. Here is a list of some other places in case of no vacancy. Hope to see you there.* —John"

I scrawled the message on a small piece of paper I had found in the kitchen and stuffed it under the door to Peter and Veronica's room. I paused to look off the porch of the second-level balcony one last time. The dawn was just breaking and a thick mist hung over the river. The sweet sound of water poured over the rocks in the shallow eddies. I would miss the gentle, soothing ambience. Soon I would be back in the smoky city of Medan, if only for a short time, before heading south to Lake Toba in north central Sumatra. My two friends wanted to stay behind for another day or two while I felt inspired to move on.

This early in the morning the kitchen was occupied by only one person. The young man seemed to still be asleep when I walked into the back office to pay the bill for my stay.

"Thank you," he said as I handed a small wad of bank notes to him over the desk. "And thank you for the music."

"Yeah, it was fun," I said. "I'm just glad I got to have my guitar back." I thought of all the times I would return from a hike to find the staff arguing playfully over who got to play my instrument next.

My host saw me out to the bridge crossing and bade me goodbye. I stood again for a moment in the centre of the bridge, listening to the river while checking my time; I was still early for the first bus to the city. I soaked in the natural sound as if trying to save some of it for my time back in Medan. The mist rolled over me, the moisture resting gently on my exposed skin. I turned and crossed the stream.

I climbed into the rugged-looking bus sitting in the small village square. I propped myself against my belongings in a corner and quickly fell asleep.

The next thing I knew, my head was bouncing on the top edge of the bench seat and I had been awoken by the sound of a shuddering metal chassis and a whining engine. Looking at my watch, I realized that I had managed to sleep away half the journey back to Medan before the rude awakening by a large patch of potholes.

By midmorning the bus was entering the outskirts of the sprawling city. The blowing dust was again drifting into the coach and the temperature by now was sweltering.

I purchased my ticket from the central office, found my bus, and prepared myself for the six-hour journey ahead. This time the likelihood of having a seat to myself was slim. Being a main route, it was advantageous for the bus companies to pack as many passengers in as possible. Departure only occurred when our vehicle was packed like a can of sardines. Seats made for three people sat five and I could hardly move with all the bodies stuffed in around me. If we had an accident the padding would come in handy. An old man sold me another bushel of rambutans from outside the window. Rumbling out of the station at just past 11:00 AM, with food vendors still exiting through the doorways, baskets balanced precariously, we were soon past the dusty streets and back on the highway.

The fresh air was again welcome as groves of coconut and rubber trees streamed by the window. Almost the entire trip was through forests of these trees. The groves of rubber trees bore the telltale coiled scarring, a long white trail of raw rubber flowing around the tree into a metal or plastic bucket waiting at the bottom, hanging from a small spout. In between the large groves of trees, crops of tapioca grew, the umbrella plant-shaped leaves catching the sun shining through the cracks in the canopy.

The remainder of the trip was marked by the sight of bus accidents on the highway. By the number I saw along the way, it seemed that they were a fairly common occurrence. A bus parked at an angle off the side of the road would cause the crowd of people inside our bus to crane their necks to get a better view of the carnage. Most of the time the damage was contained to the front corners of two vehicles which had unsuccessfully tried to pass each other on a tight curve.

Another bus had tried to take out a large tree at the edge of the road with no luck. With the front end wrapped tightly around the trunk of the still healthy tree, people were climbing out of the rear door and windows of the bus while other passengers picked up the luggage that had been thrown from the roof rack by the force of the impact. The driver of our bus hardly slowed down as he passed by the accident site, only beeping his horn and forcing bystanders to clear a path in front of him. In fact, I was sure that I felt a slight bump as the back wheels caught a corner of some unlucky person's baggage still lying in the road.

A few miles later we were forced to stop by a long traffic jam. Finally reaching the front of the bottleneck, we caught sight of the worst accident we were to come across. A passenger bus had careened head-on into a fully loaded logging truck. The first thing we saw was the payload of teak logs strewn on the highway and in the ditch. The cab and trailer had flipped into the ditch after impact. The coach, however, was still in the centre of the road. Almost all of the windows in the vehicle had been cracked or smashed by the force of the crash and the driver's cab section was caved in. Many police and others who looked like medical personnel were there, helping the visibly injured and those in shock. It was likely that the driver had been killed at the moment of the crash.


## Parapat and Samosir Island

The journey continued as we climbed steadily up through the mountainous region south of Medan. I had just begun to wonder if we were ever going to reach our destination when the terrain abruptly changed. Thick forests that had blocked my view for most of the journey now gave way to a deep valley and, beyond it, a slight glimpse of a large body of water lapping at the feet of the mountains. From here the road began to slope downward and became quite steep, weaving down along the valley wall like a huge snake.

The driver did not seem too concerned that the steep road possessed an obvious and dangerous hazard—huge cliffs. He drove down the hill at a considerable speed, slamming on the brakes only when he approached the sharper corners. A professional driver myself, I began to get a little nervous. Experience and training had taught me that this driver was creating a possible accident scenario.

Making hard brake applications in a large bus (or any large, heavy vehicle) over and over again on a steep slope causes the brake drums and pads to heat up. So much so that, if done enough, the friction and heat cause the brake drums to expand in size. An increase in drum size causes a deadly situation: the drums expand to a size where the pads can no longer make contact with them to create braking power, producing a runaway vehicle.

The driver continued to swerve around the corners fast enough to make me sweat in my seat. The further down the slope we flew, the faster our turns became and I knew why: the drums were getting larger and was taking more foot power to make contact. I stared out the window and down the face of the steep cliff wall. The dark green foliage falling away below me to the right looked to be a very ugly landing spot. I prayed that we would reach the flat valley bottom soon and not via the obvious air-borne shortcut I was staring down into. The cool tropical breeze sailed in through the windows as if to calm my fears. The worst part was that the rest of the passengers, especially the locals, seemed oblivious to the situation as they tossed back and forth on their seats. By the time we had reached this leg of the journey, a great many people had been dropped off, leaving plenty of room for involuntary motion on the bench seats. I sat holding my breath, nervously folding and unfolding my bus ticket. The bus company's name, P.M.H., blazened across the top of the paper had me imagine an appropriate slogan: "Pay Money—Hang on!"

One last sharp corner at the bottom caused me to slide sideways, slamming into the window frame. I knew that if we did not soon get to the bottom we would be toast. I finally heard the high whine of the engine start to drop. Thankfully, the land had become flat once more. The bus slowed and pulled over to let some people off on the side of the road. As the bus came to a stop, the rich smell of burning brake pads crawled in through the windows.

After only a brief stop, the driver sped off again and, in a short time, we were on the lakeflat. Craning my neck to look through the back window, I glanced upward to see where we had come from. The edge of the enormous cliff wall rose up steep and high. The vegetation was so thick that no rock was visible. The only noticeable thing was the thin ribbon of road, snaking slowly and steadily up to the rim above. As the highway came out onto the river flat, the town of Parapat sat just ahead at the shore of the enormous lake.

Lake Toba is actually the remains of a giant volcano that collapsed in on itself in the middle of a huge eruption some seventy-five thousand years ago. The explosion was supposed to have made Krakatoa seem like a hiccup in comparison. After the eruption and collapse of the land mass, the resulting hole eventually filled with fresh water, creating the largest lake in Southeast Asia, ninety kilometres long. Its steep sloping bottom reaches four hundred and fifty metres in some places. Even at eight hundred metres above sea level, the water still remains quite warm. In the middle of the lake is Samosir Island, a huge, rugged rock forty kilometres in length.

The bus rolled into a central station near the port of Parapat. This small town at the edge of the lake was a busy market centre and also the main connection to Samosir Island via the ferry boats moored by the large docks. When the bus finally stopped for the last time, I breathed more easily. My heart had been racing for a good portion of the descent and now my blood pressure was returning to normal. Gathering my bags, I stepped out the front door of the bus while at the same time eyeing the driver. His expression told me that he had no clue that his driving style would, perhaps, one day put him off the edge of a precipice and make it his last day of employment. To him it seemed to be business as usual as the burning smell poured in through both the doors and windows. Stepping onto the dusty but solid ground, I crouched beside the front wheel hub for a brief moment. As I bent close, I could feel the heat of the metal on my face. I spat onto the exposed brake drum through the hole in the tire's rim. My saliva exploded with a loud "pop" as it was instantly vapourized by the scorching metal. Hail St. Christopher!

I walked down the short road to the lakeside dock and wandered for a short time through the open market. There were plenty of people, both locals and tourists, milling about the stalls and restaurants. After a time I turned back in the direction of the dock. Along the way I was accosted by local guides, the potentially helpful and the monetarily hopeful. I arrived to find a ferry boat that was taking on passengers for one of the day's last sailings to the Tuk-Tuk peninsula, a small point of land jutting out from the edge of Samosir Island. This peninsula housed a large number of tourist accommodations. I joined the line to board the vessel, finding myself a comfortable seat. As the sun slipped toward the edge of the island's high bluff, the ferry set sail from the dock.

Despite the sun beaming through the open sides of the ship, the wind off the water was chilling. Shortly after leaving the dock I stared over the side of the vessel and already I could not see the lake's bottom. The steep slope of the land left only dark, black water to stare into. I did not notice a young man approaching me.

"Hello, where you go?"

"I'm actually looking for a place called Samosir Bungalow."

The young man smiled proudly and reached into his shirt pocket, pulled out a business card and passed it to me with an eager hand. Taking the card, I glanced on the front to see that it was, indeed, the card for the bungalow I was seeking. Sent over to Parapat to drum up business for his boss, the young porter sat down beside me, happy to have at least one customer fall into his lap.

"I am Roy," he said. He reached out his hand to shake mine.

"Hi, I am John," I replied.

"John, where are you from, John?" Roy asked me eagerly.

"Canada," I answered.

"Oh . . . Canada." He looked thoughtful. "I like to go there one day. You will like Samosir."

Roy put his arm around my shoulder and patted me on the back like an old buddy before leaving me to continue his job of drumming up more customers for his bungalow. He made himself busy, talking to tourists and handing out his cards.

The boat approached the island and made the first of several stops as we slowly sailed around the shoreline. Each of the waterfront properties possessed either a stone wall or wooden dock.

"We are here, John." Roy had returned to guide me to the hotel. It seemed I was his only customer. Despite his lack of sales, he proudly slung my luggage over his shoulders and led me to the ship's exit. He shouted something to the helmsman standing on the bridge and the ship slowed along the shoreline. As it pulled alongside the stone wall in front of the bungalow, Roy and I jumped off the ship and onto the top of the wall. I struggled to keep up with Roy as he carried my baggage up the long stairway to the main office.

## Hotel Staff

Once I had checked in, I spent some time in the large, open sitting area. Satellite TV, video, stereo, and food were always available. Kim, the resident manager, was a friendly guy and was very helpful throughout my stay. Manning the front desk, he would take orders for food and shout them down the stairs to the cooks in the kitchen. I spent time reading through the various books and magazines piled by Kim's counter. Roy was busy doing work around the room and also running about the hotel complex. Virtually everytime I looked up, however, it seemed that Roy was there to say hello to me and to give me a friendly arm around the shoulder. I took it in stride and figured it was simply his way of being friendly with the guests.

Other tourists were there as well, including two cute Danish sisters with whom I struck up a short conversation. After a time I excused myself and returned to my room to retrieve my journal.

I walked down the steps from the office and reached for the key to open my locked door. Rustling came from behind me and I sensed the presence of someone. I turned to see Roy standing on my small porch. He had seen me leave and had followed me to my door.

"What's up, Roy?" I asked.

"You sleep here tonight?" he asked.

"Well, I usually stay in a room that's booked in my name," I told him.

"I sleep here tonight?" he asked me.

"Excuse me?" I replied, not really sure if I had heard him correctly.

"I sleep here tonight?" he asked again. When I heard him say this, I understood his intentions, and I decided I had to get the idea into his head that I didn't play on his side of the fence. He was starting to follow me into my room when I held out my hand, pushing him backwards through the doorway. Standing there slightly shocked, he seemed puzzled that I should reject him.

"Sorry," I said. "I only like women, my friend." I had turned him around and gave him a pat on the back while I said it.

"Only women . . . only women," he repeated dumbly. I stood watching the wheels in his head turning as the information slowly leaked into his mind. Sending him off to try his luck with someone else, I closed the door, shaking my head.

"I have enough trouble getting lucky without this," I said to myself, laughing. I closed up my room and returned to the company of the Danish girls.

I was sitting down on the sofa across from the two young women when Roy suddenly reappeared and came back over to me, squeezing himself in beside me on the couch and placing his hand on my thigh. I looked over to the sisters as their jaws hit the table.

"I think he likes you," said one of the sisters.

"Unfortunately, I think you're right," I said to her. I looked over at my problem and grabbed his hand, pushing it back into his own lap. He firmly put his hand back on my leg. Getting up out of my seat , I forcefully pushed him away from the space he had just invaded.

"Look, Roy, I told you once. Get lost." Roy left once again, obviously in a confused state. The two Danish girls were shocked. Soon, we all started laughing.

Kim, the manager, was out of the room when this incident occurred. When he returned I pulled him aside and told him about the problem I was having. When Kim understood what had transpired, he was very apologetic and waited for Roy to return.

As we sat and talked, Roy came back into the common room and continued his rounds, this time eyeing me warily.

"Roy!" Kim called him into the back room. The sisters and I could hear him getting severe shit from the boss. The two eventually emerged from the back room with Roy looking quite defeated. From this time onward, Roy kept his distance as he did his chores. Kim left his post at the front desk and joined our group in the corner.

"I am sorry, John." Kim said to me. "This is Roy's first job and he is a little naive when it comes to dealing with people."

"You're not kidding," I laughed at his understatement and tried not to hold it against him. There were a few more incidents with Roy and it seemed that each guest had his or her own personal complaint about something he had done or said.


## Batak Village
*Wednesday, January 18, 1995*

I walked down the road that led around the edge of the Tuk-Tuk peninsula and joined the main road running along the island. The day was cool and cloudy. As I found out, the weather didn't change much here. The high altitude of the island and the mass of water in the lake created a localized weather system that was generally grey and damp. The high ridge in the island's centre was shrouded in its typical cap of cloud that never seemed to move. My destination was the traditional Batak village of Ambarita, which sat five kilometres up the coast, north of the peninsula. Bataks are the indigenous people of the Lake Toba and northern Sumatran regions, known for their unusual architecture, hand-crafted textiles, artwork, and carvings, as well as musical prowess.

As I walked along the road, a group of school kids joined me on their way to class in town. As they walked with me, they began laughing and pointing at me. I didn't know what they were saying but they seemed to be having a great time. I just smiled and walked on to Ambarita.

The "old city" was a short distance from the main road. Reaching the site, I encountered a huge, impenetrable wall of tall trees surrounding the complex. Hiking around the perimeter, it took me awhile to find the gate. I was walking quite quickly and at first I walked right past the opening. A long, narrow hole had been cut into the surrounding wall of thick trees. Crouching under loosely trimmed branches, I entered the ancient city.

A small number of people were out in the courtyard. Along with some tourists already inside the grounds, a few caretakers were busy sweeping the compound. An old woman carrying a small tin saw me enter and walked over to collect the entrance fee.

"You pay, you pay, you pay." She was adamant about the collection. Maybe she figured I was going to take a photo and run. She stood shaking the tin box in front of my face.

"Relax, I'm getting it." I reached into my wallet to retrieve the coins for her. All the while, she continued to mutter in Bahasa. I tossed the money in her pot and she left me to my visit.

The Batak architecture was striking. The roof of each building came to a sharp peak and the curved rooflines accentuated these points out from each end as if reaching into the sky as far as possible. The houses stood off the ground on short rounded posts and tiny ladders led up to the front doors. Ornate carving trimmed not only the doorways but the entire structures. The detail in the wood carvings was astounding. The ancient trees in the midst of the houses added to the mystique.

In the centre of the courtyard sat a dirt platform held in by a wall of stones. About one metre high, the platform held a number of ancient roughly cut stone chairs arranged around a circular table in the middle. The stone table sat under the boughs of a giant tree which grew within the bounds of the platform. The twisted, buckling roots of the tree made for an uneven "floor" and had begun to push out large sections of the stone wall.

Standing next to the platform, a guide was telling a group of visitors about the significance of the stone circle and the village itself. I stood behind, listening in.

"This is the council circle," the guide explained. "Conversations and meetings were very important in the lives of the Batak people. Each village had a circle similar to this where issues and concerns of the society would be addressed. Only men would sit in council and matters would only be discussed here in the sacred circle. The chairs would not be used for any other purpose." Lichen and thin layers of moss grew upon the age-old stone. A few of the chairs resembled small couches with enough room for two or three people, whereas others were made for only one.

The guide continued with his tour by leading the group behind another building to a hidden area out of view of the rest of the village. In the centre of this area we were shown another stone circle.

"This is the execution chamber . . . " The guide stopped his spiel for a moment and let the crowd murmur and whisper at the sight of this ominous place. A ring of stone slabs standing upright surrounded a short, almost square stone block sitting in the centre. I noticed that the top of the block looked to be worn down slightly, like a butcher's block.

"In this chamber the elders would stand in front of the stone slabs," the guide continued. "These elders would judge the fate of anyone accused of crimes according to Batak law. If found guilty by the surrounding elders, the person would then lose his or her head on the chopping block."

Swallowing hard, I was rubbing my throat as I walked from the chamber, thinking of the ancient ceremonies that sent criminals off to their deaths.

Walking back from Ambarita later in the day, I decided to take an alternate route from where I had come that morning. My new road took me through an area of fields and small houses. Along the way, I came across an old house that looked abandoned. An old broken door hung loosely in the jamb on the front porch and no glass filled the windows.

I had just passed the entrance to the yard when I began to hear young voices from inside and, then, singing. A chorus of voices began to pour out of the empty windows. I could hear a guitar being played as an accompaniment to the singers. The sound was great and I was inspired to take a peek in through the doorway. I crept up to the porch and poked my head in through the opening.

Inside, a group of ten young boys, perhaps around the ages of ten or twelve, were sitting in a tight circle with one of them strumming away on an old guitar. One of the boys noticed my presence in the entrance and shouted to his friends. Ten small faces turned to me in surprise as the music abruptly stopped.

"That sounds great!" I shouted to them as I stood in the doorway. I clapped my hands in appreciation of their talent. They were excellent singers with good harmonies. The fact that they were only little kids made me envious. They all began to shout with excitement as three of the friends came to greet me at the door. All at once, the three grabbed me by the arm and pulled me into the room.

I looked around to see that the house had, indeed, been abandoned. There was a musty smell to the place and huge holes in the interior walls, exposing the studs. Old furniture and mattresses sat in dusty corners. The boys were using the place as a clubhouse and I was their newest member. The musical tradition of the Batak people is very strong and it seemed that these young boys assumed everyone else in the world could also play an instrument and sing. I was glad to be able to comply with their request.

I played and sang a few of my favourite songs. They clapped and sang along as best they could. It was of no concern to them that they didn't know the words. They just seemed happy that someone wanted to share some music with them. I handed the guitar back when I was finished and another boy picked it up and the group sang more traditional songs.

I sat back and listened to the young musicians and felt very much a part of their clan. Compared to the small groups of taunting youths I had encountered on my way to Ambarita, these boys had made me feel welcome. I felt connected to their music and their playfulness as they laughed and sang.

After a time, I got to my feet and indicated that I had to continue on my way. Each boy shook my hand and smiled widely. The entire group walked me over to the door of their clubhouse. I could hear the music begin again as I walked down the dirt path.


## Hiking
*Sunday, January 22, 1995*

Peter and Veronica arrived from Bukit Lawang a few days after me. Together we enjoyed many fine hikes throughout the area of Samosir Island. There were a great number of trails that cut through the thick forests covering the cliffside wall of the island, occasional waterfalls cutting a gash in the sheer face of rock. The slopes were steep but the cool shade of the thick trees made walking in the tropical heat bearable. There was one particular canyon cutting into the cliff wall a few kilometres from the peninsula that had piqued our curiosity. The dark shadows and slightly visible waterfall overgrown by tangles of thick trees seemed worthy of exploration.

We cut across the end of the peninsula and made our way over dried rice paddies. The large, square patches of terraced land seemed like steps for a giant.

"That's the one," Peter said. We stopped briefly to spot our destination from the high hill at the end of the peninsula. It sat directly across from us as we faced the huge wall of the island. Below us the dirt road leading off the end of Tuk-Tuk snaked its way south along the edge of the lake. It led away from the canyon crevice and on to the next small village along the shoreline.

"I think that road's too far out of the way," Peter went on. "We should just cut across the rice paddies again."

"Sure, why not?" I said to him. "After all, we're getting used to it by now."

Nestled against the backdrop of the mountain were rice paddies being tended by busy farmers. The land had been tilled and terraced right up to the foot of the mountain, using every metre of space. The rich sea of green shoots carpeted the land by the edge of the lake as far as we could see. Snaking in between, the mud walls of the terraces provided pathways through the water-filled land. Getting permission to pass through the fields became a common practice, as most of the hiking destinations were blocked by someone's private property.

We sat for a moment as we picked our route through the fields.

When we had chosen a starting point, we slowly made our way down the steep slope toward the edge of the terrace. The descent included a bit of tropical bushwhacking, through dense vines and thick trees. Soon, we emerged out of the tangle and stood on the muddy edge of a rich green field of young rice.

Three woman toiled with their backs toward us and had not heard our approach, despite the noise we were creating in the forest. Up to their knees in mud and water, these women worked steadily, bent over their work as they shoved the grass-like shoots of rice into the freshly tilled muck. In the next field over, a man drove a team of oxen through an unplanted terrace. The team of animals pulled what looked like a giant comb through the flooded earth, plowing back and forth many times to get the mud to the right consistency for planting.

"Hello," shouted Peter through cupped hands.

His shout gained the attention of the three woman in the field. They stood up, turned, and smiled at us, their hands full of green shoots and forearms covered with mud. One of the women said something to us in her own language. We jokingly translated it to "What the fuck do you want?"

Using his own version of crude sign language, Peter pointed toward the mountain beyond the field and began to march in place, pointing to the narrow mud wall that we were hopefully going to use for a highway.

"Okay?" Peter yelled again. The women waved us onto the muddy maze.

We were halfway across the terrace when they stopped their work and walked over to greet us as we passed. They rinsed their hands off in the murky water and reached out to shake our hands. The three were quite old; their faces showed many years of experience in the fields of Toba. They all wore old cotton scarfs to protect their heads from the sun. Their loose cotton skirts hung to just above the level of the water they were working in.

All three began to chatter at us in Bahasa as they pointed toward the mountain wall. Nodding as if we understood what they were saying to us, we simply smiled and enjoyed their company. One of them pulled an old pipe from her pocket, stuffed a small bit of tobacco into the bowl, and struck a match. A thick curl of smoke floated around her face as she laughed and giggled with her friends.

After a short visit and unknown conversation with our hosts, we thanked them with more handshakes and pointed to the mountain. The three women spoke excitedly again as they waved and turned back to their work. Wading back out to the centre of the terrace, they resumed their bent-over position in the mud. Leaving them to their work, we made our way through the maze of narrow raised mud pathways toward the foot of the mountain.

Snaking along the walls of thick mud, I came upon a small bamboo cage just next to the trail. Hearing a lot of noise coming from inside it, I ventured nearer to have a better look. Getting closer, the sound of two very excited pigs reached my ears. These little fellows were obviously glad to see someone coming out to visit with them as they snorted and squealed, their round noses thrust out from between the cell bars to smell me and to say hello.

Knowing that pigs love to be scratched but also knowing that they can inflict nasty bites, I cautiously reached my hand into the small enclosure. My hand met with a wet licking.

As we continued on through the fields there were a few farmers in the distance who stood and stared at us as we passed. We would make sure to wave to them if they noticed our presence as if to say, "Thanks for the road."

Still in line with the ravine we were about to explore, we reached the other side of the paddy to find a large creek pouring into one end of the terrace. The water was flowing out of a thick grove of trees and looked to be the main feeder stream for all the fields that we could see.

Beside the creek a well-worn trail struck off deep into the forest. We followed and soon the land became steep. The trail that skirted along the side of the creek disappeared at the edge of a pool in the stream. Seeing no other place to go, we wandered into the water and began to climb the creek bed, scrambling over the dark grey rocks amid the cascading water.

"Ahh . . . " Veronica sighed as she stopped to take in a rich, deep breath of cool air.

"These shady places seem so mystical," I said as I stopped beside her to drink from my water supply. The trees were so thick that the sound of our voices and the water seemed trapped within the confines of the foliage. Trees hung over our heads and the ground cover along the edges of the stream was a thick mat.

"I wonder how far we can get up?" I looked up to see the top of the cliff, visible through a small crack in the forest above us. We could see the top of the waterfall as the water spilled out of the high trees and descended down the rock face.

"Let's find out," replied Veronica. She splashed through the creek and clambered up to join Peter who was standing at the top of a huge boulder.

"It gets steep past here," shouted Peter, unknowingly answering my question. I followed Veronica up the creek bed.

The moisture hung on everything like a cloak draping to the ground. The coolness splashed my face as I clambered through the water, my Tevas sticking like glue to the large boulders. The walls of the tiny canyon grew steep as small traces of sunlight fought through the tall trees. We joined Peter on the rock and glanced up at the top of the waterfall, far above us. Mist from the falling water draped a wet cloud all around us as we stood by the stream. The falling water formed another large, shallow pool. Beyond, another short trail led to the foot of the falls. Exploring a few scrambling routes up the side of the cascade, we made our way up as far as we could climb.

"I think we'd need a rope to get any further," I said.

"Yeah, for sure," Peter agreed. "The rocks are just a bit too wet for free climbing."

Veronica took a few attempts at scaling a small rock wall but soon gave up. Despite the dead end, we spent time under the waterfall's shadow, enjoying the scenery and cool water.

"Hey look!" Veronica pointed into the vegetation near the pond.

"What?" I asked her. I saw nothing.

"There . . . " she said. This time I looked and saw a slight movement on one of the rocks. A small colourful lizard had emerged from under a leaf to investigate our presence. Soon more of them began darting through the leaves and stones, bright colours gleaming in the shadows.

The humidity and shade began to feel quite cool as we finally descended back down the creek bed to the edge of the field. This time we worked our way along the edge of the farms and eventually emerged out on the dirt road leading back to Tuk-Tuk.

As the road curved toward the small point of land we called home, we decided to visit a vegetarian restaurant called TABO which sat by the lake just at the edge of the Tuk-Tuk peninsula. It was run by a German woman who had married a local Indonesian.

The log structure was octagonal in shape with laid-back seating in huge booths and open to the outside. The upper walls of the interior were covered by Batak blankets. We had asked about the blankets on a previous visit and the German bride had told us that they were, indeed, part of her traditional dowry. It was a beautiful collection of about thirty blankets, all hanging on the walls of the open-roomed structure. The patterns and colours were intricate and beautiful.

The food at TABO was some of the best I had in Indonesia. The great brown bread and salads were huge hits for most people like me who had only eaten noodles since first arriving on Sumatra. I felt really nourished for the first time in a long time.

The staff at the restaurant ranged from locals to many travellers who had decided to make the island their home for an indefinite period. One of these people included the head chef, who had travelled from Paris to Lake Toba by bicycle some months earlier.

As the day grew steadily darker Peter, Veronica, and I walked out of the log building on our way back home. As we emerged from the doorway, we could see the chef's bike leaning up against the wooden fence by the entrance. Covered with ancient mud, the machine waited quietly for its next ride; worn rubber hand grips and the rounded knobs on the tires bore the evidence of many miles of travel.

### Night Music

Many locals spent their free evenings out in the local pubs, socializing with their friends and playing music. Near our bungalow there were a number of places where one could simply walk into at any time and hear people singing and playing. Joining in with the groups was encouraged, if not expected.

I began to explore these night spots after being told about the music "scene" by a local man who ran a restaurant as well as an art gallery just down the road from our bungalow. He played guitar himself and could play a number of popular Batak songs. The music sounded almost Spanish in flavour, with keen rhythms and sweet melodies.

I began to frequent the local music houses, first as a listener, then as a participant. By the time I had been around for a few days, there were a number of local players with whom I had gained rapport and we would meet to play local music. I could never understand the words but, with the Spanish flavour in the sound, I felt as if I were at a Gypsy Kings convention. Not only were the players good, the female vocalists from the village were outstanding.

One evening I was playing some familiar tunes with my new friends when four women walked into the pub, stood right behind us, and burst into fabulous vocal harmonies on cue, as if rehearsed. I stumbled and stopped playing for a brief moment as I stared around behind me. They just smiled and kept singing. Their happy nature oozed from their music and their singing.

I enjoyed listening to the pure joy contained in the notes and chords. Watching the people interact, the music almost seemed part of the conversation. One person would start telling a story then would break into an a cappella song, soon joined by the rest. When he or she finished singing, they'd go back to the spoken tale.

This happened almost every night. I would make my way to a number of places, encounter the same fervour, and want to share the music. The local players were thrilled that foreigners wanted to join in. Throngs of singers cocooned around us as I was pulled in to join the circle. They were truly beautiful people—so open, friendly, and talented.

I began to understand the importance of music in their lives. A virtual rite of passage, it seemed expected that every man and woman learn to play and/or sing. It seemed commonplace for men to play guitars. I imagined a world run by the idea of holding art and creation in highest regard instead of the sword of power and profit. I was privileged to have known these people—they love to play, nothing more. It inspired me to play with as much feeling as I could muster. I felt the rhythm seeping into my bones. I entered the circle to join the sound of their culture's heartbeat and to feel the music running through my fingers.

### Viking
*Wednesday, January 25, 1995*
Her name was Treena. I had met the Norwegian woman down by the lake a few days earlier. We spoke only briefly, introducing ourselves as she emerged from her small hut by the lake. I would see her with her

male friend as they spent their days at the lakeside. Thinking the man to be her boyfriend, I thought nothing more of it.

My last day at the lake was spent getting things organized for the trip back to Medan. By the time evening rolled around, I just wanted to relax. I planned to eat a meal and then go out for a few drinks up the road at the local "disco."

Waiting for my meal, I noticed her slowly walking up the steps to the dining area. She caught my eye and smiled as she reached the edge of the room. Disappearing into the office for a brief moment, she came back out with a menu in her hand and walked straight toward my table.

"Hi, John," she said. She had a great smile.

"I was out hiking all day and I am starved." She sank into the chair, and just then I noticed Roy the bellhop enter the room on his way to the office. When he passed by our table, I noticed Treena giving him a look that could kill.

"Have you met Roy?" I asked her.

"Met him? The guy is an idiot!"

"What was your experience with him?"

"You wouldn't believe it."

"I'll bet I would," I replied with a grin.

"When we got here," she went on, "we asked to see some rooms for two people. So Kim told Roy to show the rooms to me. When I found one particular cabin that I liked, Roy carried my bags inside, setting them down next to the bed. Then he climbed on the bed and started writhing around, getting comfortable on the mattress. Before I could ask what he was doing, he asked me, 'You, you and your friend . . . you are, uh, fuck, fuck?' At the same time, he was shoving his index finger back and forth through a hole made with his other hand's thumb and forefinger."

"Oh, no," I said sympathetically. "Sounds like all of us have had our share of Roy here at the bungalow."

"You, too?" she asked me. I told her my story and she burst out laughing.

"I wonder how he ever got hired," she said, giggling.

"Who knows," I said. "What did your boyfriend think of him?"

"Oh, he's just a friend," she replied. "We work together back in Norway and decided to travel together. Lately, we were starting to get sick of each other so we decided to have some time on our own. He has gone to Bukittinggi for a few days. I wanted to spend some time with other people, anyway."

"Sounds good," I said to her. "Tonight's my last night here and I am going out to the pub later for a few drinks. Do you want to join me?"

She calmly smiled and said, "I'd love to."

It was later in the evening when we walked to the local dance club. By the time we arrived, the place was packed with locals and tourists. It was just about the only club with a loud music system as all the other clubs and restaurants relied on the ambiance of live players instead of recorded ones. It was a fairly small room with limited seating and a dance floor under a brilliant mirrored ball which spun from the ceiling. I laughed to myself as it seemed the complete antithesis of what I had experienced here while hanging out with the local players. Regardless, we found ourselves a place in the rear corner and spent a fun evening talking, dancing, and laughing.

Treena loved to dance. She constantly pulled me out onto the floor, dancing to song after song. Being that the dance space was small, we had to squeeze in with the rest of the crowd. The heat in the room was intense and we were soaked in sweat by the time midnight rolled around. I walked back to our table, wiping the moisture from my forehead.

"You're too hot, Treena! You're wearing me out."

She put her hand gently on my shoulder and said, "Is dancing the only thing that wears you out?"

"No, I can think of a few things . . . " I could feel myself blushing as I said this to her. She smiled and reached for my hand, squeezing it with her own.

"Let's go home," she said quietly.

The short walk to the bungalow seemed to be over in a minute. We held hands on the way back and soon stood in front of my room at the top of the steps leading down to her cabin.

"I really had a great time tonight, Treena," I said to her, holding both her hands.

There was a slight hesitation as we both stood facing each other on the landing. We stared into each other's eyes for a moment and then she leaned over and kissed me.

"I'm having a wonderful time," she said to me. "Is it over now?"

"No," I said to her. I gently pulled her close and kissed her again. "Do you want to come in?"

Her warm, wet lips answered my question as we stood, fused together for several minutes in front of my door. Finally reaching for the key, I led her into my small room and lit several candles on the bedside table. The dim light made her look so sensuous as she sat on the edge of my bed, her tousled blonde hair hanging in her face. Treena reached up, took my hand, and pulled me down onto the bed beside her. She gently held my face in her hands and kissed me for a long time. I was melting at her very touch; her lips pulled the energy of passion from deep within me.

"You are a good kisser," she whispered. "I haven't kissed like that for awhile."

"I haven't either," I replied. My words were almost slurred as if I was drunk with desire. I ran my fingers through her hair and caressed her tanned skin, damp with sweat.

I was also covered with sweat and the sight of this beauty on my mattress was making me sweat even more. I stood up, took my soaked shirt off, and threw it onto a chair in the corner.

"I think I'm going to have a shower," I said to her.

"I hope you are going to invite me to join you," she said, smiling from the bed. She stood up and pulled the slipdress she was wearing up and over her head. Tossing it into the corner of the room, she removed her undergarments and threw them into the pile. She was standing naked in front of me in an instant.

"I thought Vikings wore more clothing than that," I said smiling, my knees buckling.

"Only when we don't want to have sex," she said, pushing me into the shower in front of her.

We made love for hours. That night Treena and I shared an energy that I had rarely felt. Her warm, tender body embraced me and her soft voice drove me wild. After making love to her, I lay holding Treena close to me in the warm afterglow. I caressed her thighs and stomach, kissing her soft shoulders. She lay still in my arms making soft, sexy sounds of approval.

I felt liberated. Over the past several days, a deep sense of loneliness had grown in me, rooted somewhere in my final words with Jill.

The image of the complete and final end of that era felt heavy—a chapter of my life to which I could never go back, even if I had wanted to. Since speaking to her, I had yearned for comfort. I wanted to be wanted. I wanted to embrace my freedom.

Now these feelings were erased. This beautiful woman had taken me in, let me feed her desires and my own. I felt reconnected to my passion. She had given me the gift of intimacy and tenderness. The Viking had set me free.

# CHAPTER 12: RETURN TO MEDAN

## $top Plea$e—Roadblock in Progre$$

*Thursday, January 26, 1995*

"About time you got up," Veronica said as Treena and I entered the hotel's lobby. She was at the desk paying her final bills to Kim. The friendly manager smiled in greeting to my friend and me. Treena sat with me at a small table in the corner of the room.

"Yeah, yeah. We kinda . . . slept in," I winked at Veronica. She acknowledged Treena and smiled.

"What time do we have to leave, Veronica?" I asked. Treena and I had been up until only an hour before the alarm had sounded. I was only a little disoriented.

"You still have about an hour before the boat leaves for Parapat," she said.

"Good. Coffee time." I stood and approached Kim at the desk.

"We need the two biggest cups of coffee you can make, my friend."

"No problem," he said smiling.

Treena and I ate a light breakfast void of conversation. We were famished and fatigued from our long night together. I paid my tab at the front desk and thanked Kim for being a great host. Slinging my bags over my back, I followed Treena to her cabin by the water. We sat on her porch, talking and kissing until the time came to depart.

"Last night was amazing," I told her. "It was something I really needed."

She kissed me again, "We both needed it."

The sound of the ferry boat's engine could be heard along the shoreline as it slowly made its rounds to all the docks around the peninsula. It was almost at Samosir's stone wall.

"Boat's here, John," Peter yelled from the edge of the lake.

"Gotta go." I stared into her eyes for a long moment.

"Good-bye." Treena held me close once more in a tight embrace. I picked up my bags and walked to the stone wall.

The weathered old ship slowed, allowing us to hop onto the gunwale. I climbed up to the top deck and stood near the stern. I looked off the back of the ship to see Treena standing on her porch waving to me. I waved back until the ship drifted around the corner of the land and I finally lost sight of her. I breathed deeply and sighed as her image burned into my memory. I continued to stare at the stone wall where we had boarded the ferry. Secretly, I hoped that Treena would walk to the edge of the lake for one final farewell. I watched in vain for a few moments and finally turned my back on Samosir Island as the ship headed for Parapat across the glass-smooth surface of Lake Toba.

We walked off the dock and up the hill to the bus station, against the flow of a new crowd of tourists who had just arrived. Local salesmen were busy shouting their respective spiels to new customers. The station was crowded with outgoing passengers as well and the three of us thanked our own foresight in buying tickets a few days before.

Three buses were destined for Medan and we searched for the one with the least people in order to get a decent seat.

"Over here," Veronica said to Peter and me. We walked briskly through the compound and jumped into the back bench seat of another old rust-bucket, piling our bags in with us.

The bus looked to be in about the same shape as the one in which I had arrived. Cracked windows, rust, and the constant blue cloud puffing out of the tail pipe were its most endearing qualities.

"I am glad that this thing is going up the hill today, not down it," I said to my friends. I told them about the smoking brakes on my trip into Parapat.

"Maybe the engine will die and we'll roll back off the edge," mused Peter. Veronica elbowed him in the ribs and scowled.

"With the shape these vehicles are in, I wouldn't be surprised," I replied.

A woman began to yell at us from outside the window. We looked out to see another fruit vendor holding items up to the window of the bus, pleading with us to buy her wares. I traded a bill for rambutans and my friends bought two bags of mangosteens (a round, purple fruit that tastes like sweet rhubarb). We sat waiting for the bus to fill to capacity while stuffing our faces with fresh flavour.

After a long delay the bus driver finally sat in his seat and piloted the rusty clunker out onto the highway toward the cliff. The rim of the giant crater hung above us as I eyed the tiny ribbon of highway ascending the side of the forested wall. The bus reached the bottom of the slope and the engine began to whine as it started the long, steady climb out of the ancient crater. Almost immediately we could see a spectacular view behind us as we climbed away from the lake.

"Look at how steep that cliff is," said Veronica, her eyes widening. Rounding the corner, we caught a glimpse of the thick blanket of foliage falling away from the edge of the highway, virtually straight to the bottom of the wall. Barely a metre separated the roadway from the edge of thin air.

Before long giant Lake Toba was far below us and Parapat only a tiny speck along the shoreline. After a number of short stops to pick up and drop off passengers, the bus finally reached the top edge of the crater. I was staring out the back window as the bus reached the shallower slope of road and started to descend over the top of the rim. I caught a last glimpse of the lake below before it was obscured by thick groves of trees once again.

The remainder of the trip was filled with delays as we began to encounter a number of police roadblocks set up along the highway. I had heard that the Indonesian police were infamous for these all over the country. I had seen fully armed police cruising Medan in military jeeps and always felt a little nervous when I saw their monstrous guns and flak jackets.

There is much corruption among police in the third world and I think we all know by now that deceit and crime can exist at even the highest level of authority anywhere in the world. Here in Indonesia I had been told that the police had developed a system whereby they could make tons of money from the tourist trade as well as off the backs of the common people. The police know that buses carry foreign tourists, especially to and from high-volume areas like Toba. At one time they would stop buses constantly, pulling packs and passengers off for inspection and looking for drugs and/or bribes. With the volume of buses travelling the corridor in the recent years, these lengthy inspections created long delays. Now, instead of stopping the buses, the police simply collected large tolls from the bus companies, sort of a "no hassle" fee, to be paid at each of the roadblocks along a particular route.

We were about halfway back to Medan and I had fallen asleep against the window frame. I was right in the middle of giving Treena another kiss when my dream was shattered by Peter's voice and his hand shaking my shoulder.

"Hey, John," he said. "Sorry to wake you but you have to check this out."

Sleepily, I sat up in my seat. There seemed to be quite a bit of excitement among the other passengers. Murmurs floated through the bus along with the thick smoke from cigarettes. I craned my neck to see what the crowd was staring at through the windshield. There in front of us, standing on the highway, a lone policeman waited. He stood beside a sawhorse-like barrier that stuck out a couple of metres into the roadway. As the bus approached he began to wave his hand up and down, indicating the driver to slow down in order to make payment.

The conductor, the man with all the money collected from the clientele, saw the cop as well. Business as usual, he slowly pulled a roll of bills out of his pocket and peeled off a considerable stack of them, folding them up into a small bundle. Shouting to the driver that he was ready, the conductor stepped into the rear stairwell of the bus. Holding onto the door rail with one hand, the man leaned out of the slow-moving vehicle and passed the money into the hand of the cop. A buzz and a slight chuckle drifted through the crowd as bus began to speed up again.

"Did you see how much they paid the cop?" said Peter.

I shook my head in disbelief. "Looks like he took half the profits in one shot."

To our surprise, there was a second road block ten miles further down the road. Without a flinch, the driver and conductor repeated the same drill with the same precision as before. All in all, we encountered six of these roadblocks before reaching the outskirts of Medan.

"It's a wonder these companies can make any money at all if they are giving it all away to the cops like this," observed Veronica.

"Just as long as they don't start taking a collection from the rest of us," I said to her, laughing.


## Crunchfest

The heat and fatigue had me sleeping once again as we came to the edge of the city. Slumped by the rear window, I had some relief from the relentless temperature as a semi-cool breeze leaked in.

My fitful sleep was suddenly shattered by a smashing sound all around me. I jumped up in my seat to find that a huge dump truck had slammed into the rear corner of the coach, just where I was sitting. Ironically, as I was falling asleep, I had noticed the rough glass windows of the bus. I noted their thickness and the small chips along the edges. I had a thought of how this glass, which looked to be untempered, would probably break into nasty shards in the event of an accident. I don't really know why this had passed through my mind but it was soon forgotten.

When I leapt into consciousness at the sound of the crash, my first instinct was to look for glass falling from the window frames. Luckily, the bus had been hit in such a place that the windows only cracked. Had the truck hit the bus any further over, the damage would have included shattered glass and injuries. I felt as if I were becoming psychic, thinking about an accident before it happened. Pulling over to the side of the road, both drivers proceeded to argue and blame each other for the accident. Most of the passengers climbed out of the bus to survey the damage. The rear corner and part of the engine compartment had been pushed in by the front end of the truck. The damage looked quite bad but the engine seemed all right.

The incident caused a long delay as the drivers waited for the arrival of a policeman to take care of the official paperwork. All the rest of us could do was just laugh and make light of the situation. The police officer eventually called us back onto the bus and told the driver to leave.

"About time," said Veronica. We were all getting pretty impatient to get into the city and find a place to stay.

No more than three kilometres further down the road, the bus blew a water hose, sending clouds of steam streaming out the back end of the bus.

"What? Not again," I said, disgusted. The driver cursed loudly and pulled over to the side of the road. He couldn't have timed it better because he stopped right alongside the entrance to a garage and petrol station. A crew from the garage stood up from their shady chairs under the roof and began to help the driver with his problem.

Again we climbed off the bus and loitered along the side of the street. By now even the locals were getting pissed off with the delays. They squabbled amongst themselves and at the driver who was still busy cursing his old clunker of a bus.

Shortly afterward another bus on a scheduled run into town was flagged down and pulled up alongside the broken-down wreck. Our driver spoke to his comrade briefly and suddenly turned to us in a loud voice for all to hear.

"Everyone go with this bus! Everyone go to Medan with this bus!"

"That is the best news I have heard from this guy yet," said Peter, climbing back into the first bus to toss our luggage out to us. We boarded the new bus with the rest of the waiting crowd.

Half-full of passengers already, our count of people pushed the limit by only a few. By the time we got inside every seat was crammed with bodies so we stood in the aisle with our baggage between our legs.

With a full load the bus' air-conditioning system was working overtime to produce some kind of cooling effect in the stifling heat. A small vent just above my head was pumping out a thick mist and then started to drip water onto my shoulder. At first it was slow but eventually it became a constant drizzle and I stood there enjoying the refreshing mini-shower. I moved over slightly to allow my friends to get in on the heat relief. Not that I could move very far—I was again squeezed into a massive cushion of bodies. We held each other up as a group like a moshpit on wheels.

This new driver had his own share of close calls as he careened down the road. Other traffic cut in and around him all along the motorway. At last, we rolled into the bus station in the south of the city. Climbing down from the bus I threw my bags on the ground and fell to my knees, pretending to kiss the ground. Peter and Veronica laughed as they stepped over my crouched body.

"Better get up, you might get run over," said Peter.

"Yeah, you're probably right," I said, getting to my feet.

Peter led the way to the hostel he and Veronica had stayed in on their first visit to Medan. Sarah's Guest House turned out to be a great place in a quiet neighbourhood. We spend two nights there before going our separate ways. My friends purchased tickets for Bangkok and I reconfirmed my flight to Kuala Lumpur.

I had really enjoyed my travels with the Nelson couple. They were very down-to-earth people and I had grown to love them both. On our last two evenings together we sat in the lobby of the hostel reminiscing about all of our adventures on the island.

"Yeah, it was an awesome time," said Peter. "But I still would have liked to see that orangutan take you home with her."

"Well," I replied, "I think I prefer Norwegian girls."

# CHAPTER 13: KUALA LUMPUR

## Meeting of Old Friends
*Saturday, January 28, 1995*

I watched the crowd of people filing through the door into the main hall of the Kuala Lampur International Airport. I had no worries about recognizing my friend in the sea of faces. Being of Dutch extracion, his height would take him far above the heads of his fellow passengers.

Marvin was an old workmate of mine. We had once worked in Banff, Alberta for a tour bus company called Brewster and had managed to keep in touch over the years. When Marvin learned that he and I were headed to Southeast Asia at roughly the same time, he was eager to meet me at some point on the journey. A few brief telephone connections resulted in our meeting here in Malaysia and I was looking forward to seeing his familiar face.

After a fair number of people passed into the room, I began to wonder if he had, perhaps, missed the flight. Or maybe I had misread the date in my notebook. Just as I was about to double-check my papers, Marvin appeared in the doorway.

"Hey, brother," he shouted to me from the back of the crowd.

He walked up to me and I shook his hand and just looked at him.

"It is so bizarre to see someone from home in a place this far away," I said to him.

"Really," he agreed. "Great to see you, bud. You look like you have survived well for the last couple of months."

"It has been an amazing experience so far," I said. "And I am sure there's plenty more to come."

"Well," said Marvin, smiling, "let's get started."

We set out from the airport, jumping on a bus to the city centre. Here in Malaysia, the buses were shiny, modern, fast, and efficient. I felt like a kid going to the circus. I hadn't seen such a new machine in a long time. I felt as if I had forgotten what they looked like.

"This thing's like a Porsche compared to the buses I've been on in the last while," I said to Marvin.

He laughed, "Yeah, I'll bet. I was spoiled in Japan and now I'm going to Thailand."

"Ah, but it's not so bad there," I said to him. "It's Indonesia where you have to rely on the power of prayer."

The bus cruised past the gates of a gigantic mosque, its dome rising high above the street. Tall palm trees lined the boulevard in front of the religious building and a large pool of water reflected the ornate design carved into the stonework.

"So what did you see in Japan, Marv?" I asked. The bus took a sudden sharp corner and I almost fell into the lap of an old lady sitting beside me. She gave me a frightened glare from her seat. I just smiled and turned back to my friend.

"I was in Tokyo for the first few days and then I headed up to Kobe, just after that killer quake." He looked disturbed when he spoke about it.

"What was it like there?" I asked. "There must have been lots of damage."

"I couldn't believe the devastation," he said. "Whole areas of the city were gone. Just piles of rubble left behind. By the time I got there, they had a lot of it cleaned up but a lot remained to be removed and repaired."

"Amazing," I said. "So long to build it up and then, boom. It's gone in an instant."

"It made me feel fortunate for what I have," Marvin replied.

"I'll bet it was expensive, too," I said to him.

"It certainly was," he said to me. "The cheapest place I stayed was one I shared with a girl I met over there and we each paid fifty dollars a night."

"Really?" I said. "How big was the room."

"Oh, about the size of a closet, just enough room to sleep."

"What was it called, Villa Claustrophobia?"

During the remainder of the trip into the city centre, we agreed that we could travel together for a week. We decided to make our way to Singapore before going our separate ways.

We dismounted the bus near the city centre and began our search for a place to sleep.

"What do you think, John?" Marvin asked me. "Hilton or hovel?"

"Let's work on hovel and then we can upgrade from there," I said with a grin.

It seemed that the city was getting full. The coming of the

Chinese New Year made hotel space scarce and we were turned away at many of our first choices. As we sought space outside the city core, our search took us to the north side of Merdeka (Independence) Square, bordered on one side by the huge Moorish facade of the Sultan Abdul Samad building. Passing back into the streets feeding into the large square, we saw night market stalls being set up in the middle of the road and hundreds of people milling around every corner. I followed Marvin through the crowd until we saw a small sign saying "Rooms" and headed up a steep, narrow flight of stairs.

An old Chinese man greeted us at the top of the steps, nodding in answer to our question of an available room. He manned his post at a small wooden desk stuck into one corner of the tiny landing. Shoving a registration book at us across the desk, he was adamant about getting his payment up front.

"Thirty dollar, thirty dollar," he yabbered on like a robot.

"Okay, dude. Relax." I said this as I slapped the cash down into his greedy hands. The change in attitude from Thailand and Indonesia regarding the payment of bills had my back up in an instant. "Rude little prick," I thought to myself.

"It's not likely that we'll take off on you, you know," I said to him. He stared back with no emotion, stuffing the bills into his shirt pocket and handing over the key to the room.

He led us down the hall, pointing to the door of our rented space. He then abandoned us in the corridor, returning to his seat.

The room was simple: two single beds that looked pretty clean, an old stained sink in the corner with a drain pipe that descended straight into the wooden floor, and an old wardrobe that looked about ready to fall apart at the seams.

"Feels like home," I said to my friend.

"At least for now," replied Marvin.


## Finlandia Explores the Night Markets

"How about a drink to celebrate?" I asked my friend.

"What did you have in mind?" Marvin answered.

I reached into my packsack and pulled out a fresh bottle of Finlandia vodka that I had picked up at the Medan airport. I held it up and waved it at him.

I tossed him a juice box as he pulled his Swiss army knife out of his bag. He deftly hacked off one corner of the container and cracked the seal on the Finlandia. He mixed two gigantic vodka cocktails in our plastic waterbottles. He handed the newly made drink over to me.

"Now we're road-ready," he said to me. "Let's check out the night market while we quench our thirsts."

By now there were thousands of people milling about all the streets of Kuala Lumpur as the Malays celebrated the start of Ramadan, the Muslim holy month. During this time, things like eating, smoking, drinking, and sex are strictly forbidden for all Muslims from sunrise to sunset. Anyone breaking these rules is subject to various penalties such as having to fast for an extended period after everyone else has stopped. Now that it was well after sundown, the vendors were serving the crowds which had hung around like vultures until the time came when they could take sustenance.

Ramadan is an intensely spiritual time for Muslims. Fasting and other activities are used as avenues for worship and renewal. Marvin and I noticed a general happiness among all the faces we encountered. Many of the people that we met on the street greeted us with friendly smiles and hearty "hellos." My friend and I found an empty spot among the crowds along the stone wall bordering the large grass lawn of Merdeka Square. Marvin and I had not seen each other in person for a few years so we spent a lot of time catching up on old times.

I then shared with him the adventures I had experienced while on the road. Marvin listened intently as my descriptions of exotic destinations held his attention. I also shared what had transpired between Jill and me before my departure and during our last conversation. It felt healing to talk about it with an old, trusted friend. His support meant everything in this alien place.

Marvin, like me, had a lot to share. He had just gone through a very tough year. Aside from dealing with the end of his long-term relationship, there had been recent illness and death in his family. The stress of all this had taken its toll.

"That's why I came over here," he said. "I just needed to get away from the situation and all the reminders of those people I loved. I'm glad you're here, John. It's great to have a friend for support. I am looking forward to spending some time with you."

"I am glad you are here, too," I told him. I proposed a toast to mutual support between friends. Our plastic bottles quietly clunked together.

"I'm hungry," Marvin said. "Let's invade Chinatown." By then I was feeling a little woozy due to Marv's bartending skills.

We followed the scent of food into the crowded market streets of the Chinatown district. We picked a restaurant with outdoor seating and sat watching the colourful throngs of people.

"I love watching people, don't you?" asked Marvin.

"Yeah," I agreed. "The mix of cultures makes it even more interesting."

"And beautiful girls, too." Marvin pointed out as a group of young Malay women walked by our table arm in arm. They smiled at us as they passed.

"I have to agree with you there, brother," I said, my eyes following the flowing sarongs as they went around the corner.

After dinner we wound our way through the myriad vendors covering the pavement. There were so many people walking through these streets it became hard to negotiate without squeezing through the oncoming crowd. A few times we were pushed backward by the wave of humans.

"I'll bet this place is a gold mine for pickpockets," I said to Marvin over my shoulder, my hands tightly gripped onto my trusty waist belt, wary of any sticky fingers.

We wandered for hours, getting lost a few times in the tiny byways. Finding familiar street corners, we were again able to get our bearings. With nothing but people, lights and small stands, it was easy to lose your way in the crowded spaces.

We stopped at a small café for refreshing hot tea then re-entered the market madness. Shop-happy customers walked past us with purchases piled high in their arms.


## Batu Caves and the Little Lost Water Bottle

Just a few miles north of Kuala Lumpur are the Batu Caves, gigantic limestone caves located high in a mountainside. They were discovered at the end of the 19th century and are now a major tourist destination. The site is also popular with Hindus who use the caves for special religious celebrations throughout the year. One of the most well-known ceremonies is called Thaipusam. During this festival the faithful impale themselves with hooks, swords, and other sharp objects. Advertising posters we had seen around the city featured pictures of the long staircase of close to three hundred steps leading up to the mouth of the caves.

The bus ride was lengthy and the heat soon had us snoozing on the bench seat, despite our attempts to keep an eye open for our stop.

"Batu! Batu!" The sudden cry from the conductor had us jumping out of our sleep and out the door of the bus at the foot of the mountain. Thanking the conductor for his call, we crossed the street and gazed up the lengthy staircase leading to the caves. Many people could be seen making their way up the long set of stairs.

"Looks like a long, hot climb," I said. Marvin nodded his head in agreement. Wanting a good drink of water before attempting the hill, I reached for my trusty Nalgene water bottle.

"Shit!" I exclaimed. I turned to get a last glimpse of the tiny bus disappearing down the busy highway. I had left my bottle in the corner of the bus bench.

"What a drag," Marvin said. "Oh well, at least you can get the cheap plastic bottles."

"Yeah, I know. I just can't believe I left it behind after having it for so long." I was kicking myself and yet I found it curious that I was so upset over a simple water jug.

The climb to the caves was indeed long and hot. The humidity took its toll as we climbed the steep stairs. There were many other people ascending as well, taking short stops to rest. Their rest, however, was not too peaceful. Running among the groups of visitors were scads of mischievous monkeys. They leapt around the tourists, begging for food or causing some form of havoc. One particular monkey had the time of his life harassing two people at the top of the steps as we arrived.

A Chinese woman and her young son were making their way into the mouth of the first cave when a brash young monkey grabbed some food out of the young boy's hands. This, of course, scared the little guy and he made his upset well known to his mom. She turned around and shouted at the animal who was now chattering at them from high atop the metal fence. The food wrapper was emptied and tossed in one swift motion and, with that, the monkey jumped a few feet along the fence to where another smaller female monkey sat eating.

Without hesitation the male monkey came up from behind and started to screw the living daylights out of this little female. Pinned against the metal bars of the fence, the frightened female could do nothing, being half the size of her counterpart. After a time of being "on the job," he swung around from the fence with one arm, his quarry scurrying quickly away. With a wide grin, along with a shrill cry, the male stood proudly displaying his stiff little penis. Once he was finished letting all who looked see how well endowed he was, he jumped yet another female and carried on his shagging spree.

The Chinese woman was horrified and, before her son could ask her any questions, dragged him off into the cave opening. She left Marvin and me laughing hard enough to pull muscles.

After we entered the mountain, the cavern opened up high above us. I coughed as thick, acrid smoke clogged and burned in my lungs.

"That's gross," I said. "I wonder what they're doing?" Large barrels supported grates of burning charcoal and wood, sending sooty columns of smoke into the air. Some people prayed by the sooty fires while tourists milled around them, taking photos and talking.

"Why else would someone subject themselves to this except for religion?" I joked as I continued to cough.

We continued through the first cave to a second, further into the mountain. The stairway up into this next cave was surrounded by a metal frame with chicken wire stretched over the top.

"What's that for, I wonder?" Marvin's curiosity was aroused. The purpose was soon made clear as a small number of stones fell from the roof, smashing against the chicken wire. "Okay . . . "

We explored the furthest reaches of the cave system, cautious of any more rock falling from above, and eventually decided to head back downtown.

Emerging from the caves we breathed the fresher air once again. After descending the stairs and crossing the wide street we hailed another of the minibuses back into the city centre.

We spent time in the downtown core for about three hours before slowly heading in the direction of our hotel. Throughout the afternoon I couldn't get over the fact that I had lost my water jug. Marvin was getting sick of hearing about it by now.

"Just forget about it. You can get another one."

For some reason the lost article wouldn't let me alone. As well, I couldn't shake the idea of being distraught over a lost material item. I felt silly making a big thing out of a plastic jug. As we approached our section of the city my thoughts were still focused on the bottle. When I looked up I noticed a small minibus with the same number as the one we had taken to the caves. Knowing that there were many minibuses with the same route numbers on them, at least seven or eight vehicles serving one area, I thought my chances were very slim that it would be the same one.

But I gave into a strong feeling that I should chase after this minibus just to check. More for my own curiosity, I ran after the bus. At its third stop I caught up and hopped into the stepwell. Down beside the driver I saw the familiar blue-capped water bottle sitting under his seat. In the middle of a city of over two million people I had managed to stumble across my lost container. Recognizing me from earlier in the day, the driver reluctantly set the item back into my hands when I reached out in gesture. Marvin gave a shout of approval and laughed as I emerged from the bus holding aloft the lost water bottle.

# CHAPTER 14: MELAKA AND CHINESE NEW YEAR

## Melaka

*Monday, January 30, 1995*

This picturesque small city lies on the coast about one hundred and twenty kilometres south of Kuala Lumpur. The centre of Melaka displays a number of colonial remnants from its historic past. Plaques and signs on various buildings tell stories of past occupation by the Portuguese, Dutch, Chinese, and British. Once one of the busiest sea ports in the area, it is now one of the busiest tourist destinations in Malaysia.

As it was Chinese New Year, the city was getting filled to capacity as Marvin and I searched for a hotel room. Once accommodations were handled, we started to explore these historic byways along the seaside.

We walked over a small footbridge spanning a narrow canal and entered a village square that looked more like something in Amsterdam than anything usually found at two degrees latitude. An old windmill stood at one end of the square beside a row of large stone buildings with giant doors and louvered windows. A wide cobblestone street took us past the village square toward the ocean. Along the way we passed an ancient Dutch ship surrounded by a high fence. This old relic had been converted into an historic museum. Along the edge of the beach was a long strip of fast food restaurants, as well as a small market teeming with locals and visitors alike.

Just to the north a large hill gave a spectacular view. Sitting on the top of the hill were the broken remains of an old church built by the Portuguese in the 1500s, called St. Paul's. Walking the steep trail, Marvin and I explored the old walls which were barely standing and old cannons still on guard in the ruins, half buried under the tall grass.

"Hey, Marvin," I said to my friend who was busy inspecting one of the rusted cannons. I was reading the text on the placard bolted to the side of one stone buttress. "It says here that the British even used this place to store gun powder."

"Sounds like a good use for a holy place," he chuckled.

A governor's house sat next to the church, surrounded by a huge cement wall topped with bales of razor wire. More historic buildings lay around the other side of the small rock mountain. We passed beautiful women, dressed in fantastic saris and other traditional garments. We spent the afternoon mingling with the colourful locals and going between the hill and the beachside plaza for snacks and a few cold beverages.


## Don't Shoot Me, I'm Just a Tourist!

As we walked back to the hotel at the end of the afternoon, Marvin and I passed the entrance to a large walled compound. The wall descended from the hilltop and we saw that it was part of the same enclosure we had seen beside St. Paul's church. The coils of razor wire along the top rail looked threatening.

To our right a driveway led up to the large front gates of the compound. Next to the gated entrance sat a small blue hut occupied by a uniformed soldier.

As we walked past I glanced back to look inside the opening to the barricaded courtyard. A long winding road led up to a lavish-looking mansion in the middle of a beautifully manicured property. Trees and flowers grew in the richly landscaped contoured gardens. At the entrance the road was barred by a tall iron gate. My eyes panned the gateway and did a doubletake as they came to rest on a huge sign hanging from the bars. The image compelled me to stop and stare. The red and white sign warned passersby that the area was restricted. There was a silhouette of a soldier aiming a rifle at a man in shorts and T-shirt twisting in agony. Now I had seen everything. I pulled my camera off my shoulder and walked up the driveway toward the gate.

"Wait a minute, Marvin," I told my friend. "I have to get a photo of this."

I was almost at the gate when I heard my friend shout to me.

"Hey, John. Watch it!"

His voice made me shift my focus from the sign dead ahead of me. In the small hut beside the gate the resident soldier was now performing his duty. I had not noticed him before but he had emerged from his enclosure and was now standing on the steps next to the doorway.

I froze in my tracks. The soldier was clutching a M-16 rifle, aiming the weapon at my guts.

"Whoa, hang on, my friend," I made eye contact with the soldier and spoke slowly and directly to him. "Photo, okay?" I said clearly. The soldier hesitated briefly and then nodded approval. He lowered the barrel of the M-16 as my intestines untied themselves from the huge knot that had formed under my ribcage.

I made my way slowly to the fence to take the photograph, one eye on the soldier in case he changed his mind. I aimed my camera at the sign, making sure not to capture any part of the house inside the compound—that alone was probably worth a bullet or two. I then asked the guard if he would let me take his photo with my friend. He nodded again and Marvin had me laughing as I framed the picture. He stood beside the guard and his hut, leaning over and questioning him.

"So, you ever have to shoot anyone here?" Marvin asked.

"Oh, sure, yes," replied the guard.

"Well . . . did you get them?" Marvin asked again.

"Oh, sure, yes." The man smiled as I took his picture.

## Chinese New Year

*Tuesday, January 31, 1995*

Marvin and I met two attractive women in the hotel lobby as we were enjoying sweet morning coffee. Trish, from Italy, and Yuko, from Japan, had been travelling together from Thailand. We enjoyed a pleasant conversation and decided to hang out together for the day and explore the city's New Year celebrations.

We started off with a walking tour of the Chinese temples, seeing throngs of people praying and lighting incense, placing the burning sticks in large ornately painted ceramic pots filled with black sand. The clouds of smoke swirled in the breeze. We lit our own bunches of the burning spice. The sweet but pungent scent permeated the entire city. After awhile we swore that it was even stuck to our skin. The sounds of droning prayers and temple bells flowed through the streets, calling more people to the temple gates.

We continued on past the temples and headed into Chinatown. As we walked Trish went ahead of us and detoured down a small back road just to see what was there. With the rest of us trailing behind, she led us onward. A few blocks down she met a tiny old man on the street who grabbed her by the arm and guided her to his little shop just up the road. We could see her ahead of us talking to the old man. As he led her away she looked back and pointed to the building she was being taken into. By the time we caught up to her, Trish was having a great time. The old gentleman was cracking jokes and his English was very good. Our arrival had him happier than ever.

"Come in, come in," he shouted to the rest of us. He pulled the remainder of our group into his tiny workshop and produced small chairs for all of us to sit on. Almost as soon as he had brought us into his shop, he asked us to wait and promptly disappeared.

He returned to the room with a tray loaded with small cups of steaming hot tea. Passing one to each of us, he introduced himself as the best coffin maker in the entire region of Melaka. He touted the fine quality features of his boxes and passed out business cards to all of us. Soon neighbours were poking their heads in the door. The man began to drag his friends in to meet the prospective foreign buyers. After a stay of about an hour, we left him to his unending job.

"Talk about job security, hey, Marvin?" I said.

"No kidding," he replied with a nod.

"You call me for good quality," the old man said to us.

"For sure," said Marvin, waving the tiny business card in his hand. "If we need anything, we'll call right away." Thankful, he shook all our hands and sent us into the day with a huge smile.

"I wonder if he delivers?" pondered Trish as we wandered out of earshot.

After this we spent time on the shady hilltop next to St. Paul's church, as well as at the seaside market. As the sun get hotter we took refuge in a local movie theatre for the remainder of the afternoon.

The girls then suggested dinner at a special restaurant that Yuko had read about in her book.

"They serve dinner to you on a banana leaf," Yuko told us. "The food is supposed to be very good."

"Sounds like a plan," I said. Marvin agreed without much difficulty.

"Where is it?" Marvin asked.

"Actually, not that far from our hotel," Trish said. "We can easily walk it from here."

As we walked along the familiar path back to the Dutch village, it began to shower. The coolness of the light rain was refreshing. It was a nice break from the sweltering heat.

We followed the smell of rich spices as we approached an area filled with small restaurants. The place that Yuko had researched was the easiest to find. We could tell that the food was good from the lengthy line at the front door.

Glasses of steaming hot tea were placed in front of us by a small girl who then continued on to clean another table's mess with her now empty tray. Another woman came over to us with an armload of green banana leaves. A chunk of leaf the size of a placemat was placed in front of each of us.

The food emerged from the back almost as soon as it had been ordered. It was delivered by a number of kitchen staffers making rounds to various tables. One person carried a bowl of rice, another a dish of spicy meat or fish, followed by one carrying various greens and spices. Each food item was placed right on the leaves in front of us in small, neat piles. Once all the food was dished out, small piles of hot, fresh-made roti were placed beside our "plates," with which to eat our meals. Eating with our novice hands turned into a messy experience.

"Let's go find a night club and have a drink before the New Year comes in," suggested Marvin as we finished our meal.

"What about Chinatown?" asked Trish, sounding disappointed.

"It probably won't get exciting until midnight anyway," said Yuko. "Let's go out first, then we'll come back."

During the course of dinner, the weather had turned ugly. There was now a wall of water pouring down onto the street. People outside were crowding into the open doorway of the restaurant in an attempt to keep dry. The owners of the restaurant pulled them all inside without hesitation. Taxis and bicycle rickshaws filled the now flooded roadway. The rickshaws looked hilarious, drivers in plastic ponchos wheeling along with huge plastic covers over the passenger compartments.

We finally gave up waiting for the rain to stop and were instantly soaked as we waded across the street. We found shelter under a large awning at the next corner.

"What now?" I asked Marvin above the sound of the pounding rain as the water ran off my face. If I looked as much of a drowned rat as he did, we were both doing just fine. Just then a taxi cab came down the road, throwing water off to the side in waves.

I leaned out into the road and got the driver's attention through the torrent of rain. The car pulled up to the curb in front of us and we quickly climbed inside. The driver turned to greet his soaked passengers now drenching the rear of his cab.

I leaned over the back of his seat and smiled at him, "Night club, please. A place with good music."

"Yes . . . I know good place for night club," the man replied.

The taxi carried us into a remote industrial section of the city where we found a great number of busy night clubs, with flashing neon signs and line ups of customers. Many locals were milling around the dry doorways of the buildings, conversing amid clouds of their own cigarette smoke.

We checked out a few different places and settled on a fairly modern-looking bar with a live band. We got the idea that not too many foreigners came into this particular club as soon as we walked through the door. A wave of glances swept over us from the nearby tables as we found ourselves some seats.

The band was already playing as we walked in. They were a blues quintet that played fairly well, except that they all had the North American rock-guy look—the big hair, the boots, the tight, bulging jeans to turn on the ladies. It sure looked strange on short, thin Malaysians.

Marvin called the waitress over to the table. "One jug of beer, please."

She smiled and nodded, returning to the bar. A short time later, she returned with a tray bearing the beverages. After placing the drink on the table, she left a small piece of paper beside the empty glasses.

"I'll get this round, John," Marvin said as he stopped me from reaching for my wallet. "You can get the next one." He grabbed the small bit of paper and unfolded it in his fingers.

"Thanks, my friend." As I began to pour out the beer, I noticed the expression of generosity on Marvin's face had turned to one of shock.

"Uh, maybe you'll have to help me with this one, John. I don't think we're going to be drinking that much tonight at these prices." He handed me the paper and I looked at our total. It was the equivalent of thirty dollars. I stared down at the four glasses of amber ale and the now empty jug on the table.

"Holy bar bill, Batman!"

"Oh, well. You only celebrate New Year's in Malaysia once in your life," Marvin replied, picking up his glass as he handed the next glass to Trish. Our stay here was only as long as the pricey beer remained in our glasses.

Next door the Rhythm and Blues Pub and Grill had a talented man and wife duo act. A European man played guitar while his Malaysian wife played keyboards. They played some original material as well as cover tunes. They were great entertainers, inspiring us to remain most of the night.

"Hey, great songs," I said to the man as he walked by during one of the set breaks.

"Thanks a lot," he replied as he stopped and pulled a chair in to join us.

He introduced himself as Daniel. From England, he had married his partner a few years before. They lived in Kuala Lumpur, travelling up and down the country playing local bars.

"Do any of you play, too?" he asked the table.

"Just me," I said to him. "I'm a guitar player."

"I have an extra guitar here. Do you want to join us for a few songs?" he said.

"Hey, that would be fun," I replied.

I played with the group for almost a whole set of music. Some of the tunes stumped me. Local popular rock songs and their originals left me playing quietly in the background. Nobody seemed to notice that I had turned my volume knob to "zero" during a song I was unfamiliar with. Still I kept strumming. A kind of instrumental Karaoke. At one point I glanced over to our table and started laughing as I saw Marvin holding his lighter up in the air, the tiny flame flickering above his fist.

As the New Year's party progressed through the evening, most of the room got completely pissed. There were a few guys trying to do their best Patrick Swayze imitations but they were a far cry from the real thing. When the midnight countdown came in there was a collective roar from the crowd as the remaining people finally got up to dance the night away.

"What about the promise to go to Chinatown?" Trish said as she glanced at her watch. It was just after 12:30 AM. We paid our humungous bar bill and headed for the door. Our musical hosts saw us leaving and shouted "thanks" through the P.A. as we waved and made for the doorway.

Outside the rain had abated. The streets were still wet but were now clear of flooding water. Another taxi was called and we were soon speeding toward the old section of the city. The car let us off at the edge of a section of streets that were closed off to traffic. Beyond, throngs of people roamed in all directions amid bright lights. Clouds of smoke rose from fire crackers. We paid the fare and opened the doors into the din of celebration.

Chinatown was on fire! The celebration had only started and was gaining energy. People milled around the streets, eating, drinking, and cavorting with friends. The smoke from fireworks burned in my nostrils as I stepped out of the car.

The four of us were enveloped in crowds as we wandered through the blocks of old buildings. The streets were filled with market stalls. Food, drinks, and above all, fireworks were laid out for sale.

"I think we might just have to get into some of this, Marv," I told my friend as I started to collect a variety of bombs and crackers from one small stall. Marvin joined me in the purchase as the girls looked on.

"What is it with boys and bombs?" wondered Trish as she and Yuko stood laughing at us.

After collecting enough firepower, my friend and I looked for a decent place to set it all off. At the corner of one street an old empty lot gave us plenty of room. At one end a short cement wall marked the edge of the property.

Setting our bombs up along the top of the wall, Marvin and I created a cluster of fireworks, fuses dangling over the edge of the cement. Together, we used our lighters to ignite as many fuses as we could. In just a few seconds there were showers of sparks flying around our hands. I worked nervously, igniting any remaining fuses I could see. By now I was faced with a wall of sparks. I couldn't see clearly which ones were lit nor the ones about to reach their ends. We smartly took this as a clue to get out of the way. Marvin and I bailed out of the circle as the pile of powder started to ignite. The resulting effect of our bombs had us checking our own shorts for fires and smoke. When all the noise and flash had stopped, Marvin and I turned to look at the faces of our two companions. They were in laughter over our crazy antics and, behind them, a small crowd of locals had gathered to cheer our efforts. Not bad for tourists.

Once our private pyro show was complete, we joined the wandering crowds in the loose parade through the dark streets. Finally, we strolled home to a short sleep. It was 5:00 AM.

The doorman greeted us at the door of our hotel.

"Thanks for spending time with us," I said to our companions sleepily. "We're headed for Singapore in just a few hours and we probably won't see you again."

"It was a lot of fun," Trish said. Both women gave us hugs and kisses in farewell.

# CHAPTER 15: SINGAPORE

## Nice Digs
*Wednesday, February 1, 1995*

I woke up only because the bus had passed over a large bump in the road. The jarring motion had thrown me over into Marvin who was in the same shape I was. Luckily, we had woken on time after only two hours of rest and dragged ourselves to the station in time for the bus trip. Once onboard, we had fallen fast asleep.

I was shaken into consciousness as we entered Malaysia's densely populated border city of Johor Baharu. As I rubbed the sleep out of my eyes, I began to see large billboards marking our approach to Singapore. The familiar skull and cross bones anti-drug signs soon came into view. Another was graphic in its description of the consequences of carrying firecrackers. Huge black letters said, "**POSSESSION OF FIREWORKS RESULTS IN JAIL AND CANING.**"

A huge photo added detail to the decree. It was a picture of the rack that prisoners are strapped to while the caning is administered. The victims are draped over a wood frame like a huge sawhorse, their asses in the air, perfectly exposed for the flailing expertise of the enforcing officer. In this particular photo a dummy was set in the place of a real victim and an officer was captured at the moment his brine-soaked split rattan cane contacted the dummy. The force with which the cane would contact the victim's skin was great. The result: huge welts leaving permanent scars just to remind the criminal of his offence.

All the things I had heard about this island city and its rules were becoming clearer. For one thing, it is illegal to chew gum. In fact, it is illegal for stores to even sell the stuff. It is illegal to jaywalk, to litter, to spit, and many other things. Anyone caught breaking these laws is subject to harsh penalties. By now Marvin was awake and had joined me in the observation of the advertised penal code.

"Pretty harsh, eh, John?" Marvin noted.

I winked at my friend in jest. "Hey, I wonder if there is a hardware store around here? I wouldn't mind picking up a couple of cans of spray paint."

The bus wound up a hill into a large compound and the road turned into a long building. Parking at one end of the complex, the driver stood up and announced that all passengers were to take their own luggage through the customs area.

"This will be fun," I said to Marvin. He looked as ill at ease as I was at the Malay/Thai border. "Just make sure you've eaten all those drugs in your pockets." The joke helped him relax.

This time there were no caged walkways with dogs. Instead, groups of blue uniformed officers stood watching the passengers as they walked past their post. From the looks the guards were giving me I half-expected to have my bags torn apart. But I soon realized that the glares were the same for all of the passengers.

The bus continued its course through the north end of the island city and finally came to a stop near the centre core of Singapore. The tall, glistening towers looked like a giant gauntlet of commerce. Marvin led us through the maze of streets as he followed the map, guiding us to our destination. We had been invited to stay with Marvin's friends from Canada.

"Brenda's building shouldn't be too hard to find," he said. "She said it's right in the middle of this cluster of buildings by the bay."

"Speaking of Brenda," I said, "I am wondering if I already know her."

"Where would you have met her?" asked Marvin.

"Remember when I came to Ontario to visit you at Western University just before I left for my backpacking trip through Europe in 1983? When I was at your school I popped into a party your class was having at the student union building. I remember that you introduced me to a really nice gal named Brenda who was in your program. I have a strong feeling that this is the same woman."

"I think you might be right," Marvin said as we entered the cluster of tall steel and glass.

Marvin led us to the front of Brenda's building. We entered tall glass doors and stepped into an air-conditioned foyer leading to a bank of high-speed elevators. Blocking the way was a large desk occupied by a lone security guard. He scowled at us as we entered his domain. We were definitely not dressed for corporate meetings: sandals, shorts, and tie-dyed material didn't fit with the three-piece suits he was used to seeing. He curtly asked us what we wanted. Marvin explained our presence and asked to use the desk phone to contact Brenda upstairs. When he finally reached his friend, he left me with all our bags and went up to see her. Brenda was living here in Singapore with her husband, Sam. They were both employed by a Canadian bank and worked in corporate and investment banking, selling bonds and securities.

The elevator door closed and I was left in the lobby under the discriminating eye of the security guard. This became a hilarious experience as the old man quizzed me on where I had been. Each time I mentioned any place I had seen, he was very critical.

"Thailand no good," he began. "Penang no good. Indonesia no good." Each and every place I mentioned was slammed. Nothing short of good old Singapore would suit this unimpressed fellow. I became impatient for my friend to return.

Soon I heard the whine of the elevator nearing the ground floor. The doors opened and Marvin emerged from the small cubicle. Behind him the same woman I had met eleven years before emerged from the elevator.

"Don't I know you from somewhere?" Brenda asked me as she approached and shook my hand. I went over the story of my visit to the University of Western Ontario many years ago.

"Small world, isn't it?"

Brenda told us to go to her house and make ourselves at home. Handing us the key, she drew a map on a sheet of paper and sent us on our way.

"Thanks, Brenda. We'll see you later," Marvin said.

As we left the guard saw us to the door, as if to expedite our departure. As the large doors closed us out on the street, we left him to his cool little kingdom.

"It's nice to get out of there," I said. "That guy was intense."

"Let's go get settled in," Marvin said as he began to study our new directions. We boarded a subway train which sped us across the city into an outlying residential district.

A high brick wall surrounded Brenda's condominium complex. As we approached the gate we noticed a uniformed soldier in a small hut just inside the wall. We took care to walk in slowly, in case he was as trigger happy as the fellow we had met in Melaka. But the man only grinned and smiled as we entered.

Walking into the condo, we were shocked to see that it was a huge multi-levelled home. The living room was filled with leather furniture, beautiful carvings, shelving units, and tables.

"Nice digs," I said to Marvin who had already dropped his pack on the floor and was heading for the kitchen.

"Here," he said to me as he emerged from the back of the house. He tossed a frosty can of beer across the room to me. "Prescribed by Brenda."

"Ah, Doctor Brenda," I laughed and sat myself down on the exquisite leather couch. "Boy, do I ever feel out of place in here. This is like Club Med compared to the places I have been in the last two months."

Marvin settled into the leather armchair beside to the couch. "We even get our own rooms."

"Really? This place is huge," I said as I gazed up at the vaulted ceiling and out the huge panes of glass overlooking the central courtyard. The living room was on the first level. A large dining area and kitchen were on the next, along with two large bedrooms toward the back of the house. From here, another staircase led up to the top floor where the master bedroom was located.

"I wonder what they have to pay for this place?"

After a relaxing rest on the oh-so-comfortable furniture, I retreated for a hot shower.

I had to laugh at my rediscovery of real water pressure and really hot water for the first time in two months. I had almost forgotten about it entirely. I continued to laugh at how this simple convenience made me feel like the caveman who had just discovered fire.

Before long Brenda came through the door after a long day at work, carrying bags of groceries.

"So, how are you guys making out?" She was inspecting us as we sat in the comfy chairs. Marvin was reading and I was strumming my guitar. "I hope it's not too much of a dump for you."

"Yeah, it is, actually," joked Marvin, sipping his third cold beer. "We called and booked into the youth hostel and we're just waiting for the cab to get here."

"Well, suit yourself," Brenda replied. "I guess you'll have to miss out on steak dinner."

Marvin looked at me with a stunned look. "Steak?"

"You know, Marvin," I said. "I just realized that I lost my hostel card. Looks like I'm stuck here."

I put my guitar down and helped carry the bags of food to the rear of the house. Marvin gave his old friend a hug and they began to catch up on old times.

Sam arrived just before dinner was ready. He had just flown in from New Zealand from a few day's business. Knowing that company was present, he walked in with two bottles of wine, placed them on the counter and grected his wife with a kiss.

Sam cracked the wine and as he passed each of us a fresh glass, proposed a toast.

"Welcome to Singapore." Sam pulled the necktie from his collar and threw it onto the arm of a small chair in the corner of the kitchen. "Ah, that's better. I hate those things, you know?"

"Marvin and I were commenting on what a beautiful place you have here," I said to the couple.

"Yeah," Brenda said. "It is a pretty amazing spot, all right."

"You don't own it do you?" Marvin inquired.

"God, no! We could never afford that," she replied. "We just rent it . . . well the bank that we work for rents it."

"What is something like this worth here?" I asked.

"Try and guess," Sam said to me.

"Here in Singapore . . . " I though for a moment. "I'd say around four thousand dollars per month?"

"Try seven thousand," replied Sam. I could feel my jaw hanging from its hinges in disbelief.


## The City
*Friday, February 3, 1995*

A lot of our time in Singapore was spent in the central core of the city, exploring the British colonial structures and the areas of new, shining towers. From a small park along the waterfront we could see the Merlion, the symbol of Singapore. Half-fish and half-lion, it watches over the entrance to the harbour. As we explored the subway, with its fast efficiency, became the preferred method of transport.

Eventually we came across a large open outdoor food court. Cruising the selections for lunch, I found one that made me laugh.

"Hey Marvin, come and check this out." I was standing under a sign that read: Mutton 'N' Brain.

"Mmmm . . . can you order me a side of eyes?" asked Marvin, smiling.

This vendor's menu included a tasty delicacy—sheep's brain in soup. The photo of the still-intact organ, half submerged in dark broth, made my stomach turn. We chose another vendor and found something more tantalizing instead.

Orchard Road, the main shopping area in Singapore, was a bustling, congested place. Big sale items like watches, cameras and various electronic devices were packed into every window I could see. Jewellery was also featured. The prices were prime and there was no bargaining of any kind to be had. Making our way across the street to the other shops became tedious because of the lengthy walk to the corner crosswalks. At one point Marvin had reached his patience limit. He deftly hopped over the short fence marked with a clear "No Jaywalking" sign and cut across the empty traffic lane.

"What the hell are you doing?" I said to him as he ventured across the road.

"Come on," he said to me with a wave of his hand. I refused, still walking to the corner of the block. Later on, he talked me into doing it with him. We had seen a few other people jaywalk as well but we still had eyes peeled for any police.

## The Zoo

The Singapore Zoo is something to see. I don't normally support the idea of zoos but after seeing the design of this facility, my opinion changed. Each creature's area is designed specifically with that creature in mind, with plenty of room for movement and seemingly comfortable living, at least as far as life in a cage is concerned. The rhinos, for example, were in an enclosure bordered by only thigh-high log and pipe barriers. It almost looked too easy for them to escape. They happily went about their business, ignoring us and the other humans.

The lions looked very serious as they watched the crowd from their perch. They had a large stone den fitting five or six adult lions. They were in a huge pen with trees and grass. On the spectator side of the enclosure was a deep moat in front of a very high cement wall. This was our viewpoint into the pen. We noticed the concentration of two younger lions stalking a young child walking with his parents at the viewpoint. As the child walked back and forth with his family, the lions tracked the boy along the length of their den.

Zoo workers showed up with lunch for the lions. They began

tossing raw, plucked chickens into the pen. Each beast gulped down at least three apiece. Only three bites and the food disappeared. We both wondered how many bites would have been needed for the kid in the front row.

Particularly memorable were the Komodo Dragons. Lying in their pen in the hot sun, they looked mellow but frightening. These beasts have a nasty reputation as deadly hunters. Tourists travel to see live goats fed to the giant reptiles on their native island of Komodo, west of Flores in the Indonesian island chain. Their jaws are extremely powerful and a nearby information booth showed films of the creature literally ripping its prey apart in one bite.

"It says that they can move really fast." I was reading from the information sign under the video screen. We walked back outside to see the live specimens again. The pen they occupied was quite spacious.

"Hey, look! I sure hope he gets paid well to be in there," I said. At the far end of the pen I saw a brave soul at work. A lone cleaner was busy sweeping the pen with a broom. We could see him carefully keeping an eye on the locations of the beasts and occasionally pausing to count with a pointed finger so that all of the monsters were accounted for. He would then return to his cleaning.

Near the entrance to the zoo a crew of orangutans were being exploited by their owner. The man was selling the chance to have a picture taken with his red-haired friends for a price. A sad-looking lot, the apes would be placed in the laps or around the shoulders of a human subject.


### Indiatown and the Bay of Bars
To thank our hosts for their hospitality we took Sam and Brenda out for a meal in the East-Indian section of the city. It sat on the edge of the rich and developed area of Singapore.

The first thing I noticed was that the clean and gleaming look of Singapore that I had become accustomed to over the last few days was replaced by what I had seen in previous cities: old, worn buildings, grime, and run-down shacks in the alleyways. It actually had a nicer feeling to it and it was here that I noticed the people smiling a great deal more. Amid the breakdown, litter and dust, the humanness of life was showing through. The rest seemed so cold, sterile, and heartless.

Before having dinner we took the opportunity to wander through some of the many shops and to encounter a few of the friendly locals who were more than glad to throw a smile our way.

After eating a huge feast of spicy Indian delights we returned to the small bay behind the city centre. Along the waterfront small shops lined the sidewalk and small ships converted into pubs were moored against the sea wall. Climbing into one of these floating bars, we sat for the entire evening, listening to live music.

"So how long do you think you will stay here?" Marvin asked his friends.

"Well, after being here for almost two years, we are really hoping to get transferred to London, England," Sam told us. "It has been great being here. We have great jobs but we both feel that we would like a change."

"We also want a break from the inherent attitude of the people here," added Brenda.

"Pretty snobbish?" I asked.

"Yeah, sometimes it can be extreme," said Sam. "I mean, the whole deal with this city is corporate entities and making money. That's the main focus. It shows in how the people interact, even socially."

"How so?" asked Marvin.

"If, say, you're invited to a party here in Singapore, first of all you had better dress well." Sam nodded in the direction of a few business-men near to our table who were dressed in very expensive custom three-piece suits. "Then, when you arrive at the party, you get asked three standard questions: 1) How much is your house worth? 2) What kind of car do you drive? and 3) How much money do you make per year? After you answer the three questions, then the people can decide whether they want to have anything to do with you at all or if they will just move on to the next guest to continue their analysis."

"That sounds ridiculous," I said. "What a bunch of snobs. I could probably never survive here. I hate the attitude that can accompany a lot of money."

"Yeah, there is a definite attitude," said Brenda, "but we've managed to ignore it for the most part. Especially with all of the perks of the job."

"Good luck to you both," said Sam as we toasted our gathering.

We thanked our hosts for their fine hospitality.

"Oh, Sam," mocked Brenda, "we forgot to tell them about the bill!"

# CHAPTER 16: JAVA

## Night Flight

*Saturday, February 4, 1995*

I sat slumped in the uncomfortable chairs of the Jakarta International Airport terminal, trying my best to kill some time. A mechanical delay in Singapore had caused me to miss a connection to Semarang by only about thirty minutes. I now sat with my books and local maps, considering my next move.

During the flight delay Sempati Airline discount coupons were handed out as an apology for the inconvenience. Deciding to skip the dusty roads of an overland journey, I dug the coupons out of my bag and proceeded to hunt down a ticket office open on a Saturday. This, I discovered, was no easy task. It only took a mountain of section managers to find someone who could take care of my exchange of traveller's cheques and coupons. During my search I managed to find a flight schedule and discovered the next flight was not for another six hours. I decided to wait at the airport, despite the boredom factor. The clock slowly turned until the time had come. The only thing that I wasn't looking forward to was arriving after dark. Night-time was slightly intimidating but I soon relaxed and turned it into a challenge. With this my excitement grew and I soon heard the announcement to board crackling through the speakers.

I descended the flight of stairs along with the other passengers and emerged on the tarmac in front of the Dash-8 aircraft. As soon as the outer door opened I got a chill. The weather was turning ugly with brisk wind and rain. I wondered how the smaller plane would stand up to the windy conditions, handed my bags over to the steward, and kept my guidebook for reading.

I climbed into my slightly cramped seat near the cockpit and strapped myself in. The din of the prop engines was soon relieved when the cabin crew locked the doors down. But the noise and vibration grew as the plane started its course to take-off. The small craft tossed quite a bit as it climbed into the night sky. The turbulence soon calmed as we drifted away from the storm front.

Unfortunately, another storm was waiting for us further along the coast. Its effect wasn't felt, of course, until dinner time. I was about to drink some water when the plane entered an air pocket. As the plane suddenly descended, my water decided to stay behind, still in the shape of my glass. My eyes widened as it floated in front of me. At the other end of the air pocket, a majority of the liquid thankfully decided to return to the container. Only a few big drops escaped the rim and landed in my lap.

After dinner had been served and cleared away I struck up a conversation with the only other English-speaking person on the aircraft, an American. He sat with a group of women a few rows behind me. I had looked in their direction once or twice as their conversation was loud and quite jovial. Noticing me looking at their group, the man spoke to me.

"Come back and join us if you want." He indicated an extra seat available beside him.

"Don't see too many tourists on these local flights," he said to me as I took my new seat. I noticed he was looking at me rather intently, as if studying me. I decided to ignore the judging glance.

"Well, you don't look too local yourself," I joked to him, fastening my seatbelt.

"Actually, I have lived here for ten years," he replied. He started speaking to the women around us in Bahasa and, by the sound of it, he was fluent. He pulled a bottle of Scotch out of his small carry-on bag and poured out a serving. "Would you like some?"

"No, thanks," I said.

"When you sit with me and my friends you have to have some." He sounded demanding and belligerent and was obviously getting a bit too loaded for his own good. Deciding to keep him cool, I accepted his offer. He called to the flight attendant to bring him another glass.

"Drink up," he said to me as he passed the shot into my hand. I normally find Scotch too harsh to drink but, again, not to insult my host, I endured the amber fire.

"So, what do you do here?" I asked him.

"Business," he replied, giving me a strange glance once again. It was as if he were analysing me and what I said to him. I simply took it as an effect of the Scotch and didn't ask him to clarify.

"Do you live in Semarang?" I asked.

"Yeah, I've been there for a long time," he said nonchalantly.

"Well, perhaps you can give me some help," I said to him. "There are a few hotels that I have researched in the city and maybe you can tell me the best way to get to the area I am looking for."

He nodded but looked quite bored with the whole idea, "Mmmhmm . . . " was his only reply.

"Funny chap," I thought as I walked back toward my seat to retrieve my guide. "Oh well, at least I might get some information from him."

I opened the book to the detailed map of Semarang and pointed to the small dots on the page that were my potential destination. He looked at the map with a critical eye and started to flip the pages forward and back as if searching for the proper map.

"This map is all wrong," he said.

"What are you talking about?" I asked him. "I have always found those maps to be very accurate."

"No, it's wrong. There are no hotels in this part of the city." He continued to look at the page as I began to get very suspicious of him. Finally, he ran his finger across the page and let it come to rest on a remote spot on the paper. "I know of a good hotel right here where you can get a good rest."

I craned my neck to see where his finger was pointing to. He was pointing to an area outside the limits of the city where no road lines were indicated at all. The terrain looked hilly and, for all I know, could have been nothing but jungle.

"There are no roads there," I said to him. "How can there be a hotel where there are no roads?"

"I told you. The map is wrong!" He was adamant that my book was in error.

"Well, every other map is pretty damned accurate from what I have experienced," I told him. "I find it hard to believe that this is the only map that is out of whack."

"Hmph . . . " he said. He began to read a small column with other information about the city itself. "The population figures are wrong, too," he growled. "It says that there are just over one million people here. There are six million!"

His comments about the maps and the book were beginning to ring alarm bells. My trust in the accuracy of the *Lonely Planet* book series won out over the distrust I felt for this man as he began to get drunker from his bottle of Scotch. His insistence that I go with him when we got to Semarang, combined with the loss of inhibitions, had made him obnoxious.

"No, thanks, I think I can find my way all right." I graciously declined the offer, suspecting some bullshit at the end of that road. The vision of a shallow grave in the forest came to my mind.

"Just what the hell is your problem?" he fumed.

"What are you talking about?" I replied.

"You come back here. I give you booze. You don't accept my offer. What the hell is your problem?" The man was pissed off with me and the other passengers started to notice the performance.

I looked him straight in the eyes and said, "I don't trust you." That twisted his nose out of joint a little more but I didn't care. My intuition was telling me to be wary. I decided to listen. Enduring a few insults, I returned to my seat in the front of the plane.

Approaching Semarang, the turbulence became more intense. The final dive onto the tarmac was very rough and a few times I wondered whether the plane would stay in the air. My seat was so near the cockpit that I could lean out into the aisle and watch the pilot and co-pilot fighting to outmaneouvre the stormy night. From my position I had a clear view through the front windscreens. As the plane's nose dropped, Semarang's lighted runway could be seen far ahead in the night. The lights bobbed up and down while the plane pitched and rolled. Heavy rain slammed against the windscreen on our steep descent. At last the nose of the aircraft suddenly lifted and the wheels touched ground. I let go of the breath that I had held and loosened my grip on the edge of my seat.

## Wet Feet and Lodgings

The rain pelted down onto the tarmac as I exited the plane and collected my luggage from the attendant on the ground. I ran inside the terminal building to seek temporary shelter from the elements. Digging through my papers I searched for a contact phone number given to me by my friend, Danny. He and his fiancée, Wiwied (pronounced "wee-wid"), a local Semarang resident, were supposed to arrive from Canada any day. Their plan was to look for and purchase various arts and crafts from different areas of central and east Java, shipping them back for sale in Canada. Danny had given me the number of a family friend before I left home and had told me to call them upon my arrival. If I could reach this contact it would be possible to stay with her until my friends showed up. The prospective list of hotels I researched in the guidebook was my back-up plan.

I called from the small phone booth in the corner of the terminal and let it ring for almost a minute, hoping that I would get an answer. But no one picked up. I was left to find my own place in this stormy, wet night.

"Hey," said a voice behind me. The drunken man had met his friend and had seen me hanging on the phone line. "This is your last chance for a ride." I watched him leave the terminal, shaking my head in refusal. The two men got into one of the taxis lined up outside the door and disappeared into the night. I turned back to my book. I scribbled the names and addresses of five different cheap hotels in the city centre onto a scrap piece of paper. I then re-sealed my valuables, put on my Goretex coat, and walked outside.

The first waiting cab pulled up to me and I jumped into the back seat. The driver was friendly and spoke fairly good English.

"Where you go?" he asked me. Holding the scrap paper up so he could see it, I pointed to the hotel name at the top of the list. After negotiating a fair price he agreed to take me to my destination. I had selected five hotels in close proximity in one area of town. Surely one of them would have room for the night.

The cab driver made his way out into the night's flooded streets and the busy flow of traffic. Car tires were half-submerged and the rain was coming down so hard that windshield wipers could not move fast enough to clear the flow. The view out the front of the car was a total blur. Speeding through a number of traffic circles, the cab finally reached the hotel and pulled into a flooded driveway.

Stepping out of the cab with a loud splash, I thanked the driver and walked toward the entrance. A group of people sat in the doorway and watched my approach with curiosity. Walking through the door, I looked for someone working the front desk. It wasn't long before an old man emerged from a back room, prompted by one of the young men who sat in the lobby.

"Kamar?" I asked the man behind the counter for a room. My Indonesian language skills remained in one-word elements, learned from my tiny dictionary.

"*Penuh* (full)," he said to me with a shrug of his shoulders.

I didn't want to go back outside but I had no choice. As I turned for the door I remembered the cab driver who had dropped me off. I rushed outside to see if he was still outside. As I splashed into the driveway the car was only just backing into the roadway. I ran up to the window and started to knock loudly on the glass. The driver jumped from the sudden surprise. He rolled down his window despite the heavy rain.

"Do you know how far these other hotels are?" I showed him my list again. After a brief moment he pointed down the road.

"Not far, you can walk." He showed me that the others I wanted were all just down the street. I waved thanks and tightened down my rain hood.

Walking out of the driveway into the road, I met a wall of water thrown at me from a passing line of cars. Evidently, Indonesians didn't prescribe the idea of driving for the conditions and carried on at their usual clear weather speed. Aside from my Goretex coat, I wore a pair of tie-dyed cotton pants and my sandals. The wave of water went straight through my pants and the material now hung heavy and wet against my skin. I could feel the cold water straining down through my underwear.

"Fuck!" I yelled the word out in frustration. It was drowned out by the pounding rain and passing traffic. Just then another passing car sent a second wave toward me. This one was a little smaller than the first but it didn't matter anymore. I never even bothered to get out of the way. I was simply thankful for the coat over my head. I began to walk along the street, facing the traffic toward the next possible hotel. The ground around me was covered by deepening water. I waded through the flood that was now halfway to my knees.

I inquired at the second, the third, and the fourth hotel only to be turned back out into the rainy night. I was not surprised. With the severity of the storm and the time of day, all the rooms would have been snapped up early. I stood in the rain wondering what the hell I was going to do. I had to get dry. I finally told myself that the best thing to do was to keep moving, despite the miserable wetness. I could feel myself getting cold and, by now, even my rain jacket felt wet all the way through. My body began to shiver and I felt an urge to cry out of sheer frustration. Then I got mad.

"You're not giving up, man. You're not!" I screamed at myself out loud. "Just keep moving and focus on finding shelter!" I felt helpless and scared but I knew I had no choice but to keep looking. My water-logged baggage hung heavy on my shoulders. The flood was almost up to my knees in some spots as I pressed on. Slosh! Slosh! My legs dragged through the cool, muddy water. I continued to be splashed by the passing traffic. It did not matter. I couldn't get any wetter now. My body's shivering, however, concerned me.

I continued on along the edge of the road. Cars were passing quite close to me by now. Here in the dark and rain the headlights would only illuminate my presence at the last moment. Upon seeing me there at the edge of the track, the drivers would suddenly swerve out and around me. I looked for a place to get off the road before getting run down.

At the end of the block I found two more hotels. Unfortunately both were full as well and I felt totally defeated. I was still shivering and felt a wave of nervousness. I was ready to give just about anything to get out of the rain.

I glanced further up the street and saw a bright neon sign flashing in the darkness. It was another hotel. The sign flashed its advertisement in English and it was like a beacon in the night: Rooms—Hot Showers. It looked to be a more expensive hotel compared to the other hotels I had just checked out. At this point I would have gladly signed over all of my remaining funds for a dry space.

The only thing keeping me in the storm now was the busy road I needed to cross to reach the dry lobby. Patience was a virtue as I waited for a hole in the traffic. I had never seen rain like this in all my life. Water was now dripping off every part of my body. It had even managed to run inside my hood, running down my chest and back. My body shook uncontrollably. I prayed that this place would have a room. If I was turned away again I would certainly lose it. Finally there was a hole in the flow of cars and I rushed through the dirty waves.

"Hello!" I shouted. The front desk seemed deserted. "Hello! Anybody here?"

A man appeared from the rear of the office and greeted me with a smile. His friendly glance turned to concern when he saw the state I was in.

"I need a room," I said sharply. "Please, do you have a room?" I let my bags fall to the floor in a heap.

"Yes, yes." The man calmed me down as he quickly pulled out his registration book and began to write. "You need a hot shower, too?"

"Absolutely." The sound of the word "yes" from the man's mouth had me breathing a sigh of relief. I had found shelter at last. The man pointed to a door just across from the lobby.

"There is your room," he said as he passed me a key. "Breakfast is served here in the morning."

"I get breakfast, too?" I was elated. "Thank you . . . thank you very much." The man stood behind his desk as I picked up my heavy bags and walked across to my door. My shaky hand placed the key in the hole and turned the knob. The room was dark but revealed a single bed with a side table and a small black and white TV. At the opposite end of the room was the shower room and commode.

The first thing I did was empty my packsack. Everything I had in my possession was soaked with the exception of my books and documents wrapped securely in thick plastic bags. The room soon resembled a laundry with, every possible space used to hang clothes. Even my guitar was drenched. I stood in the shower stall when I opened the gig bag. A puddle of water formed at my feet as I extracted the soaked instrument. I knew that instruments needed to be kept in a humid atmosphere but this was ridiculous.

Peeling off all my clothing at last, I stood in a steady stream of hot water coming out of the showerhead. I shook for the first few moments as my body temperature returned to normal.

At last I crawled into the warm, dry bed. I was totally exhausted. The struggle through the storm had expended all of my energy. I fell fast asleep to the sound of heavy rain pounding on the roof.


## Semarang

*Sunday, February 5, 1995*

Fuelling up on a few cups of thick, rich coffee, I headed out into the day. The streets looked totally different now that they were no longer rivers. I soon discovered just how different. A wide pool of water I had noticed the night before as I waded down the flooded road was, in fact, a flood channel to draw all the rain out of the city, back to the sea. I looked down into the huge, empty hole with widening eyes. The ditch was eight metres wide, four metres deep, and as long as the block. I remembered the moment when I considered walking here to avoid the crazy traffic and thanked myself for choosing to stay on the edge.

Studying the maps I found my way to the markets and got a feel for the city. The markets and streets of Semarang were as I had expected, congested with people. Indonesia had a population of about one hundred and ninety million in 1994. The island of Java is about twelve hundred kilometres long and two hundred kilometres across at the widest point. It supports one hundred million people. I tried to wrap my head around that number and compare it to something I was familiar with. It was something equivalent to, say, fifty million people living on Vancouver Island.

The locals found me to be a curiosity. From the reaction I received as I explored the tiny alleyway stores, I guessed that not too many tourists shopped in this area of town. I haggled with the fresh fruit vendors and made a pig of myself, eating loads of rambutans, mangosteens, and star fruit. At one point as I was walking past a large fruit stand, I noticed a familiar symbol out of the corner of my eye. Among the piles of fruit and food, I discovered a large wooden crate filled with shrivelled and sad looking BC apples. The only things that looked fresh were the BC stickers hanging off the wrinkled skins. Despite their appearance they seemed to be a popular item. I wanted to laugh as I watched local shoppers pushing each other out of the way for a chance to grab some of the sick-looking fruit. I figured the locals, unable to grow them here, thought them to be delicacies. I gladly skirted around them and chose a large bunch of succulent rambutans.

The friendliness I experienced from some of the locals was offset by contempt from others. At lunch I sat alone in a crowded restaurant. Suddenly a young girl slid onto the bench beside me and was very friendly. She told me that she wanted to practice her English as she ordered her lunch. We had a nice conversation and she became quite excited when she found out I was from Canada, asking me all kinds of questions about my home. At the end of the meal she handed me the bill for her meal and insisted that I pay it because she had been so friendly.

"Sorry," I said to her as I handed the piece of paper back to her. She suddenly turned quite indignant and, making a huge scene, complained all the way to the counter as other patrons looked on. She slammed money from her pocket down on the counter and stormed out of the restaurant in a huff. The owner laughed as he looked over at me from behind the counter.

"No worry, sir," he said in broken English. "She do that always."

Later that afternoon I encountered a group of young men hanging out on the edge of a side road. I could sense that they were watching me and heard them laughing among themselves. I thought nothing of it as I passed by.

"Fuck off, man," one of them said.

"Go home, man," added another. A chorus of insults was hurled at me as I continued past the group. They started to follow me, continuing the barrage of words. I ignored them.

It was then that I was nearly hit by a small rock. The throw was long and the stone flew over my shoulder and landed in front of my path. I wanted to react, to walk over, and confront the thrower. At the last minute I decided to be discreet, swallow my pride, and keep walking. Any reaction by me on their turf could prove to be a hazardous choice. They soon tired of their game and left me to my day.

Later in the evening I wandered back into the market area to have dinner, and ran into the same group of youths near a central market. After eating I slid into the shadows as best I could, hoping to avoid them. I returned to my room feeling very unwelcome.

I was getting a taste of prejudice. It was a feeling that made me want to hide away from everybody. I could understand that they would do it, however, knowing what the majority of tourists are like. I had met a few on this journey who made me feel embarrassed to be white! I was seen as rich, ignorant, and uncaring. I longed to see my companions. For now, the small hotel room provided solace.


## Mom's Digs
*Monday, February 6, 1995*

"So, you made it." Danny's voice crackled through the old phone in the lobby.

"Yeah, I decided to head straight here to meet you," I said to him. "I figured that you would eventually get here, so I was going to stay put until you called."

"Well, we just got into town," he replied. "We got stuck in Jakarta for a couple of days on business. So, do you still want to give me a hand while you are here? We will be heading to Bali eventually and you are more than welcome to tag along."

"Sounds great, Dan, I would love to help you out," I replied. It felt good to connect with another person from home.

I had just enough time to pack up all my belongings and pay all my bills at the front desk before a small taxi rolled into the driveway. Danny and Wiwied sat in the rear seat. After I climbed in to join them, the car sped through the city to the southern suburbs and we soon arrived at Wiwied's mother's house.

Having just arrived from Canada, Dan and Wiwied's luggage filled the house. I set mine down in an empty corner.

"Thank you for letting me stay in your home," I said to Wiwied's mother. After looking at me curiously, she waited for her daughter to translate what I had said. Once she understood, the tiny, unassuming woman nodded her head and giggled, pointing to the spare room in back.


### Ramadan and Sleep Deprivation
*Tuesday, February 7, 1995*

Getting used to Muslim sleep cycles during the height of Ramadan was a challenge. During the Holy Month the faithful rise very early to the sounds of prayers from the mosques. Modern technology has aided the efforts of the holy men to get their brethren to join in the ceremonies by amplifying the morning prayers through very loud speakers.

So far during my journey, my exposure to the sound of these chants had been at a distance. For the most part, they created a sooth-ing sound that would wake me only temporarily, then send me back to sleep as I listened to the eerie voices in the night. Wiwied's moth-er's house, however, was about sixty metres from one of the Semarang's mosques and, unfortunately, the speakers on the minarets were pointed directly at our windows. The beginning of my first night's sleep in the house was very peaceful, with the exception of a few roaming dogs wandering the dark streets. These beasts occasion-ally barked and howled as they searched for shelter or food. However, just after 3:00 AM, the semi-silence was completely shattered by the beginnings of a chant that would plague our sleep each night. When the noise began I swear that I was almost shaken from my mattress.

"*Saur! Saur! Saur! Saur!*" (pronouced "saa-oor") the voice cried out in the darkness.

"What the . . . ?" I sat bolt upright in my bed.

This first shout continued for a few minutes, followed by the low refrains of the holy men.

"*Allah Akbar . . .*" Cries from other, distant mosques joined the mix of sound drifting into the night, calling the faithful to rise and begin the day.

"Tee hee hee . . . " The small spaces between blaring voices were filled with the distinct sound of laughter. As I concentrated, I could hear the familiar giggle that could only be Danny, laughing at the ridiculousness of the volume. It prompted me to begin laughing as well. Soon both Dan and I were in our separate rooms, shaking with uncontrollable fits of laughter. In no way was it meant to show any disrespect for the religious practice. It was simply an automatic response to the stimulus and the lack of sleep we were experiencing. Once the chanting ceased the first time, the sound of a recorded air raid siren filled the early morning. They played the tape so loud that the speaker cone could be heard distorting in the mix. Once finished, the chanting continued with added energy and volume, carrying on for close to an hour.

Inside the house, the phone began to ring off the hook. The entire household was now buzzing with the sounds and movement of Wiwied, her mother, and several young relatives and friends who began marching in through the front door from across the street. Wiwied chattered loudly on the telephone with her friends and the children began to play with toys and games. Mom sat herself in front of the television and cranked the volume up high. Drifting in and out of limited slumber, I finally surrendered to the fact that trying to sleep through this was to be a lost cause. The cacophony prompted me to get up with the rest.

Sticking my head out of my door, I watched the activity in the living room. I checked my watch—4:30 AM. Looking across the room, my half-opened eyes caught sight of Danny, looking as sleepy as I did.

"I guess they want us to get up," Danny said to me as he again began to giggle loudly.

"How did you ever get that idea?" I said. The kids were screaming and shouting with excitement, running throughout the house. The volume of the TV was reverberating off the walls.

"Does that thing have to be so loud, Wiwied?" Danny asked his fiancée sleepily.

"What did you say?" she asked him, yelling above the din, her other ear glued to the phone.

Danny only looked at me and started to laugh. We would have to live with the noise.

## Monkey-Class Driving School
*Friday, February 10, 1995*
Danny planned to visit various art studios and galleries throughout central Java and Bali over the next month; both he and Wiwied had a number of good contacts throughout the area. Dan had rented a van and the three of us began preparations for many short trips near Semarang and eventually to Bali, from where I would eventually return home. Excited to join them on the overland excursions, I was glad to have the opportunity to see many places off the beaten tourist track.

On the morning of our first trip to Jogyakarta (pronounced "Joag-Jakarta"), I began to joke with Danny about the local traffic.

"So, you really want to go one on one with the drivers here, do you, Dan?" I laughed.

He laughed nervously, saying, "It's going to be the ride of your life, boy." I was more apt to agree with him when I noticed that the van he had rented had only two seat belts—in the front bucket seats. My place, as I was the third passenger, was to be on the rear bench seat, free of safety belts. I accepted the risk with slight trepidation. The images of careening buses raced through my mind, as did visuals of fast exits through glass. I placed my faith in Dan to have good reflexes and a keen eye for any narrow escape routes.

"Just hang on and pray," he said to me. I felt nervous at the very sound of his words.

Jogyakarta was about one hundred and forty kilometres to the south of Semarang, near the south coast of Java. We left mid-morning and fought our way out of the city through snarling traffic that did not end for the majority of the trip. As a result the travel time was extended for much longer than we had originally expected. At best, the average speed on the highways ended up to be only about fifty kilometres per hour. Twists, turns, and a ton of tiny vehicles filled every possible space along the busy highway.

"There are only two road rules in Indonesia," Dan told me. "Biggest goes first and fastest goes first." We both laughed.

The worst of the culprits, by far, were the buses. The drivers of these smoky beasts seemed to possess an unspoken hierarchy on the local roads. The rulers of the highways wielded their power over other smaller vehicles with a single tool—terror!

First of all, the look of the buses can intimidate an observer. The chassis are very high off the ground, built with a nose sloping from the high front bumper down to the front axle. The shape reminded me of the under-carriage of a military amphibious vehicle. On the front bumper are extremely bright flood lights capable of trashing retinas even in the daylight. Next to them on the chrome bumpers, sets of horns blast a warning of imminent approach. Furthermore, most of the drivers dodge madly around any and all traffic in front of them, flashing lights and blaring horns until the car or truck in front of them moves out of the way. I began to observe that this also included oncoming traffic. Wiwied called the buses "monkey-class," one step below third-class.

Far down the road buses could be seen pulling onto our side of the highway. With bright lights flashing rapidly and horn exploding, the giant heaps of hurtling steel would force their way in front of numerous cars. Without enough room for the buses to make the maneouvre safely, the oncoming traffic would have to move to avoid eating ten metric tonnes of undercarriage. This adjustment included driving onto the shoulder of the road, then returning to the pavement once the monster had passed by.

Dan had experience with this style of driving. He and Wiwied had been on Java the previous year. After a few close calls Danny soon got his driving rhythm and his nerve back on track as I lent an eye to the flow from the back, holding my breath along the way.

"Are you all right back there?" asked Dan.

"A Valium would help," I replied, laughing nervously.

The high stakes game of chicken continued without end. Dan had to remain sharp at all times to keep pace and to survive.

"It's like playing PacMan with only one man," I said.

"Yeah, and I'm goin' for the high score!" Danny swerved onto an exit leading to another smaller highway and headed south.

Apart from the wild driving, the countryside was beautiful. Lush green hills covered with coffee and tea plantations, mingled with fruit crops and rice fields. Small stands found along the road sold all kinds of produce. Star fruit, rambutans, coconuts, durian, and jack fruit, among others, could be seen piled at various roadside booths.

Mount Merapi, the most active of all the volcanoes in Indonesia, came into view, its tall, smoking summit reaching into the sky out of the jungle. The sharp peak constantly belched heat, steam, and a thin column of grey smoke. Our destination was on the opposite side of the smouldering giant. The road snaked its way over the contours of the land. Black soil, rich in nutrients, sprouted thick, full plants. Coffee beans hanging along the road's edge glowed a rich red. By early afternoon we entered the outskirts of Jogya.


## Gong Factory & the Tin Can Man

*Saturday, February 11, 1995*

East of Jogya lies the city of Surakarta, also known as Solo. Throughout Indonesia, certain areas and towns are known for a particular kind of artwork or artistic discipline. Jepara, north of Semarang, for example, is known best for teak carving. The art in Solo does not feature any particular type of art but borders on creative genius in a variety of disciplines.

Among the national instruments of Indonesia are gangsas, xylophone-like instruments, as well as large metal gongs. These and other percussion instruments are combined in large orchestras called Gamelans. The brass gongs, keys, and the intricately carved teak frames for these instruments are produced in only a few factories in the area. On their last visit here, Dan and Wiwied had done business with one of these local instrument manufacturers.

Danny's attempt to relocate this particular factory met with a slight problem—we got lost in the process. We drove around the outskirts of Solo for a good hour. Danny was sure that he could retrace the route he had taken the precious summer. Finally giving up, Wiwied was set to work, speaking to as many locals as we could come across and asking for directions. She inquired as to the location of the factory. Some inquiries met dead ends, others gave just enough instruction to guide us on to the next available guiding hand. Each person she asked seemed to have an entirely different idea of where this particular factory was located. After a time Dan and I sat in the vehicle in fits of laughter as we were guided right, left, back over the hill, over the river, and around the bend until, finally, we reached the front gate of the factory.

We were greeted by the factory supervisor who remembered the couple from their last visit. I was introduced as another foreign art buyer and Dan asked if it were possible for us to see the actual production line.

"Yes, of course, welcome," the supervisor said, shaking my hand. "Please come inside." We were led through the courtyard and in the corner sat a man busily shining a small, newly made brass gong with a sheet of emery paper. He worked silently and diligently, his young son playing nearby. The man raised his head and smiled at us as we approached. Just beyond where he sat, the forging room sat behind two large closed doors. Near the doorway a giant gong hung from a large roof beam by a thick rope.

I choked as I passed through the soot-covered doors, entering a world of intense heat, darkness, and smoke. A hot fire raged in the centre of a room full of grime-covered workers, standing around the large fire pit and holding hand tools and hammers. The air was hot and hard to breathe. My first thought was the fact that these men worked inside this place all day, ingesting the smoke on a constant basis.

One man using long metal tongs was flipping a large gong-shaped brass plug in the coals of the pit. With deft skill he handled the hot disk like a toy. Once the fire had transferred enough heat and the metal grew red-hot, the man lifted the gong out of the pit in front of the waiting men. Two men with gripping hooks pulled it closer and began to turn the gong clockwise on the dirt floor. On cue the men holding long-handled hammers began to pound the disk into the proper shape with timed precision, striking the glowing brass gong in turn, continuing until the metal had cooled and needed to be softened again. All the while these men worked with the hot metal and the flying sparks from the fire pit in bare feet.

"How long does it take to make one gong?" Dan asked the supervisor.

"Almost two hundred man-hours of labour for one that size," he said.

The heat inside the building was becoming unbearable. We soon left the forging room and carried on to another small building next door.

"Once the work in the forge is complete," the supervisor said as he led us through the doorway, "the gongs are shaped by hand and then tuned. This is the tuning room."

About six people worked in this room, filing and shaping large gongs and small brass keys, similar to those on a xylophone. Piles of brass shavings covered the floor all around them as they peeled bit after bit away to attain the right sound. I watched the workers carefully comparing the tone of their work to a master tuning bell beside them. I lagged behind to observe, while Dan and Wiwied were shown a storeroom full of completed pieces ready for sale. By the time I caught up to them, Danny was already emerging from the room with a large gong he had picked out.

"This is a beauty," he said to me. The large brass gong gleamed brightly. The supervisor carried the wooden stand as we were led back to the entrance of the complex.

"How does it sound?" I asked him.

Before putting it into the back of the van, Danny hung the instrument in its teak frame and handed me the padded hammer included in the sale.

"Go for it," he told me. I swung the hammer against the metal face and a rich, low note floated through the air.

"That's great," I said as the sound slowly dissipated. "Are you going to buy a bunch of these?"

"Only one for now," he said. "This is for a friend back home."

The supervisor followed us back to the van as we lifted the gong and stand into the storage compartment. The man thanked us, turned, and went back inside.

"Okay," Dan said to us, turning the key in the ignition. "Now let's go see the Tin Can Man."

"Who?" I asked.

"The Tin Can Man," repeated Danny. "You won't believe his artwork. He makes everything he sells out of old tin cans." I tried to imagine what this art might look like.

We drove around the hills surrounding the slopes of Mount Merapi. Everytime I looked at the peak I was mesmerized by the thin clouds of steam and smoke rising into the sky. Danny negotiated narrow paved roads until we reached another small village. He pulled the van into a driveway beside a house and small workshop.

A man sat in the shop surrounded by tools and materials. When we entered his driveway he looked up and his face brightened when he recognized his friend.

"Hello, Danny!" he stood up and came over to the window, shaking Dan's hand. "Come in."

He was at work creating some of the art pieces Danny had described. We followed him into his shop to see his progress. Dan had tried to explain his technique to me as we drove from the gong factory but I had to see it to understand it. His method was to transform long strips of discarded tin cans six to eight centimetres wide. Using tin snips, he would then make thin crosscuts along the length of the metal strip. Each thin cut was then twisted with pliers into a fine coil, like a ringlet. The end result looked like long strips of coarse steel wool. Once a great number of these strips were produced they were applied to the outside of a carved wooden core. Finally, a coat of paint covered up old labels and any bits of rust remaining on the exposed metal.

Using this technique the Tin Can Man made birds and animals, using the twisted metal as layered feathers or fur. His art looked really great and he had a number of different pieces to show us, among them eagles, peacocks, and a horse rearing up on its hind legs that stood more than a metre tall. The horse really impressed me as I ran my hand over the head and mane of the creation. With its wooden core, the whole statue felt very solid.

Danny placed orders for more items to be picked up later in the month. He also handed over some photographs of animals that were new to the artist, namely bears and loons.

"Do you think you can make some of these?" he asked his friend. The Tin Can Man studied the photos for a moment and nodded his head.

"I think it will be okay," he replied to Dan with a smile. He was looking forward to applying his technique to this commissioned work.

After buying a few more pieces from the artist, including the horse, Dan presented his friend with some brand new tin snips to help the creator with his work. He had purchased them in Canada specifically for his friend. The look on the artist's face made me think he was going to burst into tears of joy at the sight of the tools. The state of his present tools left much to be desired and he excitedly began to test the snips on a few pieces of scrap left over from another project. It was like watching a little kid in front of a Christmas tree.

"Thank you, Dan, thank you." The Tin Can Man was one happy fellow.

"See you in a month or so," said Dan.


## Teak Mills and Art Galleries

Danny was searching for a teak mill that could produce yard furniture. If a cheap enough price could be found, he could have items produced and shipped directly to Canada. There were a few mills on the outskirts of Solo that we visited. Wiwied was indispensable in these situations, dealing with the mill owners, translating into English the prices and details. This part of Dan's overall plan didn't seem to pan out very successfully. Mainly, the prices ended up to be too high to be worth the trouble. Aside from that, one mill owner seemed a little too ruthless with his employees, making Dan refuse his business.

As we had the tour of this particular factory, some of the workers were painting metal I-beams for a new section that was being added to the mill's structure. The long green beams lay on large bricks close together. One of the men climbed over one of the beams to paint the other side, causing it to roll. When it did, the beam pinched his foot in the space of a moment, breaking a few of his toes. He hit the ground screaming his head off. The can of paint and brush he carried flew onto the dirt beside him.

"Ouch!" I said out loud. "That's gotta hurt." I knew his bones had been broken when I saw them bent at a right angle to the rest. The other workers helped this poor fellow up and brought him into the main office where we were in a meeting with the boss. The injured worker continued to cry out loudly as his workmates set him gently on a wooden bench near the open door.

The boss was pissed off and spoke sharply to the group of workers. I leaned over and asked Wiwied to translate what the boss was saying to his employees.

"He says that he is very upset that the man has hurt himself. It sounds like he is more upset that his work is not going to get done."

"You mean he doesn't give a shit that the guy has a smashed foot?" I was shocked.

The workers protested the boss's response and Wiwied again translated the conversation.

"The men want the boss to call an ambulance, but he will not," she told us. "He says that the young man is on his own and someone from his family will have to come and get him." Dan and I couldn't believe what we were hearing.

"This guy is psychotic," I said, looking at the boss man. Wiwied also overheard that the owner refused to provide steel-toed boots for his employees. Any men who were too poor to buy them risked this kind of injury all the time.

Meanwhile, the injured fellow continued to lie on the bench in excruciating pain. Medical help would have to come out of his own pocket. Now unemployed, he wouldn't have the money for this, let alone enough for his family to eat, until he was healed and could work again. I could see the stress of the situation in this young man's face when his boss told him he was on his own. He was at the point of tears. My guts wrenched at his plight.

"This is bullshit!" Danny was disgusted with this man's treatment of his workers. "Let's get out of here. I am not giving this man any of my business."

The boss man seemed slightly perplexed at the fact we were now heading for the door. Without a word Danny passed all the various information sheets given to him when we had arrived into the hands of one of the assistants standing off to the side. We marched past the owner as he watched us leave the mill in disgust. Passing by the injured young man, I looked in his eyes.

"I wish there was something I could do for you, bud." He had no idea what I had said to him but I think he understood by my facial expression that I was concerned.

By now the other men had stopped their work to contact one of the man's family members by telephone and to help him rest more comfortably while he waited for someone to arrive.

The ride back to Jogyakarta was quiet, all of us still upset by the events we had just seen.

"What a bastard!" I thought to myself. I wondered just how common this kind of employer/employee relationship was. From the fact that the country was so poor, I guessed it to be rampant.

Batik factories were commonplace in Jogya. This city is best known for this type of art and textile design. We stopped into a few of the biggest factories when we returned to the city. Danny and Wiwied spent time purchasing dozens of pieces from the owner while I toured the building, looking at the works and also observing production techniques of this beautiful craft. I watched as the women used large wooden frames to hold the fabric tight, painting the cloth with tiny pen-like implements filled with hot wax. Once done, large vats of dye were used to colour the remaining areas of the cloth. Looking at some of the final product had me shaking my head as to how they did the colour blending and fading. The complexity of colours was amazing. I watched as the works appeared almost before my eyes. The whole building smelled of paraffin and dye. These batik paintings were then hung on racks to dry and then framed for sale by the boss and his wife. The factory carried every style of painting: landscapes, flowers, fish, animals, and beautiful abstract art.

Other galleries held things ranging from model ships full of soldiers made of soft rubber to beautiful carvings and masks. The bows of the ships could be bent and twisted and would pop back into shape again. One place sold stone tables made from coloured stone fragments pressed together with resin. Wood carvings were plentiful and magnificently detailed. The drug-like smell of sandalwood filled some of the galleries and these carvings carried ridiculously expensive price tags. Sandalwood carvings are sold not only according to the work's intricacy but by the weight of the wood as well.

As I walked through one gallery a large art piece caught my eye. I recognized the style to be that of the Tin Can Man. It was a huge ornate dragon that stood almost three metres off the floor. The work put into this piece must have been considerable, seeing how much twisted tin was layered over the body of the creature. It felt eerily like scales. I reached down and turned the price tag over in my fingers to see the numbers. It was the equivalent of twenty-five hundred American dollars.

## Borobudur

*Sunday, February 12, 1995*

Heading back to Semarang, Danny made a detour to see the temple of Borobudur, northwest of Jogya. Borobudur is a giant temple built by the kings of the Sailendra Dynasty in the 9th century. It was resurrected out of the jungle and the ash of countless eruptions from the nearby volcanic chain, first by the British in the 1800s and then by Dutch colonists just after the turn of the next century.

Walking up to the enormous edifice, I couldn't believe the size of it. It rose up out of the forest and possessed an amazing view from the top level, many steps away.

"It's the biggest stupa in the world," explained Danny. "It's also the biggest ancient monument in the southern hemisphere." I looked up to see that the structure covered the entire hill above and around us. We started up the long, thin staircase along with other tourists and a number of Buddhist faithful heading up to pray.

The steps took us up through three outer levels of the stone structure. These levels were filled with hundreds of small stupas (bell-shaped monuments) and stone carvings depicting figures of gods, men and animals. The carvings depicted the story of the life of the Buddha.

"When they rebuilt this temple from the ashes," Dan went on, "they had to put the whole story back together, piece by piece, fitting the pictures back in place."

"What a job it must have been for western Christians to rebuild a Buddhist story with any accuracy," I was impressed by the intricate detail of the stone pictorials.

Further up the stairs we encountered another three levels leading up to the centre of the temple. These three levels were much more open and created huge rings around the highest point of the edifice, inside the rectangular outer structure. Larger stupas covered each of these three levels. These structures were hollow inside, interlocking stones creating a lattice-like outer cover. Peeking in through the diamond-shaped holes, I could see each stupa held a seated Buddha. I observed that each one of the Buddhas had a different hand position as I strolled from one stupa to the next.

Passing the top two levels of the temple, we reached the large, central stupa. This central monument was solid on the outside but was apparently hollow inside. Danny understood that it represented nirvana.

From the top of Borobudur I looked out over the land surrounding the temple. Rich, green forests and farm fields stretched out into the distance. Across the valley, Mount Merapi could be seen in the haze, a barely audible rumble coming from its belly, the plume of smoke constant.

Exploration of the entire structure took a couple of hours to complete. As we came around to the main staircase and began to climb down through the top levels of hollow stupas, Danny caught my attention.

"That one particular stupa has special significance to the faithful," he said.

"How so?" I asked, noticing a huge crowd of people surrounding the monument.

"It is said that if you can reach in and touch the hands of the Buddha inside, your prayer will come true," Dan told me. The crowd of people included mostly Chinese tourists. One of the men was trying his hardest to stretch his arm into the opening, any opening, to reach the statue. Unfortunately for him, his arms were just too short to reach. I watched him as he tried desperately to get his fingers closer to the stone hands. After a great deal of effort, he finally gave up and departed disgruntled, trailing behind his group.

I gave a silent prayer for peace and harmony for myself and others in my life as I reached in through one of the holes until my hands met the texture of the Buddha's palm. I felt the worn stone, closed my eyes and breathed deeply.

## Stranded

*Monday, February 13, 1995*

These next few days saw us exploring the various towns near Semarang. Jepara is a small city north along the coastline and was the farthest distance we travelled, only about sixty kilometres. The speciality of this area is teak carving, mostly furniture. One particular gallery on the outskirts of town was owned by a friend of Wiwied's family. They were makers of a large collection of varied work.

Their gallery had many rooms that led to other rooms and seemed to go on forever as I strolled through the building. Wall boards, cabinets, and large bed frames filled the halls of the large barn-like structure. Adjoining rooms off to the side were filled with masks, carvings, chairs, benches, jewellery boxes, and chests. Another entire room was dedicated to musical instruments of all shapes and sizes. This particular family had a heritage of carving brilliance spanning many generations.

Dan's main focus was on smaller items like jewellery boxes and small chests. He purchased almost the entire collection of these as the owner gave him a very good deal. To thank Dan for purchasing such a considerable amount of merchandise, the owner gave each of us a few small teak boxes.

We had almost packed up the van and were about to make our way to Semarang when the sky opened up and the most incredible rainstorm began. Reminding me of my arrival after the night flight from Jakarta, the roads began to quickly become covered with flooding water.

"We had better get going," Dan said, "or we may never get home."

By now it was well past sundown and the night was pitch black. The gallery driveway was already a small lake as we slipped out onto the main road. Dan began to slowly make his way along the street, attempting to retrace our route back toward the highway. The headlights didn't help at all and the windshield wipers were a joke. At one point Dan parked in the middle of the road staring ahead into the dark, flooded landscape. Finally, he turned to look at me over his shoulder.

"Can you tell if that is the road or a flooded rice paddy?" he asked me. I stared out in front of the vehicle. All I could see was a huge lake with a few small shrubs and one lone stop sign sticking out above the water line.

"No," I replied. "Do you think we can make it back to the highway?"

Danny drove slowly ahead. By now the front bumper of the van was pushing water like the prow of a ship.

"We might need some pontoons," Dan said as he began to giggle. "Tee hee hee, this is ridiculous."

"The rain here is unbelievable," I said, staring out the window.

"Yes, is very bad, Danny," said Wiwied. "We cannot go home tonight."

"Yeah, I think you are right," answered Dan. "We'll have to get a room for the night." He turned to me with an apologetic expression. "Sorry about this, John."

"Why?" I replied. "I think this is great! Stranded in a tropical rainstorm where we can't tell our way from a hole in the ground—literally—now this is an adventure!" The sound of the rain on the metal roof of the van was deafening as we sat contemplating our plans. Slowly we crawled along the road and felt our way into the centre of Jepara.

By the time we got to the town centre the rain had levelled off but was still steady. The streets here were not as badly flooded as the road leading into town. We hunted down a small motor inn and took refuge for the night.

"It's 10:00. No wonder I am hungry." Danny had taken the words right out of my mouth.

We went down to the small restaurant attached to the hotel in hope of finding some food. The place was filled with locals watching TV and drinking tea. I looked in the glass case below the counter and saw nothing but empty shelves. Unfortunately for us, there had only been a certain amount of food prepared for the day and by this time of the evening, everything had been eaten up by recent customers. The only thing left was a plate of sweet desserts sitting in a corner of a cabinet in the kitchen. Since there was no food left in the place and it was late, we just decided to sleep and leave early in the morning.

The next day the sky was bright and sunny. The roads were now visible and there was fresh food in the restaurant. We ate a large meal before heading back to Semarang at mid-morning. Taking a detour, Dan managed to find some interesting backroads. We had to cross quite a few old wooden bridges that had me ready with one hand on the door handle for a fast exit. A few of the crossings were completely out, forcing us to backtrack to other bridges, weaving our way through the forest and the farms.


### Monkey-Class Driving School II
*Friday, February 17, 1995*
We were finally headed for the island of Bali. Our three-day journey included visits to art galleries and mills along the way. We stayed with Wiwied's relatives in the city of Bojonegoro as we made our way through the northern highways of East Java. One of our main destina-

tions was a volcano called Bromo. Danny had promised me that it would be something to see. I longed to get close to one of these smoking giants but for now we had to contend with slow-paced traffic and the horrid driving skills of the local populace.

Driving through small towns in Java required skill and patience since the path was often blocked by the people milling along the roadway. Honking horns gave pedestrians a warning as cars drove by. I never saw anyone get hit during my journey but I did see quite a few close calls. Once again, the monkey-class bus drivers created the most havoc.

Heading through one town in the middle of the day we came across a large group of school kids walking down the road. Their classes had just been let out for the afternoon. I saw a sea of blue and white uniforms. Filling an entire intersection in the centre of the village, the students were laughing, talking, and joking. They were not holding up the traffic on purpose; their sheer volume was taking a long time to clear the street. Suddenly, the group received a reason to clear off a little faster.

"Oh, oh . . . " My eyes widened as I stared down to the end of the visible stretch of highway.

Around the distant corner came a huge bus at full speed. It was one of the infamous "Express" buses. These were known to career through villages and towns with no intent to slow down nor to give any courtesy whatsoever to anyone or anything in their path. The giant beast barrelled toward the crowd of school kids. Upon seeing the speeding missile on wheels, Danny pulled the van off to the side of the road, having no intention of playing chicken.

I had expected a scene similar to a Japanese sci-fi movie in which a panic-stricken crowd stampedes away from danger. The exact opposite happened. The kids, as if well-practiced at the art of avoiding this kind of death threat, simply observed the speeding bus and casually created a wide space in the centre of their group, through which the vehicle could pass.

The bus approached, its lights and horns working hard to give any stragglers one last warning. The speed varied only slightly as the huge machine raced into the opening in the centre of the group. "He must be going one hundred kilometres per hour," I said as I watched the bus rocket past the kids, within inches of squishing them flat.

The resulting wind generated by the bus kicked up a huge cloud of thick dust which enveloped the children. The giant vehicle sped past our van parked safely on the gravel shoulder.

"That guy is insane!" I was shocked at the callousness of the twit behind the wheel.

"Yes . . . ," said Wiwied as she, too, followed the bus with her eyes as it passed. "He is monkey-class."

As the dust cloud slowly settled, the crowd of kids nonchalantly carried on with their day, as if nothing at all had occurred.

## Kuwu and a Lesson in Humility

Kuwu is a geothermal mud flat located in East Java. Wiwied was adamant that we should visit the area, not just for my sake. She persisted in asking Dan to make the detour until he finally agreed. He wanted to reach Mount Bromo before the sun went down.

We followed the scarce signage and the directions of locals with the help of our handy translator. Soon we were parked next to a giant moon-like landscape of mud. Far out in the middle there were plumes of mud and steam that would burst upward as sub-surface pressure was released. With at least two large, steamy belches per minute, the huge field of grey mud looked like a wasteland. Near the entrance an elevated observation post stood at the edge of the open field. The wrinkled mud stretched out before us. Small worn paths led out into the muddy mass and I watched as people walked out on the surface, seeing the plumes from a closer vantage point. I was inspired to join the pilgrimage out onto the plain. As we stood watching a few local guides persistently asked us if they could take us out onto the surface of Kuwu.

For some reason I became incredibly stubborn. I turned and made my way toward the edge of the plain, ignoring the men who wanted me to pay them their fees. One of the men followed me down the platform's steps, calling after me to wait for him.

"No!" I shouted back at him. I just wanted to do something on my own without someone hounding me for guide fees.

"But sir, wait. You must have a guide." He continued to follow me out onto the mud surface. I still refused. Here at Kuwu I had finally lost my tolerance for the constant hassling I had encountered in

Indonesia. It was on the mud flat where I learned an important lesson about accepting assistance.

I wanted to do it alone. The feeling was so strong and it was strange that it came upon me so quickly. I was so sure that I could just walk out onto the mud to the same place I saw others go and not have any problem. I had seen so many tourists back in my hometown of Jasper hurt by the natural hazards encountered in the wilds, and thought them idiots for being so careless. Feeding bears or getting too close to dangerous waterfalls was all too common. I knew what I was doing. I wasn't going to do anything stupid in an unfamiliar environment . . . until now.

I followed a worn path that formed a crust of many footprints pressed into the thick mud. As I walked the trail weaved through the muddy wrinkles. At one point the track forked. I took the left path and walked further out onto the grey earth.

"Come back, sir. Come back!" he cried out to me but it was no use. I stubbornly kept on toward the other people I could see ahead of me. Then, stepping onto what I assumed to be solid crust, the surface gave way under my feet. I quickly sank knee-deep in the thick grey muck.

"Holy Shit!" I yelled in surprise. By now my adrenaline was pumping at full speed. Luckily the mud wasn't too soft and I managed to pull myself back onto the harder crust behind me. As I squirmed and twisted around, I noticed the guide standing a few yards away. The small man began to jabber at me in Bahasa.

"Too soft, sir. Too soft." As he pointed at the ground, he started lightly hopping up and down. As he did so, the entire crust of mud he was standing on jiggled like a giant bowl of jello. It was this action that made me realize what a shithead I had been and that I could have easily gone in over my head had the mud I stepped into been any softer than it was. The guide reached out to me. Taking my hand, he pulled me back up to the surface beside him.

Out of the danger zone, I now had to deal with the thick, sticky mud clinging to my feet and sandals. Trying to scrape it off was a joke. It stuck like glue to my skin. Squishing between my toes, it was as thick as the clay used in making pottery. In fact it was probably the same stuff. My feet looked Neanderthal with the bulky mud caked on them. The weight of my legs had me clomping back to the viewpoint. A chorus of laughter was coming from the other guides and my companions who were at the lookout post, watching all the action.

I looked up to see Danny capturing all the exciting events with his handicam recorder.

"Way to go, John," he laughed. "Now you are a real tourist, tee hee hee hee."

I quietly ignored all the attention I was now receiving from the crowd of amused spectators to look for water. Water was so scarce in Kuwu that I had to pay a premium price for a pail of the stuff to clean my legs off. I also paid the guide who had led me back to safety.

"Thank you, my friend," I said to him as I headed for the van with my companions. I had been humbled.


## Mount Bromo

The mountain lay dead ahead of us. I craned my neck to catch a glimpse of the summit, only to see a thick cap of cloud shrouding the peak. Mount Bromo itself was hidden in behind two other giant massifs that were like protecting walls. The crack of a narrow valley was the only access into the steep slopes leading up to the rim of the distant crater.

We had just turned to follow the mountain road, bearing right at a small, conspicuous sign posted on the side of the street, and passing through the coastal town of Probolinggo. A wooden board hung crookedly on a tall stake next to a small intersection. "Bromo" was all it said. The sharp, cut side of the sign provided the only indication of direction.

Danny swerved through the streets of town, avoiding potholes and pedestrians amid the gravel and dust. As we passed through Probolinggo the landscape changed abruptly. The road wound up through dense forest, through a long procession of steep switchbacks. Looking up above the trees, I watched as we entered the narrow gap between the surrounding mountains. It was not long before we gained spectacular views of the coast behind and below us.

By now the road had become very steep. The switchbacks had ended and the road snaked along the tops of richly overgrown lava ridges leading up to the summit. The steep slopes on either side were covered with thick green foliage and rich crops which terraced up the side of the mountain. Soil, blacker than black, sprouted yields of cabbages, coffee, and tea.

"I can't believe that the plants don't just fall off the slope," I observed. Perfect rows of vegetation hung onto the jet-black hillsides. Occasionally, a farmer or two could be seen leaning on a hoe, staring at us as we sped past field after field.

At one point the road levelled out. We had just driven onto the shoulder of the mountain. I looked ahead and saw another steep climb in the distance. This would take us to the rim of the crater, an elevation of about three thousand metres. The van strained up into the thinning air and we finally came to the gates of the small village perched on the edge of the caldera.

We passed through the dirt streets of the small village. Many small hotels and houses lined the roadsides, their inhabitants observing our passing. It was close to sundown and a thin bank of clouds drifted over the tops of the trees as Danny drove to a viewpoint next to a hotel at the edge of the rim. The van lurched to a halt within a few metres of a wooden railing. Beyond the fence the land fell away and I got my first view down into the giant caldera.

"What do you think of that?" Dan had shut the engine off and had turned to see the look on my face.

I sat mesmerized for a few moments. Then, without speaking, I fumbled for the door latch to get out. The cool air made me shiver as I stepped out of the vehicle. I staggered around the body of the van until I reached the wooden rail and stared off the edge, holding my breath.

We were parked on the rim of the Tengger Crater, about ten kilometres in diameter. Once a giant volcano itself, the bottom of this ancient formation was now a flat sea of black sand. In the centre of the caldera were two other volcanoes. On the right was Mount Batok, a dormant, sharp-ridged cone. Thick vegetation grew in the deep crevices leading up to its flat top. On the left was the smoking crater of Mount Bromo, its rim attached to another larger dormant crater behind. There was a long stream of white smoke trailing up and out of Bromo's crater, ash strewn for hundreds of metres in all directions. Far in the distance, the largest of the volcanoes in the area, Mount Semaru, continuously belched clouds of grey ash from its cone at just over thirty-six hundred metres.

On the floor of the black sand sea I could see a trail of white stones outlining a path across the barren land. It led straight to the bottom of the active crater.

"What are the stones for?" I asked Wiwied.

"When you go to the mountain, you go early in the morning before the sun rises. The stones guide you to the side of Bromo. There you will find the stairs to the top of the crater." She continued to stare as if hypnotized.

I turned my gaze once again toward the volcano. I strained to hear the sound of the rumbling mountain, but the distance was too great. I felt drawn to the edge.


## Crater

*Saturday, February 18, 1995*

In the darkness I woke to the sound of doors being pounded upon. I groped in the dark to search for my watch. It was 3:15 AM. One of the hotel staff had been sent around to all the rooms that had made a request for a wake-up call. By the noise outside, which hadn't even reached my door, I supposed the rest of the guests here got the same call, wanted or not.

Bang! Bang! A fist pounded on the door near my bed. "Bromo, Bromo!" A voice shouted through the cracks.

"Okay!" I said, sitting up in my bed.

Danny and Wiwied stirred in their sleep and grumbled at the noisy intrusion.

"Go on ahead, John. We are too tired to go with you." Danny spoke to me as if he was still half asleep, his words slurred.

"No problem. I wanted to do it solo, anyway. I will be back for breakfast." I threw on layers of clothing, packed my flashlight, water, and my journal and walked out into the dark morning.

I could hear many voices and the sound of horses neighing in the darkness. The local guides were saddling up their mounts at a nearby corral in order to carry tourists to the mountain in long horse trains. Despite my experience at Kuwu, I was determined to take this journey without a guide. With all the other people making the trek, I was certain to have contact with them if I needed it. I would simply follow behind, with the group but alone enough to feel the solitude of the mountain.

A number of parties had already left for the floor of the caldera. I could hear them far down the trail in the darkness. I made my way to the trailhead that was actually a barricaded service road. I discovered the barrier when I nearly tripped over the thick chain strung across the path. I stepped over the chain and began to descend into the darkness. As I wound down the trail, following the beam of my flashlight, my pace soon had me catching up to one of the horse trains. The animals plodded along with their passengers heavy upon their backs. The guides spun around to see who had caught up to them in the night. I passed the long procession with a series of quick steps, trying not to disturb the animals. I continued through the semi-darkness until the forest opened and the trail turned onto the dark dunes of the wide sand sea.

Ahead of me I could see two parallel rows of large painted stones creating a wide guiding path toward the distant mountains. I strained to see the volcanoes ahead of me and could only make out a faint outline of the cones and the grey ash strewn around the slopes of Bromo. In the centre of the rows of stones the path across the sand sea was well worn. I could hear more parties of people ahead while others coming from behind were slowly emerging from the forest trail. Turning from the pathway, I plunged into the darkness at the side of the trail. With the white stones still in view, I walked far enough away to allow myself as much private space as possible. I traversed across the rolling black dunes, managing to separate myself from the other humans crossing the barren landscape.

I turned my attention to the dark land surrounding me. I stopped and placed my pack on the ground and stood still, breathing deeply. The air felt cool and fresh as I stared toward the volcanoes ahead of me. The moon was trying to shine through a thin layer of cloud blown quickly across the sky by a silent wind. The holes in the cloud layer allowed patches of moonlight to slip across the ground around me. The only sound was that of my feet shuffling in the sand and the horse trains off to one side. I could feel a few light raindrops as the breeze began to pick up.

Suddenly I was overcome by a strange sensation. At first the feeling was like a heaviness, a feeling of being pulled down toward the earth. I attempted to adjust my stance, discovering that my feet felt heavy, like lead weights. At first I thought my imagination was working overtime but the feeling continued. I wanted to fight the sensation but soon allowed myself to experience what was happening. The feeling grew stronger until I felt my whole body become heavy and, to an extent, immobilized; I strained to lift my arms out to the sides. It was as if I were turning into a statue. The intensity of the feeling slowly faded and soon all of the "weightiness" disappeared.

And then I experienced a feeling of incredible loneliness. Intense, so much that I started to cry. The tears poured from my eyes as I sobbed and began to grieve. Clear pictures began to flash rapidly through my mind's eye. Images of Jill and me together in happier times, others where we were locked in confrontation. Our entire life together passed my vision, the vivid scenes pouring from my memory. Other images flooded into my mind as well. Times when I had made mistakes and felt regret and sorrow throughout my life, along with childhood and adolescent memories, created a kaleidoscope of rapidly changing imagery.

I felt as if all my grief was being drawn out of my body. I had a sensation of a very strong energy flowing through my bones. It felt like a surge of electric current. I relaxed and let the energy pulse through my body in rhythmic waves.

Suddenly, as if it had never occurred, my sadness and grief lifted. The feelings had vanished. I now became aware of an inconceivable amount of energy all around me. The only way to describe it was that the air seemed stiff or thick, as if filled with static electricity. I stood silent for a long moment, my skin tingling, as if sparks would fly if I turned around too quickly. From the initial feeling of heaviness, I now felt light as a feather and full of energy. I felt awesome, as if I could take on the world with my own hands. The captive energy of the volcano far beneath my feet was flowing up through the hardened crust of rock, pulsing through my soul. I jumped up and down with excitement, feeling as elated as a child on Christmas morning, even though I was not sure what had just happened to me.

I picked up my bag and continued across the sandy expanse. By now I could start to see the faint details of the surrounding caldera. I walked fairly quickly; I wanted to be at the peak of the crater before the sun reached the horizon. I looked back to see the sky brightening slightly with the approach of dawn. As I marched toward the foot of the mountain, I had the feeling of being watched or followed. I ignored the sensation only until I began to hear something behind me. The sounds of snuffling and growling reached my ears as I finally realized that I was being followed by a dog. Stopping in my tracks, I shone my light behind me. Sweeping across the horizon, the beam suddenly caught the reflection of a pair of yellow eyes, tracking back and forth toward my position. I felt a surge of adrenaline run through my system as I turned to find anything that would deter my stalker. Finding a good-sized rock, I turned the light back out to find the approaching creature. It was not long before I relocated the set of wandering eyes. He was close enough now that I could pick him out without the light beam. He was sneaking around like a coyote through the dunes of sand, growling as he got closer to me. Discovering me standing alone on the sand, he must have figured I was an easy mark.

When he was within range of my pitch, I threw the stone at him, missing only by a few centimetres. I saw him stop and step back a few paces, uncertain if he should continue his pursuit. Another rock soon convinced him to quit his hunt as it struck his body with an audible thump.

"Yelp!" The creature turned away as I began to run after it, yelling loudly. This convinced him to lose interest and he retreated across the plain.

I turned and continued my trek toward the crater wall. I reached the bottom of the mountain and began to climb as the trail wound up onto an ancient lava flow and up to the outer edge of the crater's slope. I came upon an area where many guides waited in the twilight with their horses, their tourists already at the top of the crater. Just beyond, a long staircase headed straight up the side of the crater to a viewpoint at the edge of the hole.

I counted two hundred and forty-five steps to the edge of the Bromo viewpoint. A good bit of exercise this time of the morning was unusual but enjoyable. Once at the top, my wish for quiet solitude was shattered by a noisy group of Chinese tourists. Even at 4:20 AM they talked so loud that anyone else would have to yell to be heard above the volume. Furthermore, they stood at the edge smoking cigarettes. The stench made me feel sick. I made my way to the fence and stared down into the giant crater. It was still fairly dark but I could see the ashen slopes dropping steeply down toward the bottom. In the bottom sat a small lake of muddy water. Further up the side of the cone, the plume of white sulphur smoke emerged and floated straight up into the dark sky. Even though I felt a little disappointed not seeing any lava bubbling in the bottom, the sight had me awestruck.

"I wish I could get away from this noisy lot," I said to myself. The other tourists continued to chatter and shuffle around the fenced lookout with what seemed to be little regard for the incredible sight before them. They seemed to be more concerned over how many cigarettes they could ingest before the sun reached the edge of the sky. It was then that I remembered some advice from my friend, Mark, who had been here two years earlier. He had told me about a thin path that followed the top edge of the crater rim. If one was careful to stay on the narrow crest, he told me, one could hike right around the volcano. Reaching for my flashlight, I quietly backed away from the noisy group, hoping that no one would notice me disappearing into the shadows. I slowly wandered to the edge of the viewing platform, turned, and vanished into the darkness.

The beam of my torch revealed the path my friend had mentioned. I followed with care as the edge of the cinder cone was very narrow and the steep slopes dropped away at a sixty degree angle on either side of me. I carefully concentrated on the trail, trying to ignore what I could hardly see. One misplaced step would have me either tumbling into the giant pit to my right or left onto the black sand sea far below.

It remained dark enough that I could only see the round spot of light guiding my progress. At one point I reached a slope so steep that I began to slip backwards. My sandals had found an unseen layer of loose earth. I crouched on all fours to regain my balance, preventing myself from sliding off the edge into the night.

I walked a quarter of the way around the crater and checked my watch: 4:30 AM. I sat on the edge for a brief time, the sound of the tourists back at the viewpoint in the background. I also got a few whiffs of strong sulphur gas. The white plume of smoke was being blown in my direction fairly constantly. Not wanting to take a chance of being overcome by fumes, I decided to head further around the rim. I could see the highest point of the crater ahead of me. It was exactly opposite the viewpoint.

"That's where I want to be for sunrise!" I said out loud. I clambered over the rugged terrain in a dash for the summit. The sky was brighter now and I was in a race with the sun. As I reached the final peak of the crater, the dawn was ready to break.

It was 5:00 AM and I was alone at the edge of Bromo. Stars and planets shone brightly above me and a widening band of light spread up from the horizon. The sky was still black, the Milky Way twisting through the cosmos. I perched myself on the edge of a large rock close to the edge. Pulling my journal and water jug out of my bag, I quenched my thirst and began to write.

The sun finally rose, lifting the veil of night from the bleak, desolate landscape below. From my crater-top seat I could clearly see the long line of white stones marking the path across the flat plain below. The white smoke drifted up out of the crater and off to my right. Slowly the land got brighter and more distinct. The sharp grooved face of Mt. Batok became more prominent as the morning emerged around me. The sun rose quickly and lit the surrounding mountains like a giant torch. I could feel the heat of the sun warming my skin almost as soon as it broke the horizon.

Sitting at the edge of the crater, I felt so small, so insignificant. I felt smaller again when I stared behind me toward the larger distant caldera of Mount Semaru. Every few minutes, a large grey puff of ash would slowly be pumped into the sky from the bowels of the bigger mountain. Each column of ash looked like a nuclear explosion, a grey mushroom cloud floating skyward. I scanned the view all around me and thought about our attempts to control the natural world around us, thinking that the Earth is tame under our thumb. I laughed out loud at the thought.

Man is nothing compared to what I saw here in the crater. The planet, formed from fire, now waited, narrow pressure valves along crustal fractures holding back the awesome inner fury. I was mesmerized . . . I felt as if I was staring off the edge of the world.

I left my perch to walk the remainder of the thin path around the rim. Again there were steep sections where my traction was poor. A few times I came too close to the outside edge and had to scramble back to the centre of the trail.

At another point the trail had carved a deep trench in a steep uphill section of the climb. The edge of the trench was shoulder-deep in places. As I walked through the middle of the trench I suddenly noticed my foot steps had become decidedly hollow-sounding.

"Oh, oh!" I just about jumped out of my skin when I realized that the crust I was standing on was very thin. I didn't want to guess just how deep the empty space under my feet was.

I nervously grabbed the sides of the trench. Composed of nothing but layers of ash and cinders, the edges of the trench crumbled under my touch. I climbed out of the trench as quickly as I could, exerting as little weight as possible on my foot falls. Emerging out the top end, I lingered to investigate the hollowness. I found a point where a tap of my foot sounded solid and just next to that, another tap revealed the sound of a large hollow chamber hidden beneath the surface. Further along the trail I passed a small group of hikers, speaking to them briefly as they passed.

"Whatever you do," I told them, "don't walk through that trench all together." I went on to describe to them the hazard that lay ahead. They continued onward with caution.

The contour of the rim now dropped steeply as I hiked down toward my starting point. Finally at about 7:30 AM, I reached the viewpoint at the top of the long staircase. The loud tourists were long gone, replaced by groups of other people just arriving. I stood once again at the edge of the platform for one last look into the giant crater below. The smell of sulphur was strong and the white plume continued to belch skyward, floating occasionally over the viewing deck. I could hear a faint rumbling from deep within the mountain.

I savoured each final moment at the edge of Bromo. I was loath to leave. The magic of the volcano had reached to the very core of my being. At last I turned and walked to the top of the steps.


### Forest of the Last Tiger

"Hey!" Danny shouted from the driver's seat as he hung his head out the window. "Are you ever going to unglue yourself from that fence?" I was standing next to the high viewpoint in front of the hotel where I had first set eyes on the smoking mountain.

"Sorry for holding you up." With one last glance I turned away from the Tengger Crater and climbed into the back seat of the van.

Dan was eager to make the ferry to Bali as soon as possible. The road had less traffic now and so we were able to make up for lost time.

The highway followed the north coast of East Java and its path took us along the edge of the Baluran nature reserve.

This protected area is supposed to be one of the last remaining habitats for the Javanese tiger. This animal is a lot smaller than the Bengal of India and its population has fallen dangerously close to extinction. The number remaining alive is said to be small, maybe only a few hundred. The forest itself was very bright as the thin leaf canopies allowed more daylight onto the forest floor. I kept my eyes peeled for the remote chance of seeing one of the striped cats, knowing my chances were minute. The only life we did see were locals making their way down the thin roads on loaded bicycles, firewood piled high above their heads.

## Race for the Ferry

Emerging out the other side of the park, we were only a few kilometres from the ferry at Banyuwangi. The highway turned south and the island of Bali could be seen just off the coast, across a narrow ocean channel.

As Danny negotiated the winding highway, his attention suddenly became focused on the rearview mirror.

"Oh, oh," he gripped the steering wheel tightly. "Here comes monkey-class."

Both Wiwied and I turned in our seats to see the fast-approaching enemy of the roadway. Another fully loaded bus was fighting its way past the slower traffic behind us. Slowly and steadily the beast bullied its way through the crowd of cars in its path, creeping closer to our bumper with bright lights flashing.

"No way, monkey-class. Not this time." Danny wasn't going to let the bus past. Dan's foot hit the floor like lead as we sped to escape the marauding grill of steel trying to run us off the road. The bus tried in vain to pass Danny as he sped along the narrow highway. With the sound of the monkey-class horn scraping paint off the rear of the van, we flew into the outskirts of Banyuwangi and rushed toward the ferry dock.

Swerving into the ferry lineup, we were held up behind a long row of cars. Unfortunately, all the buses had assured loading and so the monkey-class was allowed to pull in front of us.

"After all that he still beats us on the boat," said Danny, disappointed at his turn of luck.

"Yeah but the ride was worth it," I said to him, laughing. All the adrenaline in my system made me feel like I had just pounded back an entire pot of coffee.

The vehicles were finally guided onto the rickety-looking ferry boat, jammed into the smallest spaces possible. As the vessel filled to capacity, we were one of the last cars to board.

I climbed to the upper deck of the ferry, found a seat next to a railing and stared out over the gentle sea. The sun hung low in the sky. I remembered all that I had seen in the past days and watched the Java coast drift slowly away into the distance.

## CHAPTER 17: BALI

**Family, Friends and Hospitality**
*Saturday, February 18, 1995*
A forty-minute drive along the Bali's south island highway brought us to the city of Tabanan, northeast of the capital, Denpesar. We had been invited to stay with Wiwied's relatives, giving us a break from the constant bustle of the main tourist centre to the south. Passing by endless acres of rice and coconuts all the way from the ferry port, I could see a distant volcano, Ganung Batur, looming on the horizon.

When we reached the family home a slight state of pandemonium broke out as Wiwied and her relatives hugged, kissed, and shared all the latest news. Wiwied had been away in Canada and hadn't seen these family members for a long time. Danny was welcomed again and I was introduced.

Nyoman, the head of the house and Wiwied's cousin, reached his hand out to me in a firm handshake. "Welcome, welcome to my home." We were quickly ushered inside.

"How long will you stay with us?" he asked Wiwied. The two began to speak in a mixture of English and Bahasa Indonesia as Wiwied told him of the plan to be here for roughly a week. Nyoman told us we were more than welcome to use the house as a base from which to collect our artwork.

Downstairs the three women of the house were busy fussing over a brand new member of the family. Nyoman's wife had just given birth to a beautiful baby girl. The new mother and her sisters sat cuddling and cooing with the new arrival, only a few days old. She was very cute and she was very loud. I saw her being loved and welcomed by her entire family as they passed her around, a precious bundle of human being.

We all gathered in the kitchen where we enjoyed a welcoming feast of tasty treats, as well as plenty of beer prescribed by Nyoman.

We accepted the hospitality from Wiwied's family and made plans to concentrate on looking for material from one particular area of Bali known as Ubud. This seemed to be a particularly talented region of this island kingdom. Many well-known artists from Bali are from this village. I was eager to see their work.

## Sandalwood Kingdom

*Sunday, February 19, 1995*

The artwork of Bali was impressive. The most intriguing was the carved sandalwood. The work was astounding in its intricate detail. One of the many galleries we visited boasted giant pieces carved out of the root balls of entire trees with price tags reading thousands of dollars US. The galleries were thick with the smell of the sweet wood, so rich it was like a drug. Balinese sandalwood is a precious and sought-after commodity. Shop owners would put gloves on their hands, handling it with utmost care as pieces emerged from the display cases.

Apart from sandalwood, galleries displayed other beautiful and less expensive artwork. Paintings, carvings, batik, masks, ceramic . . . you name it, you could find it here. One gallery had an entire floor dedicated to masks, some more than two metres tall. Some smaller masks were made into mirrors. A roadside store displayed huge handmade quilts in amazing designs, hanging on lines like freshly cleaned laundry. Another sold handmade kites of various sizes and shapes.

We met one family whose reputation came from the production of detailed paintings. During our visit we discovered that even the little children were part of the process, painting parts of the work along with their parents. It seemed that, as the group painted together, the whole process was like an assembly line. One person was perhaps good at painting birds, another good at flowers. One artist would paint something on the small canvas or paper, then pass it on to the next, who would then proceed with their own speciality. The young children were very talented and amazing to watch. One four-year old kid handled paper and brush like a professional of many years.

Again, the designs were unique, never made the same way twice. The only exception to this rule were the mass-produced plates, bookends, mirrors, stools, statues, and knick-knacks, with ever-present themes of cats, frogs, moons, and suns. After awhile it all began to look like typical tourist junk.


## Gunung Batur

Taking a break from art shop visits and orders, Dan drove up the thin road which ascended toward the centre of the island. A long, steady climb was eventually rewarded by a view one of the island's main volcanoes. The road cut left along the contour of the caldera and led us to a spectacular high view, directly across from the tapered cone. Far around to the right side, Batur Lake filled a vast section of the crater. A small village sat perched on the edge of the ancient caldera. A thin road snaked its way down the crater wall and across the volcanic plain toward several small villages nestled along the shoreline beneath the shadow of the great mountain. We looked down from our viewpoint onto the barren terrain, strewn with geological junk, rocks, hard lava veins, and ash. I listened intently and could hear the low rumble coming from the bowels of the mountain. I could see small showers of pumice being thrown a few hundred metres into the air from one large vent.

Standing and enjoying the view without being disturbed lasted only a few minutes. A crowd of vendors soon discovered us at the viewpoint and surrounded us on all sides. Merchants, some of them small children, pushed their way up to us, thrusting carved and painted items into our hands.

"Please, mister, you buy! Please, mister, you buy!" The cries flooded over me as each person tried to have me purchase something from them. As they pushed each other, the momentum moved us as well. Being close to the edge of a cliff, we had to start pushing back to hold our position.

"No," I said as I gently held my ground.

"Please, mister, please, mister!" I was pushed back again, this time almost losing my balance.

"No!" I shouted. Their insistence had worn a hole in my patience.

Wiwied began to interject, talking to the group, trying to get them to understand that we were not interested in their merchandise. The group only shoved their wares in her face and began to push her toward the edge as well.

"They just don't know when to give up, do they?" I knew that they did this in order to survive but their tenaciousness had me fatigued.

"Let's find a quieter place. This is ridiculous." Danny pushed his way back toward the van.

With Danny in the lead, the three of us fought our way back to the vehicle, the crowd still pushing us and pulling on our clothes to gain our attention. I climbed into the rear seat of the van and had to literally push two or three people back out of the van. I closed the sliding side door to regain solitude. As the van began to move, the crowd blocked our exit in an attempt to have us remain.

Honk, Honk! Danny moved slowly ahead until the group finally gave up their attempt to keep us captive. Seeking a quieter place to observe the volcano, we continued up the hill to the top where a small café sat at the edge of the volcanic moonscape.

"I think we left the vultures behind," Danny said as he scanned behind us to see if we were being tailed.

"I was just glad you didn't have to resort to running them over, Dan." I looked behind as well, double-checking our privacy.

Finally, away from the crowd of eager businessmen, we sat watching the rumbling mountain. The sun was bright and we could see for miles. Again the noise of the mountain was unearthly, the eerie, awesome power harnessed below the surface.

"I am still amazed when I see so many people living this close to an active cone." My eyes were following the thin road to the edge of the lake inside the caldera. I imagined a giant steam bath in the event of an eruption.

"They love the mountain." Wiwied's simple statement made perfect sense to me.

The Balinese have great respect for this old mountain and its power. There are many ceremonies performed by the faithful, designed to quell the anger of the god who dwells within. Another of the island's main volcanoes, Ganung Agung, possesses a mountainside temple for such worship. In the early 1960s, a few days after a significant sacrificial ceremony, Agung erupted with brutal force, killing at least one thousand people. I shivered at the thought of lava landing in the beds of parents and their children.

It was obvious that the island's people were closely bonded to the mountain in a precarious existence. The skin of the Earth separated men from the fire that could, in an instant, wreak havoc and destruction. I could never expect to understand their connection to the powerful force that provides so much bountiful life from the rich, dark soil. The roots ran too deep.


**That'll Be Five Million Please . . .**
*Tuesday, February 21, 1995*
Ubud is a small village just south of the giant volcano, almost in the

centre of the island of Bali. Well-known around the world for the prowess of its artisans, the small centre boasts various shops and galleries of every description. A rainbow of rich, vibrant colours filled the store entrances all along the roadside, in the forms of hanging mobiles, carved mirrors, furniture, and painted fabrics. On and on. Once again, the themes remained constant: suns, moons, cats, and birds prevailed.

Dan had selected one particular store carrying a wide assortment of the things he was looking for. The owner of the shop became fast friends with Dan as my friend and his fiancée began a buying spree that was guaranteed to fill their vehicle to capacity.

"Ten of these . . . two dozen of these . . . six of these . . . " Danny slowly took stock of the items for sale, choosing his favourites. As he walked through the collection with the owner, another man followed behind, quickly pulling items from the shelves, taking them into the back for packing. I knew that the process would take a great deal of time and, eventually, money. To kill time, I wandered through the shop on my own, still within earshot of Danny's continuous shopping spree.

In the back of the gallery I discovered a room entirely filled with carved masks. The detail of these works was so beautiful that I wanted to take the whole room home myself. Selecting a few pieces, I was particularly taken by one, unpainted but intricately carved. The face of a horned beast, a cross between a lion and a dragon, looked menacing with its large fangs and waggling tongue. Feathers and ornate curls framed a face that must have taken many hours to carve. I studied the mask for a long time, finally setting it back in its place. As I reached the other side of the room, something was screaming at me to purchase this mask. I returned to the same shelf and once again held the work in my hands. It was as if it were speaking to me.

"Take me with you." The wooden eyes implored me to hold on. There seemed to be a playfulness behind the menacing, toothy grin. Not sure why, I returned to the front of the gallery with mask in hand.

Back at the front desk the accountant was busy tallying up the cost of Danny's spending spree. Once done with his calculator, the fellow scribbled a figure onto the bottom of the sales form sitting by his work space. He then got up to help in the final packing of the merchandise.

Curious, I wandered closer to the table and pretended to examine a jewellery box as I scanned for the number written at the bottom of the form. My eyes widened as the figure registered in my sight. The final figure was over five million rupiah, approximately thirty-five hundred Canadian dollars.

I caught up to my companions as they were still adding items to the final tally.

"I saw you looking at the total over there. It must be big by now, tee hee hee hee." Dan was totally okay with the high cost. He knew that these items would sell at home and so he had no concern about the money he would invest at the outset.

"It's actually a pretty good price for the amount of stuff you are buying," I told him. "It is just that the price tag in rupiah looks ominous."

"What are we at now, anyway?" he asked me.

"You don't even know yet?!" I looked at him like he was nuts to not know by now.

"I've been too busy ordering," he told me. "So what is it, four million by now?"

"Try over five million."

"Oh well, we're on a roll." My jovial friend accepted the price with happy abandon.

Danny pulled a mountainous wad of faded bills from his wallet and forked over the vast amount of local currency needed to purchase all the items he had ordered. Meanwhile, the happy owner's eyes grew larger as he watched the pile of paper grow higher on the surface of the desk.

Wiwied approached me and gently grabbed the mask I had chosen from the other room.

"Barong—a very beautiful one, too," she said to me. "Do you know what it means, the Barong?"

"No, what is it?" I was curious.

"It represents the cleansing forces of the universe. Getting rid of the old and bringing in the new."

I instantly knew why I had such a strong feeling from the work. Relating it to my present circumstance, it was the perfect purchase.

The pile of large boxes and bundles were finally covered with plain paper wrap to protect them on the journey back to Semarang and beyond. Making use of every space possible, we managed to pack the van up tight as a drum. Wedging myself into the remaining space, I felt like a sardine in a can that was about to be sealed as Dan stared in through the open side door.

"Can you still breath in there? Tee hee hee." He laughed at me, stuffed in with the parcels.

"Good thing I'm this thin," I replied. "Otherwise, I'd have to walk."

"Or ride on the roof," Dan suggested. "Just be glad you aren't going back to Semarang with us."

"True enough," I agreed. A thirty-minute trip to Tabanan would be enough of a pain as I already felt my circulation being challenged. The trunk of a heavy wooden elephant dug into my ribcage. I adjusted my weight, attempting to acquire some semblance of comfort.

## Hairless Dog

Part of the background, part of the dirt of the road, the dogs remained dejected and forgotten in the streets. I had become used to the sight of these beasts throughout my travels; however, some were so skinny and pitiful that it was hard to believe they were still alive. Living on the fringe of society, looking in from the outside, these sullen creatures were simply accepted as a temporary, transient part of everyday life.

"I'm gonna have to show you the most hideous hairless dog that you will ever witness, John." Dan had seen it over four months ago on a previous visit to Denpesar and wanted me to have visual proof of its existence.

"Maybe he's already dead," I said to Dan as he began a diligent search through the back streets and alleys where he had once encountered the vile creature.

"He has to be here. You just have to see this . . . " He scouted the alleys until, at last, the mangy beast was found, standing behind a small four-by-four vehicle. "Over here!" Dan shouted to me as I followed his lead.

Across the street, just under the fender of the small jeep, a grim apparition stood sad and decrepit. When I saw the animal, I had to do a double-take to make sure I was not imagining this thing in front of me. Not one hair remained on the dog's wrinkled hide. The black skin was rubbed raw with infection and its body was covered with open, fetid sores. Barely standing, the poor dog would constantly lick its sore-looking feet. He stood aimlessly beside a hot dog vendor's cart, obviously smelling a good breakfast. His hopeful eyes scanned for any spare morsels falling into the dirt.

As I approached the animal from across the road, he may have thought I was about to drop some food into his lap. He looked at me as his feeble tail wagged slowly back and forth, his feet making awkward steps toward me.

"You poor bastard . . . " The sight of his state of existence made me feel ill. Keeping my distance, I watched him for only a few minutes, unwilling to even give him a pat on the head.

Finally realizing that I was not going to produce any food for him, he slowly wandered off toward the lane from which he had emerged. Once there, he mingled with a large group of mangy dogs congregating at the mouth of the alley. He blended in and soon he was lost from view.

# CHAPTER 18: HOMEWARD

## Flight Over Borneo
*Friday, February 24, 1995*

"Thanks, Dan, and you too, Wiwied. It was a pleasure to spend time with you." I hugged my departing companions as they prepared to make their way back through the monkey-class traffic of Java and home to Semarang.

"You're welcome." The two of them wished me luck in my return to Canada and to my new life ahead. These were two people who really enjoyed life together. Engaged to be married, the final paperwork was being prepared for a licence. The next time I saw them, they would be husband and wife.

Dropping me at the gates of the airport, they then headed back into the city. I watched them drive away until I could no longer see the van. It melded into the bustling rush-hour traffic as they made their way back to Tabanan to load the mountain of artwork into the van.

I checked in and waited impatiently for my flight, enjoying strong coffee and a bite to eat. I was not looking forward to the long journey ahead of me. I would be travelling for the next twenty-one hours.

Finally my flight was called and I claimed my seat. I watched sadly as the jet taxied to the far end of the runway, the gentle swaying of the coconut palms in the light morning breeze. The giant engines whined and the plane began to thunder down the asphalt strip. With my face pressed against the glass, I watched as the Earth suddenly disappeared and Southeast Asia dropped away under my seat. As the jet banked to the right in a long turn, I could see the crowds already gathering on Kuta Beach for another day in the hot sun. Further ahead, Ganung Batur sat smouldering in its ashen cradle. My last view was looking down on the top of the great volcano. We climbed higher and the island of Bali slipped away from under the flight path. The Bali sea was a beautiful blue.

## Home
Hong Kong was cold and misty for the second time. I got the same feeling from some locals here, gawking at my strange presence. I spent

the waiting time in a quiet corner chair writing in my journal.

At last my homeward flight was announced. Descending a flight of escalators, I joined a crowd boarding another of the large buses used to carry passengers to their aircraft. The vehicle drove to the far end of the airport and pulled up alongside a Cathay Pacific 747 which was still being loaded with large containers.

As I climbed the staircase from the tarmac, a cool breeze sent a chill through my body. A thick band of clouds blanketed the surrounding hills and laid a pale layer of grey over the entire city. With a final look back I ducked into the plane's rounded doorway and took my seat by the window. I sat, staring blankly through the window, lost in thought. Before long, the thrust of the aircraft pushed me into my seat as the plane lifted into the sky. Next stop, Canada.

I had come full circle. I remembered boarding the Bangkok-bound jet just fourteen weeks ago. I recalled my anxiety, wondering what adventures would befall me. I recalled the intense excitement of the unknown journey ahead. Now, as I looked back, my experiences lay behind me and I felt enlightened. I had experienced inner growth and a re-connection with my self and my own life. In this short span of time, that in some ways seemed to last a lifetime, I came to be in touch with all aspects of my being, both positive and negative. I had experienced times when my confidence showed me that anything was possible, when my sense of intuition kept me aware of and away from trouble, and other times when I felt like the loneliest man in the world.

It had been a rainbow of emotions and I could feel that they had made me a stronger person, ready to better stand on my own feet and to take on what was next in my life. I felt anxious about going on alone. Yet, at the same time, I thought it funny that I feared something that was completely natural: we all come into the world alone and leave it alone. My experiences with the rich cultures and the wonderful people of Southeast Asia were rewarding beyond words. The ancient monuments, exotic places, colours, smells, tastes, and flowing consistently through all things modern and ancient, the eternal smiles and warm hearts of friendly locals. I felt honoured to have experienced all of this.

I thought of all the people I had met and travelled with during these many weeks, each one of them adding their own individual energy to my experience. I believe strongly that none of these meetings were coincidences, every person appearing at the right time and place for a specific reason, bringing a specific lesson to light. The humour, the wisdom, the wildness, the support, the real humanness of these friends and companions came back to me as I stared out into the open sky. All of us there to put pieces into our own puzzle, to dig our own wisdom from the ancient land, to see a part of ourselves that would otherwise remain undiscovered. I felt blessed to have been in their company and to have learned from them.

After many hours the jet neared the edge of North America. I saw large, choppy waves in the freezing waters of the Pacific Ocean far below my window. I had returned to chilly latitudes. The airliner's wings took large slices out of the thick cloud banks as we slowly descended out of the sky. I recognized familiar landmarks of BC's Lower Mainland through small holes in the cloud cover. A bumpy landing signalled the return to Canadian turf. The Boeing 747 braked and turned off the end of the runway. I looked out to see puddles of fresh rain pooling by the edge of the asphalt. The sky was grey and the rain falling.

I breathed deeply as I lifted the latch of my seatbelt. I looked out the window onto the rainy tarmac and felt a sudden wave of apprehension and excitement holding me to my seat. The world outside was familiar, yet brand new. A new path awaited me under a crying sky. As the cabin lights were turned on, I shifted my focus to see my own face staring back from the reflecting glass of the window. I was home.

## Acknowledgments

I would like to thank the following people for their existence and assistance on this journey and during the creation of this book:

All of the friends and companions who shared the best of times with me in Thailand, Malaysia, and Indonesia. Hats off to Marvin. Your support and your sense of humour allowed me to see a new perspective. Danny and Wiwied, thank you for shelter, transport, and companionship in Java and Bali.

I also wish to thank Doug Elliott, my childhood friend, for opening his home to me, allowing me to get resettled upon my return, and for allowing us to strengthen our friendship. Thanks, brother!

I would also like to thank Thomas Wharton and Janice Dickin for their literary expertise and assistance.

Above all, I would like to thank God and my Guardian Angels who kept me safe upon this journey, allowing me to learn from these experiences and for granting me the memory to recall the events which occurred.